Political Education and Political Literacy

Edited by
Bernard Crick and Alex Porter

The report and papers of, and the
evidence submitted to, the Working Party
of the Hansard Society's
'Programme for Political Education'

 Longman

Longman Group Limited
London

Associated companies, branches and representatives
throughout the world

First published 1978

Printed in Great Britain by
Richard Clay (The Chaucer Press) Ltd,
Bungay, Suffolk

Contents

Contents

ACKNOWLEDGEMENTS

We are grateful to the following for permission to reproduce copyright material:
Guardian Newspapers Limited for articles by Peter Cole, 21st January 1975, Peter Hildrew, 18th March 1975, Adam Raphael, 16th December 1973, Your Own Reporter, 19th December 1973 which appeared in *The Guardian*; Times Newspapers Limited for extract from article 'Ministers Now Look to Conciliation' which appeared in *The Times*, 7th June 1976. Reproduced by permission.

Preface

The Hansard Society for Parliamentary Government in association with the Politics Association (the professional association of teachers of politics in schools and colleges of further education, founded in 1969) obtained a grant in 1974 from the Nuffield Foundation, for three years, to launch a general Programme for Political Education consisting of curriculum development and of assessment of innovation in political education aimed at enhancing political literacy in secondary schools and non-degree classes in colleges of further education. The Hansard Society also obtained funds from the Leverhulme Trust to make and publish a survey of levels of political knowledge and ignorance among school leavers, and the research officer in charge, Dr Robert Stradling, worked in close cooperation with the Programme. Some additional funding came from the Schools Council to make a report on how the Programme's conclusions could be diffused. And cooperation was close, as will emerge, with the jointly funded Political Education Research Unit at the University of York under Professor Ian Lister. The Society thanks all these bodies warmly for their patient and imaginative support; it also thanks Birkbeck College for the continued use of premises and facilities; and the very many teachers, lecturers, educationalists, local authority officers, and others who have helped the Working Party and their staff, far too numerous to mention by name. Neither the Society, nor these other institutions and persons, however, should be held responsible for the opinions expressed in this report: the Society issues it, like its other recent reports on 'Electoral Reform', on 'The Consequences for British Representative Institutions of Joining the EEC', and 'Parliament and the Public', simply as an important contribution to public debate in a somewhat neglected field. Lastly, the Working Party wish a special word of thanks to be given to Miss Frauke Hansen who was secretary to the Programme throughout and who supported it with diligence, skill, understanding, and enthusiasm.

1

The report of the Working Party: objects, methods, findings and recommendations

1.1 Origins and control of the Programme

Political education has been a neglected area in schools, and the need was plain both for more of it and for a greater clarity of purpose about its objectives and methods. The subject is inherently both important and difficult to handle. Therefore a broadly-based Working Party was established under the chairmanship of Professor Bernard Crick to try to produce three things: (i) a general programme of the minimal contents of what should constitute a political education (not a single best syllabus, as for instance in Nuffield Science programmes); (ii) examples worked out in depth for a series of different situations, ages or institutions to include small politics components for a variety of subject areas; and (iii) help and advice to teachers both in their existing work and in launching new courses. The content of both the general programme and of the particular developments were to be discussed with teachers at every stage. The whole Programme was designed to begin in a flexible way so that the response of teachers to early documents would be a major factor in determining what to attempt to work out in detail. As part of the same grant, an independent Research Unit was established at the Department of Education, University of York under Professor Ian Lister in order, it was hoped, (i) to monitor the effectiveness of the main developments of the Hansard Working Party when they were tried out in schools and colleges; (ii) to study examples of good teaching practice, quite independent of the Working Party's main developments; and (iii) to produce case studies of good teaching practice for the use of teachers.

The main aim of the Programme has been to enhance 'political literacy' by which we mean the knowledge, skills and attitudes needed to make a man or woman informed about politics; able to participate in public life and groups of all kinds, both occupational and voluntary; and to recognise and tolerate diversities of political and social values. A politically literate people should know what the main political disputes are about, what beliefs the main contestants have of them, how they are likely to affect them, how they relate to institutions, and they will have a predisposition to try to be politically effective while respecting the sincerity of others. Obviously political literacy is relevant to everyone. It is not to be limited to or confused with time-table slots labelled 'Civics', 'Politics' or 'British Constitution'. While not ignoring A levels, we concentrated on the needs of the full range of the thirteen to nineteen age group; both school-leavers and those who continue either in school or further education. Nor did we begin with an assumption that 'political literacy' is best gained by teaching about politics directly. Of particular importance, we thought, was how political literacy can be advanced through other subjects, for instance, History, English, Geography, Social studies, Sociology and Economics.

We limited our considerations to what was directly relevant to England and Wales. Both the practice of and the research into political education in the United States and in the Federal Republic of Germany are particularly impressive, yet while they may furnish many detailed suggestions for future developments and even examples of how political education can form part of Public Law, they did not seem directly relevant to either the general guidelines or the specific curricula of our Programme. However, we have benefited directly from the example of the Modern Studies curricula in Scotland, a multi-disciplinary approach in which politics plays a large role and which has produced many materials readily useable or easily adaptable to schools and colleges in England and Wales.

The Working Party consisted of: Mr Tom Brennan (Head of Division of Social Sciences, Bingley College of Education), Professor Bernard Crick (Department of Politics and Sociology, Birkbeck College, London University), Mr John Dickie (Department of Modern Studies, Aberdeen College of Education), Dr Linda Dove (then of Trent Park College of Education, now Institute of Education, London University), Mr Derek Heater (then Head of History Department, Brighton College of Education, now Dean of the Faculty of Social Studies, Brighton Polytechnic), Mr Cliff Jones (St Catherine's Secondary Modern School, Liverpool), Professor Denis Lawton (Institute of Education, London University), Professor Ian Lister (Department of Education, University of York), Mr Henry Macintosh (Secretary of the Southern Regional Examination Board for the CSE), Mr Alex Porter (then Head of Politics and Economics, Solihull Sixth Form College, now of the Institute of Education, London University), Mr John Robottom (then a Lecturer at Crewe College of Education, now with the BBC), Mr John Sutton (Headmaster, Southwood School, Corby), Mrs Maureen Whitebrook (Trent Polytechnic). [John Robottom withdrew at an early stage due to pressure of work. Mr John Slater, HMI, was appointed by DES as an assessor. Henry Macintosh was deputy chairman and took the chair at meetings in the middle section of the work.]

Mr Geoffrey Petter (a former HMI) was Development Officer in the first year of the project, responsible for setting up the administration, for assisting the working groups and for coordinating with schools, LEAs and other bodies; and Alex Porter was Development Officer in the second year of the project, responsible for observing and helping the cooperating schools. Geoffrey Petter's services were retained for a second year, separately funded by the Schools Council, specifically to obtain the cooperation of schools and teachers' centres for diffusion of the Programme's results. (This work has now been taken over by Alex Porter and the Institute of Education and forms part of a general application (now before the Schools Council) sponsored by the Association for the Teaching of the Social Sciences, together with other subject associations.

The Working Party held six meetings, necessarily limited to matters of principle and broad strategy. The detailed direction of the Programme was in the hands of a Steering Committee which consisted of Bernard Crick, Ian Lister, Henry Macintosh, Derek Heater (who had to withdraw after the third meeting) and Alex Porter, with Geoffrey Petter, Robert Stradling of the Hansard Society and Mr Garth Allen of the Political Education Research Unit, University of York, in attendance.

Bernard Crick, with the help of Mr John Malone of the Teachers' Centre at the Queen's University, Belfast and Dr Paul Arthur of the Polytechnic of Northern Ireland, made several attempts to set up a working group of teachers in Northern Ireland, as if to test in the most difficult circumstances the Working Party's belief in tackling real issues, but though some real interest was stimulated, nothing lasting could result from our limited and largely borrowed resources.

1.2 The status of this report

Section 2 consists of the Project's own papers, written before any field work was undertaken. Then follow the reports of the various groups and individuals mostly commissioned by the Working Party. These reports are, however, theirs. We offer comment on them in this first part of the report. Their status is akin to that of evidence commissioned by a public committee of enquiry. We think them all worth considering and print them *in extenso* as being directly useful to teachers as well as evidence for our conclusions. But the opinions of the group reports are not necessarily those of the Working Party.

The Working Party intend their own report in Section 1 for all interested parties, public authorities, educationalists, press, politicians and parents' organisations, not simply for teachers. The recommendations are those of the Working Party as a whole. Comments on the field work and reports of the groups (in paragraphs 1.6 and 1.7) are necessarily more subjective: the Working Party endorse them in general, but reserve their individual opinions. The first draft was prepared by Bernard Crick and Alex Porter jointly.

1.3 General aims and objectives

We must make clear what we have been doing. New enterprises go right or wrong in their basic assumptions rather than in their complicated methods and equivocal results. Politics as a subject of disciplined enquiry has no need to hide its light under a bushel, nor to find melodramatic excuses for being taken seriously and forming part, as John Milton said, of the education of the whole man. Its antecedents are good, fathered by Aristotle as the supreme union of practice and philosophy; and if some of its children are a little delinquent and embarrassing in their behaviour, it is widely admitted to be better in theory

3

than in practice – which is as much as can be hoped from any education that remembers that education is part of life, an important part of life, but neither a substitute for life nor an adequate protection from life.

Civilised life and organised society depend upon the existence of governments and while governments cannot, however wise, dedicated and popular they may be, make us good and make us happy, they can effectively prevent our betterment. To take a Greek or Jacobinical view of the matter may now appear to go too far: that a man is only fully a man when he or she is taking part in public life. But it remains true that we think less of a person who either has no public spirit or is so fastidious that he will not take part in all those jostlings of interests and ideals that constitute politics. There are no clear grounds for saying that society would be better if everyone took part in politics. However, there are overwhelmingly clear grounds for saying that societies are bad which prevent or even merely discourage popular participation, and there are reasonably clear grounds for thinking that distaste for or distrust of politics can threaten any kind of just and tolerant life. Politics is concerned with the creative conciliation of differing interests, whether these interests are seen as primarily material or moral. To say 'creative conciliation' is to try to convey that in a political tradition we try to resolve disputes as well as possible and as far as possible, but that we never hope to resolve or to solve them all.

To start from this abstract but basic perception of politics is simply to show that the first task of any possible political education that is of educational value is to convey some sense of the naturalness and variation of politics. Political education must begin by showing what conflicts there are: it is not a scheme for solving them. This is not quietism. On the contrary, we may not have the poor with us for ever; but even in a society of equals, it is likely that political disputes will continue.

EDUCATIONAL VALUE

Hence the political part of education is primarily, as in any possible moral education, an education in what differing viewpoints are held, who holds them, why, in what context and with what restraints. This may seem platitudinous. But how often is political education, if approached at all explicitly, approached primarily through a study of constitutional rules and institutional forms? The cart is put before the horse. Those rules and institutions which exist because there are disputes and issues are thought to be prior to those disputes and issues. The British Constitution is only meaningful as a summary of the way we contain pre-existing, actual problems: it was not something either given to us by King Alfred or Gladstone, nor yet invented like croquet. Rather it developed, like football, to such an extent that it proved convenient to have generally recognised rules; but these rules are derived from practice, they did not make the practice. And it would be an odd way to learn football to begin by learning the rules.

GCE examinations in British Constitution have not been our concern. Rather we have tried to define the nature of a minimum political element in all education, not staking out another territorial claim for the already grossly over-

4

crowded timetable, particularly for the more able alone. Politics (as the perception of differing interests and differing justifications about the allocation of resources within, or the direction of, society) both affects everyone and can crop up in many different parts of the timetable. History is involved in politics at every step. Geography will, through environmental and local studies, necessarily touch on the political factors. English Literature has a distinctively English involvement in social and political issues, and Use of English draws heavily on social and political materials in the attempt to find motivation to enhance language skills. Economics begins to return from a perhaps excessive mathematical abstractness to its fertile, Scottish origins as 'Political Economy'. And, of course, a good deal of explicit discussion of political and social problems already takes place in many of those hours variously designated 'Social Studies', 'General Studies', or that ever-deceptive 'Free Time'.

The question is not really whether it is done at all, but whether it is done well or done badly. It should be done: there is no need to fear what is one of the greatest parts of our cultural heritage (even if one still the least fulfilled in terms meaningful to the many) because of fears of bias or indoctrination – of that in a moment. But it can be done better than it often is. There is sometimes need for greater professionalism. There is need for greater system: some simple set of basic concepts should be used with a reasonable consistency. There is need for a small core of political education to be part of teacher education at every level (all children become citizens, as well as workers, husbands, wives, parents and pedestrians, all of which can find a place in the curriculum). There is need not simply for a modest requirement of timetable hours in Politics but also for helpful booklets, teaching notes and resources which will help the existing teacher of other subjects (or children) to enhance, through what is done already, the political literacy of children at school.

THE FEAR OF BIAS

It would be a dubious gain to move from the neglect (of which Derek Heater has written)[1] of civic education in this country into an arid constitutional, institutional and purely descriptive approach. This is often done out of fear of bias – just as 'sex education' can be reduced to anatomy. But part of the activity itself is a consideration of what *should* be done – even if answers vary and alternatives abound. Some bias is not only probable but, if we are moral beings, unavoidable. While we share the fears of LEAs and parents that there can sometimes be gross bias in the classroom (whatever the subject), we do not share the hopes of those who believe that methodologies can be produced which are guaranteed value-free and will eliminate bias.

One should be dispassionate, rational, sensible, in a phrase, professional and responsible; but nothing can guarantee that one can be without bias. To think otherwise is self-deception, and it may not even be a sensible desire. For there is bias and biases. Teachers should be aware of their own biases, and being aware of them, increase their empathy for the plausibility of other biases. While

[1] *The Teaching of Politics*, editor D. B. Heater, Methuen Educational 1969, pp. 1–21.

it is right to seek to contain prejudices, it is not always either right or possible to seek to eliminate prejudice. Part of teaching is to make pupils aware of their own biases, the biases of others in the class and outside, and to alert them to the implications of particular prejudices or perspectives. Such bias is human, venal, inevitable and actually educational. At some stage the teacher does have to convey that these things matter. While there are classrooms, we cannot destroy example. But bias of a kind that excludes the plausibility of the other viewpoints, or that gives unrecognisable accounts of them often by not recognising one's own bias, is unprofessional and indefensible. Teachers can actually go beyond 'mere bias' into positive indoctrination (whether conscious or unconscious) if something is taught as the truth regardless of consideration of evidence and if the pupil is not introduced empathetically to alternative viewpoints and alternative sources of evidence or information.[1]

Since politics is about conflicts and alternatives and acceptable ways of resolving or containing them, we should start by identifying what the main issues of our society are thought to be. We should show who holds different views and why, and draw the class into all this, particularly to imagine or reconstruct the justifications and motivations of people holding viewpoints other than their own. For we can, after all, dispute not merely about goals, but about values and methods too. At every level, the first main task is to create an understanding of the plausibility of those differing political perspectives that every pupil is likely to encounter in his life, and how these viewpoints define not merely objectives but priorities among problems too. If this kind of knowledge is created, then problems of bias become far less acute. Many would feel that teachers have done their main business as educators of citizens if their pupils can come to understand what the issues are commonly felt to be, who holds what viewpoints, why, and what reasons they offer.

POLITICAL LITERACY

An emphatic knowledge of differing viewpoints is, however, not enough. Plainly if we want citizens, we have to tolerate some of the unpredictable inconveniences of action and participation. We have to teach or let the pupils learn skills relevant to political action. There are many ways: gaming and simulation, perhaps just old-fashioned debates, or perhaps some voluntary share in communal tasks; and a political education is surely something to do with the whole organisation of the school, although it does not imply reorganising the whole school. Informed and orderly participation, not any old participation, is needed. A citizen is not a docile subject but he is not an ever-angry activist either, he seeks to get rid of bad laws, but to abide by better ones. Teachers have to teach what are the conventional laws and rules. But teachers must also stimulate the imagination of the pupils as well as their experience, for their relevant experience is limited. Perhaps an experience of something like politics

---

[1] I. A. Snook, editor, *Concepts of Indoctrination: Philosophical Essays*, Routledge and Kegan Paul, 1972, and his simpler *Indoctrination and Education*, Routledge and Kegan Paul, 1972; and B. R. Crick, 'On Bias', *Teaching Politics*, May 1972.

can be created in small groups, even in schools, but many of the factors of national politics will necessarily be lacking.

Fortunately academic research into the formation of political attitudes does tell us something. It tells us very clearly that the basic social factors conditioning children's partisan political attitudes are far more present outside the school than within. Teachers should neither hope to influence nor fear to influence political attitudes too much. But the school may have a great effect on two things far more important than a proclivity to vote one way or the other: not what the biases are, but how they are held (peacefully and tolerantly or violently and blindly, for instance); and if we perceive injustice, are we equipped to and temperamentally likely to try to do something about it? All we feel fairly certain about is not that political values can ever be inculcated by any form of school organisation (deliberate indoctrination seems more likely to cause apathy and cynicism than enthusiasm), but that some practices in schools can negate political values – if it is obvious to the pupils, for instance, that a head teacher never consults with his colleagues, habitually interrupts lessons in progress (perhaps on Civics), or draws up an agenda for a School Council without consultation.

Thus a person who has a fair knowledge of what are the issues of contemporary politics, is equipped to be of some influence, whether in school, factory, voluntary body or party, and can understand and respect, while not sharing, the values of others, can reasonably be called 'politically literate'. It is common sense and common prudence to develop political literacy as a general educational and cultural goal. Obviously political literacy, like general literacy, is both relative and functional. It must be applied not as a rigid general formula, but in relation to the abilities, concerns and situations of very differing people and very differing schools and colleges. Some such moves are, however, long overdue.

POLITIC WORDS

Recently there has been a great breath of what the poet called 'politic words' about the need for political or civic education. The Government's Green Paper on *Education in Schools* of July 1977 only spoke in very general terms of the need for there to be in schools a greater awareness of the community at large and of the role of individual participation in a democracy. But some of the statements from organisations invited to take part in 'the great debate' were far more specific. We have read all the submissions to one of the four regional conferences, that held at Peterborough on Friday, 11 March 1977, with Miss Margaret Jackson, M.P. in the chair, and we find the following statements. The NUT said: 'the complexity of society makes it increasingly important to understand the nature and origins of society and the influence of historical, social economic and political factors...' The Council of Local Education Authorities: 'the aims of a "core curriculum" should be to provide a framework in which all pupils can develop ... an understanding of simple scientific facts ... a knowledge of social, historical, geographical and political bases of the world in which they live.' The National Association of Teachers in Further

7

and Higher Education: 'If we are to develop greater participation in political, social and industrial life, and the Association thinks it desirable, it is necessary for schools to equip young people to play their part. This involves a curriculum wide enough to give young people the basis for such participation.' The Head-masters' Association also: 'Included in this should be an awareness of the major social, political, and moral issues that our society faces.' The National Consumer Council remarked: 'It is open to question how far schools are able to encourage the development of a critical and analytical approach to ... social issues. Should not the importance of doing so be emphasised if pupils are to achieve the necessary high standard of what is now coming to be known as "politeracy"?' The National Association of Head Teachers: '... due attention should be paid to the study of aesthetic and cultural values no less than those which provide the knowledge and skill necessary for the pupil's future life as a political and economic member of the community.' The Church of England Board of Education named as among the seven issues towards which a debate should move: 'How far is the educational system, not only "fitting" children for life in our society, but enabling them constructively to criticise and reshape it?' Lastly and not least, the two giants: the CBI said 'In summary, what the schools can do to help in this general area is to ensure that (i) pupils are much better prepared for the change from school to adult and working life; (ii) pupils have an understanding of the social and economic aspects of industrial society'; and the TUC said 'If there is a core curriculum which all young people should share equally, then it must include a thorough preparation for playing a full part in democratic life – both political and industrial. In other words, all young people must be helped to become politically and economically literate, and understand the basic structure of our industrial society.' Much of this was platitude, but a little of it found its way into the Green Paper and schools have recently been asked by the DES to report on what they do for political education as part of the questionnaire on the educational needs of industrial society.

That political education, indeed specifically our coinage 'political literacy', was so widely mentioned, shows at least worry and some clear recognition of a need, even though few of the bodies that said these things have yet shown much sign of trying to implement them. But at least the nervousness is not now so great that it cannot be mentioned, or that it can be regarded as something quite improper to form part of a whole and humane education. Several LEAs have sponsored teachers' meetings or short courses on political education in the last three years, as well as the Hansard Society and the Politics Association. At Easter 1976 two important organisations, the National Association for Adult Education and the National Association of Youth and Community Officers, both chose 'Political Literacy' as the subject of their opening, key-note addresses and the chairman was the speaker. The BBC ran in 1975, and repeated in 1976, a series on 'Political Education' for teachers, and in 1978 begins a series for schools. Dr Stradling's recently published survey, *The Political Awareness of the School Leaver*, Hansard Society, 1977, however, has shown how desperately low are the levels of political knowledge and information among the young at the very point that they move from being pupils to becoming citizens. The coverage of his survey in the Press and broad-casting media was remarkable. Several foreign papers seemed to take the view that 'things aren't what they used to be' in Great Britain. We doubt if they ever were, but they need to be more than before. Finally, the Secretary of State for Education and Science, perhaps in response to that publicity and our preliminary findings, authorised the publication of an unofficial paper on 'Political Competence' (*Times Educational Supplement*, 25 November 1977) prepared earlier by two of the HMI's in History (which we reprint as Appendix B), a paper very much on the same lines as most of our own thinking.

1.4 The strategy of the Programme

Our original strategy is set out in document 2.1. It will soon emerge as one of our findings that the original strategy did not work as intended, but was amended both for practical and educational reasons. From the beginning we intended to advance in two ways: a massive frontal attack combined with permeation and infiltration aimed at specified targets behind the lines. The frontal attack was to be 'a generalised programme or outline of curriculum development for local adaptation' as a two year course and the permeation was a strategy of infusing political literacy into the curriculum through other subject disciplines ('for example', we said, 'History, English, Geography, Social Studies, Sociology and Economics'), and we intended to monitor the progress of the advance by Hansard producing materials, both for the big push and the infiltrations, getting schools to try them out, and then for York to monitor and assess the results.

This quickly proved, within our very limited resources, to be both over-ambitious and partly misconceived. To have produced five or six curricula in a year (as distinct from guidelines for curriculum development by teachers in actual classes), to have got them adopted and then monitored, was quickly seen to be an impossible task with only one full-time Development Officer at the Hansard end and with one assistant at York; and rapid inflation following the oil crisis made it impossible for the schools who were willing to cooperate with the Hansard end to be regularly visited from York. Also most of the teachers' groups (as will be seen in more detail later), meeting after work, purely volun-tarily and with no leader able to devote definite and substantial time to drafting, proved unable to produce anything in time, or in some cases even to keep going at all. Only the History group worked as planned and possibly the further education or general studies group. With hindsight, we could perhaps have negotiated some such arrangements beforehand, with five or six friendly LEAs, as we have now been able to do in hope and preparation for diffusion. But would they have been willing to cooperate in such a sensitive field until we had something definite to show? It is at least doubtful. (There are now so many official expressions that something needs to be done about political education, but a general reluctance to give a lead until it can be seen what happens else-where.)

However, York quickly realised that of their main two objectives, to monitor the Hansard innovations and to monitor any other examples of good teaching practice, the latter was the most practicable and certainly the most cost-effective. And in the first year, as we at the Hansard end tried to get our groups going and to look ahead for cooperating schools for the second year, it became clear that the only schools likely to cooperate (without long delays and official negotiations) were those doing something already. Some of them indeed had already been influenced to some extent by the articles in *Teaching Politics* or in Derek Heater's pioneering anthology, *The Teaching of Politics*, Methuen, 1969, which led to the setting up of this Programme.

Therefore, the direct link we had originally hoped for between production of materials and assessment of them broke down. In its place, we think more usefully, Hansard concentrated on (a) clarifying the principles (as in documents 2.1, 2.2, 2.3 and 2.4); (b) turning them into clear guidelines for the local production or adaptation of curricula (as in documents 2.5, 2.6, 2.7, 2.8 and 3.1); and (c) producing some *examples* of curricular modules capable of being slotted into other subjects or forming part of General Studies (as in sections 3.2, 3.3, 3.4 and 3.5). But at the same time they produced some detailed observations on the way in which teachers in five different schools and one college of further education attempted to put into practice the project recommendations, together with some commentaries based on the development officers' observations of how successful (in a particular sense) the attempts were. It may well be this Section, 4, which will be examined most closely by Chief Education Officers, Advisers, Head Teachers and members of Management Committees. York was then to concentrate on a more elaborate assessment of examples of existing teaching practice and on the diffusion of papers and advice likely to be of immediate help to teachers. We will comment later (paragraphs 1.6, 1.7 and 1.8) on how well we think our revised strategy worked; but there is an inherent dilemma in any project of this kind in Politics or Social Studies. Clear guidelines are needed, both to help the teacher and, by setting standards of professionalism, to act as safeguards in the public interest. And we became more and more intellectually aware that our key document 2.2, Political literacy, with its diagram, 'the political literacy tree', is not to be seen simply as an outline for developing curricula, rather than as a check list to assess whether any or all of many different kinds of actual curricula are likely to enhance political literacy. But teachers also want actual materials to use and, in the pressure of work, often with no time for preparation except their own leisure time, will often welcome ready-made lessons. Yet a ready-made package can rarely fit local circumstances if, as seems widely agreed, issues must be discussed which touch upon or are closely analogous to the experience of a particular group of pupils. The danger of producing examples for local adaptation is that they never get adapted. The danger of not producing them is that, like Milton's rebel angels, we beat our wings in the empyrean void in vain. So, like the famous translators of the Authorised Version of the Bible, we have tried to steer a middle course between being too precise and too free, too concrete or too abstract, too homely or too remote, indeed between offering too much or too little.

1.5 The status and summary of the working papers

THE STATUS AND SUMMARY OF THE PROJECT PAPERS

The documents (reproduced in Section 2), which have been widely circulated already, serve different purposes. Document 2.1 was our original statement of intent, somewhat modified in practice as we have just said. Document 2.2, though written speculatively by Bernard Crick and Ian Lister, was firmly endorsed by the Working Party who made clear, which to us is very important, that the objective of general political education should be 'political literacy' and neither simply knowledge nor simply skills of politicising or participation; and, indeed, we all hold that certain attitudes are involved if a person is truly politically literate rather than, say, politically aggressive, effective, reliable or even knowledgeable or wise.

Document 2.3 on Basic Concepts by Bernard Crick reflects the Working Party's firm view that political literacy implies some basic vocabulary of terms used in a reasonably consistent manner over and above the slogans of political rhetoric and debate; it reflects their view, also, that having said that, someone must offer the ordinary teacher a plausible and sensible answer to the obvious question, 'Yes, perhaps – but what concepts?' But the detailed content of his schema is not endorsed by the Working Party.

Document 2.4 on Procedural Values is of a similar status to document 2.3 – or we might say, 'ever more so'. The Working Party does hold that attempts to study politics which purport to be free of values are mistaken and self-deceiving, but not all would agree with how Bernard Crick has tried to show precisely what values are necessarily involved in political literacy. Document 2.5 Issues and Political Problems and its Appendix, Constructing a Programme and Teaching Issues and Political Problems (document 2.6), reflect the Working Party's firm recommendation that political education is best approached initially through political issues, not, as is so common, through learning about institutions or being taught what, according to some elaborate theory, are 'the basic problems'. But the suggestions as to how to identify issues in a reasoned and reasonably objective way (for choice of issues worries many people more than discussing issues as such) and to build them into a curriculum, while relatively technical are also relatively personal to Alex Porter and Robert Stradling.

To these documents, the original policy statements of the Programme, have been added a paper by Robert Stradling, Notes for a Spiral Curriculum for Developing Political Literacy, and one by Alex Porter, Outline of a Civics Syllabus, which although originally submitted in evidence, were felt by the Working Party to be logical extensions of document 2.5 and its appendix, document 2.6, and so should appear together with them as if they were original commissioned and circulated papers of the Programme, and with the same reservations attached. The speculative nature of all these documents can be seen, for instance, in how Robert Stradling takes issue with and would change some of Bernard Crick's proposed concepts in document 2.3 when it comes to trying to adapt them to a curricular proposal. A summary of these papers will help those who have not read them understand better our findings and

11

our recommendations, but those familiar with the papers could well go straight on to 1.6.

(Document 2.1)
We have already repeated most of this in what is written above on the need for political education, the general philosophy behind the Programme and its original strategy. But three paragraphs in this introductory paper (11–13) have been somewhat lost sight of in subsequent work or possibly taken for granted and should be stressed.

The Working Party identified three different possible objectives of political education which are often seen as political alternatives, and as mutually exclusive:

a. The purely and properly conserving level of knowing how our present system of government works, and knowing the beliefs that are thought to be part of it.
b. The liberal or participatory level of development of the knowledge, attitudes and skills necessary for an active citizenship.
c. Beyond both of these there lies the more contentious area of considering possible changes of direction of government or of alternative systems.

We said that the last was, indeed, a perfectly proper area of educational concern, capable of treatment without gross bias, but only when taken together with some consideration of the previous two. We are inclined to doubt the alleged stimulating effect of starting the teaching of politics by dealing with extreme or minority 'rousing' viewpoints – as some have argued. The educational justification can be that dealing with this third objective is habituating the pupil to the critical use of partisan sources, such as he will meet in the real world, whereas the second only habituates him to, at the best, conflicts of values or more often simply to following through the implications of his own beliefs. The original paper suggested that these three different objectives can be seen as a sequence of stages or levels through which a full programme for political education in secondary schools could move. But it is now felt that no strict temporal sequence should be implied. To be relevant and to arouse interest, the experience of many teachers suggests, an immediate consideration of alternatives can sometimes stimulate students into appreciating how specific and significant are the ordinary institutions (of the first category) which otherwise they would take completely for granted or regard as banal. However, equally obviously, any prolonged consideration of alternative institutions or societies should only be returned to after facts and opinions about conservation and the opportunities and limits of participation have been considered in some depth. The safest generalisation, in other words, is that all three objectives must find their place in a curriculum together and not be taught in isolation or to the exclusion of the others.

Right from the beginning, then, we stressed that theories of the aims of political education are necessarily close to the main doctrines of politics, of conservation, participation, and of change. Perhaps it is for this reason that we prefer to see the objective of our whole Programme as to enhance 'political literacy' rather than 'political education'. Strictly speaking, political education could be seen as instrumental: working towards realising certain pre-conceived political objectives. The politically literate man or woman would be somebody who (however he or she may act in a personal capacity) can appreciate the plausibility of, give some good account of the nature and implications of, each of these three doctrines. It is hard, indeed, to see how any account of politics can be plausible which does not draw, in different circumstances and for different purposes, on each of these three theories or doctrines.

POLITICAL LITERACY (Document 2.2)
This paper discusses the central concept of the project. It explains that by political literacy we mean a compound of knowledge, skills and attitudes, to be developed together, each one conditioning the other two. To meet the needs of the vast majority of young people, basic political literacy means a practical understanding of concepts drawn from everyday life and language. To have achieved political literacy is to have learnt what the main political disputes are about, what beliefs the main contestants have of them, how they are likely to affect you and me. It also means that we are likely to be predisposed to try to do something about the issue in question in a manner which is at once effective and respectful of the sincerity of other people and what they believe.

The paper emphasises that we do not mean something only attained in one way. We are not postulating some universal role or model. There are alternative ways of attaining it as of attaining any skill. But there are common elements which exemplify and typify politically literate persons, what they know, their attitude to what they know and their skill in using what they know.

By way of further explanation three questions are posed and answered:

What kinds of knowledge would a politically literate person possess? (i) The basic information about the issue: who holds the power; where the money comes from; how the institution in question works. (This may apply to Parliament, a committee of the County Council, a factory, a school, a trade union, a club or a family.) (ii) How to be actively involved using the knowledge of (i) and understanding the nature of the issue. (iii) How to estimate the most effective way of resolving the issue. (iv) How to recognise how well policy objectives have been achieved when the issue is settled. (v) How to comprehend the viewpoints of other people and their justifications for their actions, and always to expect and to offer justifications oneself.

Such knowledge is used at different levels by different people. Someone who is highly politically literate will possess the ability to apply sophisticated political concepts. He is also aware of what he does not know, but he knows where that knowledge can be obtained. Basic political literacy for a majority means grasping concepts which grow out of situations which lie within everybody's personal experience.

What are the attitudes of a politically literate person? These must of necessity vary. It is no part of this project to expect that all the values of Western European liberalism will be taken for granted or can be applicable everywhere. What we have inherited as part of our tradition must be subject to criticism and sometimes scepticism. There is in our view no *correct* attitude to be inculcated as part of political literacy; nevertheless, attitudes will inevitably be adopted, and they will be based consciously or unconsciously on values. The author of Document 4 identifies 'freedom', 'toleration', 'fairness', 'respect for truth' and 'respect for reasoning' as what he calls 'procedural values': values which are presupposed in political literacy.

What skills would a politically literate person possess? The politically literate person is not merely an informed spectator: he is someone capable of active participation or of positive refusal to participate. At the same time the politically literate person, while tolerating the views of others, is capable of thinking in terms of change and of methods of achieving change. We recognise that the chief difficulty lying in the way of educating for political literacy is not that this might encourage bias on the part of students or indoctrination on the part of teachers, but that it should inevitably and rightly encourage action. We are confident that political action is worthy of encouragement if it is based on knowledge and understanding. Knowledge and understanding cover not only the facts which go to make up the conflict, but the views of the disputants. Empathy with different viewpoints is greatly to be encouraged. All of this is summed up in what has become known as the 'Political Literacy Tree', reproduced in full in document 2.2.

Finally we stress that the media, not the school, inevitably supply much of the information about politics that a person needs: the role of the school is to help pupils handle this information in a critical way, and to help them to form their own opinions, to appreciate those of others, and to give them the will and the means to participate in an effective and responsible manner. We assume that, as part of a general education, pupils acquire some general knowledge of the kind of society in which they live, its people, its history and the broad economic and geographical factors that define and limit that society.

BASIC CONCEPTS (Document 2.3)
This paper first appeared as 'Basic Concepts for Political Education' in *Teaching Politics*, September 1975. It argues that a politically literate person should possess a vocabulary of concepts from which he or she could construct very simple and elementary frameworks for political understanding; and that these need not be and should not be drawn from the technical concepts of political science as a discipline, but rather from terms used in everyday life, yet employed more precisely and systematically than is usual. The paper simply attempts to suggest one set of possible basic concepts and to offer working definitions of them for the teacher to apply to whatever materials he or she is using.

The paper argues that concepts as such, broadly and usefully defined, can be for all practical purposes regarded as 'value-free'; but when concepts are put to use either in argument or in explanation, then they inevitably take on some bias, slant or value.

The concepts chosen were treated as genuinely *basic* or *primary*, that is those from which others more complex can be derived and on which theories, generalisations, explanations and moral judgements can be based. But these primary concepts are not necessarily what people regard as the most important or the most widely used terms. For instance, 'Democracy' is plainly a most important concept, but it is a compound of more basic concepts. Anyone who understands what is meant by 'individuality', 'liberty' and 'representation' can build up the concept of Democracy, although some usages of Democracy also build into themselves notions of 'welfare'. Plainly it is not much use teaching in a pseudo-Socratic manner by asking conundrums of the kind, 'what is *the* definition of Democracy or of Equality?' for straightaway one is faced with several different and plausible theories and doctrines about what should be done or how things should be done. One can better begin by trying to establish common usages of basic concepts from which these more complicated and value-laden concepts are derived.

So we developed what is essentially the oldest and simplest model of politics: the perception that it is about the relationships of rulers to ruled, the few to the many, 'them and us' and the possible relationships between them. Diagramatically thus.

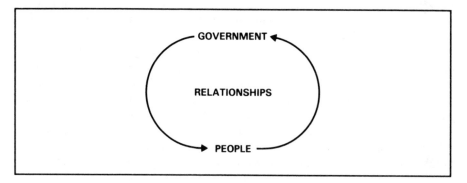

But a more elaborate model was developed, though still extraordinarily simple compared with most conceptual frameworks in political science – thus:

GOVERNMENT			
Power	Force	Authority	Order
RELATIONSHIPS			
Law	Justice	Representation	Pressure
PEOPLE			
Natural Rights	Individuality	Freedom	Welfare

Implicit in the paper is an argument that the study of politics should begin not with considering general theories but with clarifying simple concepts. This a class can do, with the guidance of the teacher, very much for themselves – a matter of discussion and exploration. Theories, however, whether of Liberalism, Conservatism, or Socialism, whether of élites, class or status – as in political sociology – will always have to be taught to and learnt by the age groups we are considering. Better that they come to form some general explanations themselves, however incomplete or tentative, after gaining some understanding, than that classes of fifteen to seventeen year-olds are given the illusion of general explanation which can rarely correspond to their own experience or abilities.

PROCEDURAL VALUES (Document 2.4)

The paper makes the specific claim that 'freedom', 'toleration', 'fairness', 'respect for truth' and 'respect for reasoning' are 'procedural' values in that there cannot be any reasonable process or progress of study or practice of politics, other than simple indoctrination, which does not presuppose, however minimally, such values. The study of politics cannot be neutral towards these values: its own existence depends on encouraging them, indeed it presupposes their existence. The politically literate person, in so far as he is genuinely literate and not simply accidentally effective (i.e. by having the right kind of narrowness and intensity for a particular situation), will be able to act, change his mind, appreciate other points of view, weigh evidence and arguments fairly and recognise the difference between truth and ideology. And if he cannot always draw such distinctions in practice, he will at least recognise that through education there are such distinctions to be drawn.

The paper criticises any attempt, whether Marxist or Liberal–Capitalist, or whatever, to build into the whole activity of political education the very assumptions that they wish through practice to universalise. For example, this paper itself has been criticised both for omitting 'market values' as basic political values, and for not adopting a 'critical stance' to the frequent association of these very procedural values with 'Bourgeois Capitalism'. But our argument is that even such theories themselves when they are at the theoretical and formative stage (ignoring what may happen in practice), must presuppose something like our procedural values if there is to be intellectual activity at all.

We hold that it is both proper and possible for the teacher to nurture and strengthen these procedural values precisely because they are educational values, rational and public. It is a quite different matter from the teacher attempting 'to impose his values' upon a class – this usually and often all too correctly means imposing his doctrines. People who seek literally to impose doctrines are rarely respecting procedural values.

Working definitions of the procedural values are then elaborated much in the way that the basic concepts were.

ISSUES AND POLITICAL PROBLEMS (Document 2.5)

The theoretical basis on which the Programme for Political Education is based is rounded off in a paper Issues and Political Problems by Robert Stradling and Alex Porter with contributions and comments from many of the teachers working with the project. The authors regard it as very much open to amendment.

This paper describes issues as disagreements over:

> **goals** – where are we going? What purposes would a given action serve?
> **values** – in what way should we act or not act?
> **methods** – how should we do it?
> **results** – was it the right outcome? the fairest? the best? the one that was required?

Not all issues are necessarily political. Some may be purely technical, scientific, artistic or moral. An issue is political only if it creates the kind of conflict within the group which threatens the continued existence of that group. Conflict arises, they say, under the following conditions:

a. when there is a dispute amongst the members of the group concerning the allocation of resources or over values;
b. when the disputing members of the group demand a common decision to be taken which will be binding on the whole group;
c. when this common decision has to be taken if the group is to continue.

They see five ways in which teachers can select issues. The first three are objective measures: the findings of national opinion polls; use of the media at national and local level; and material issued by a political party in the form of manifestos, electoral addresses and party political broadcasts. The last two are more subjective, they represent the politics of everyday life, either issues which in the teacher's judgement are close to the experience of a class or issues actually selected by the pupils themselves.

The appendix to document 2.5 (section 2.6 in this report) makes some suggestions about the construction of a course or teaching programme on the above lines. The author warns that certain guidelines should be kept in mind when choosing examples. Issues must be appropriate to and manageable in a particular context; there must be sufficient resource material on them; above all, they must be of a nature which can kindle the interest of pupils. While national issues are clearly important, they are not always issues which have especial relevance in a particular locality.

These two papers try to show that issues for classroom discussion can be chosen according to clearly statable criteria, not the whim or prejudice of a particular teacher. But the criteria are not concerned with whether issues are contentious or not, or indeed with whether they are particularly important or not, but with whether they can be handled in the classroom in such a way as to enhance political literacy. And political literacy is best enhanced by exploring in depth a few issues rather than trying to cover everything in a short time. What seems most suitable for a lesson, however, can often be modified by the motivation of the class. Elsewhere we note (Section 4) that when classes have a hand in choosing which issues to discuss, the success of a lesson seems greater. The issue is, however, always less important than the manner in which it is discussed.

NOTES FOR A SPIRAL CURRICULUM (Document 2.7)
This paper was written during the final year of the project and has not been circulated to teachers on as wide a scale as the other five documents. It is also more tentative. The author emphasises that the paper outlines only one of several possible frameworks for developing a 'spiral' approach to teaching politics. Ultimately, a suitable spiral curriculum will only emerge through a process of trial and error in the classroom. However, for one example of how this approach might be put into practice, see the outline of a Civics syllabus by Alex Porter (document 2.8).

The paper contends that a key aspect in enhancing the individual's political literacy is the development of a structured mode of thinking about political problems and situations. It argues that this can best be achieved through a curriculum which revisits and refortifies continually the central organising ideas and concepts of politics, firstly in simple, concrete and familiar contexts and then 'spiralling' outwards to a wider framework and building upon these ideas until the student has grasped the structured mode of thought which underlies the political literacy approach. To this end the paper discusses which ideas and political concepts might be thought of as fundamental and why; and it considers the relationships between them. Some of the problems connected with this approach are also considered.

1.6 Group reports and findings

What has been already said about the Programme's general strategy needs some further explanation concerning what we commissioned and what we actually got.

We wanted (a) to set up working groups to produce curricula in each conventional subject which could show how political literacy could be enhanced through it; and (b) to produce a model of a two-year programme with two or three periods of its own a week, which we would call 'Civics'. We also wanted (c) to look at two special problems defined by type of institution rather than subject: teacher training and low-level further education.

Experience of several groups showed the difficulty of keeping a curriculum development group alive without LEA support and/or considerable backing in terms of time off and greater resources for documentation and replication than we could offer. To try, indeed, to produce curricula in order to stimulate demand can prove difficult if the producing groups are not already convinced that there is a clear demand. Perhaps the only curricula worth publishing in permanent form are those that have been revised after appraisal and assessment in use. This means keeping groups alive with expert help for assessment for several years. It is plainly difficult enough, with the tremendous pressures on time, for an individual teacher even to re-do completely a single course that he or she is teaching, let alone join in such complicated exercises.

The most effective groups in terms of production were those who, somewhat against the grain of the Programme, either had a definite examination as a target, as in the N and F group, or assumed an examination context, as is obvious in most of the History modules. However, the work of these two groups at least shows that there is no formal contradiction between the objectives of political literacy and possible examination syllabuses.

The Civics group proved abortive. This could be blamed on accident and resources. The first convenor made some attempt to begin, but had not constituted a group before leaving due to pressure of work, leaving us insufficient time to start again. With the task of running the most active group, together with having three or four other groups to service and many schools and LEAs to contact towards arranging trials or observation of existing teaching, no one full-time officer could pick up these lost threads himself. Resources are involved. Looking at it again, we plainly needed a full-time development officer and a full-time field officer right from the beginning, and working together. Or perhaps our working groups should have been set up before the funded Programme began. We received funds to meet as a Working Party to amend and resubmit our original application, perhaps we should have tried to set up the groups at that stage. But this would have given the groups of teachers far less say in what they were to do.

However, there were differences of opinion about what the Civics group should do, or about the value of a 'two-year over-arching programme', which somewhat inhibited action in trying to get this group going again or reconstituted. Some of us seemed wedded to 'political literacy by indirection', the strategy of permeation, to the exclusion of the 'big push' strategy – a comprehensive model programme purely of politics or civics. And those of us who believed strongly in the big push, did not do so exclusively, so could not pursue it with a single-minded zeal. Besides, like many curricular projects, we were certainly not blinded, but were made a little short-sighted by our own rhetoric. The rhetoric was, of course, that particularly in political education, particularly in our political literacy approach with its stress on skills and the 'politics of everyday life', principles (such as in our five or six basic documents) *must be interpreted in local situations*. Some of us thought that this merely meant that any detailed curriculum we provided as a model would be so interpreted and heavily adapted in actual teaching, whereas others thought that the provision of a detailed two-year programme would necessarily be something rigid, even contradicting our stress on adaptability, i.e. the teacher must choose what issues to tackle himself and assemble his own documentation etc. Here again are two theoretical positions which, in practice, can be reversed: for knowing how hard pressed most teachers are, some of those against over-specification can yet admit that initial over-specification, the ready-made lesson, is the only way in; and those in favour of providing the ready-made lesson will, nevertheless, in practice, appreciate how intensely difficult it is to provide materials that fulfil the sort of criteria of relevance and interest detailed in document 5 and its appendix (Section 2.5 and 2.6).

At the end of the day, both the experience of the Programme's officers and the opinions of the Working Party do seem to indicate that even if we could have produced a detailed marching plan, it would have had to include a great many gaps, a great many areas where virtue would have been made of improvisation by the teacher and the alleged greater closeness to a pupil's experience of local rather than national politics. The sensitivity of the whole area points towards being as specific as possible, so that everything is above board and, however contentious, defendable in public; but the difficulties of teaching point to the need for a great deal of flexibility and local experiment, but within definite guidelines.

So the paper, Alex Porter's 'Outline of a Civic's Syllabus', which we have included with the basic documents in Section 2 (document 2.8), is very much guidelines and even then not the product of a group, although it emerged from the general discussions and policies of the Working Party. We think, indeed, that it could form the starting point for the work of the local groups who (as described in Geoffrey Petter's report to the Schools Council in Appendix C) stand ready to produce detailed curricula adjusted to local needs and conditions. Robert Stradling's 'Notes for a Spiral Curriculum' (see document 2.7) gives more guidance to the same end on possible teaching methods. He shows that what matters is less the particular institutions or issue tackled (which are difficult to specify in advance of meeting and appraising a particular class), than whether certain basic concepts (on which he has his own views) are exemplified in any such material in such a way that they keep on recurring and reinforcing themselves: not the 'now that's done' attitude to an examination syllabus, but 'these same ideas need amending or elaborating a bit' in tackling this new problem.

Only the History and the Further Education groups, worked more-or-less as planned. The History group limited themselves to materials immediately usable by good sixth forms, but there seems no reason in principle why the same kind of materials cannot be used lower down the school. Derek Heater's report carries its own self-criticism about the difficulty of actually keeping the group together, so that some of the material was produced by corresponding members and none of the material produced, so fully and helpfully produced, got the final full-scale criticism of the group as a whole which was originally intended. History as a discipline and history teachers as a group are plainly still the most likely and effective allies – allowing for very many local exceptions. But as yet, despite the keen interest of some of HM Inspectors and advisers in history to encourage the application of history to political education, progress has been limited. Our History reports show that a great deal of effort can have its rewards in the short-term in convincing history teachers that a few lessons, mainly drawn simply from the concepts in the political literacy diagrams, can be used in a lively and effective way to revise already familiar or semi-familiar material. But this has its limitations as political education. It can seem more like the application of the methods of our political literacy ideas to the goal of learning history, than the application of a sense of history to political problems. In the long run, we hope that history teachers can apply their way of looking at things to our full specification of political literacy which must surely involve some topical or contemporary issues, not simply historical issues; and involve some skills of participation in issues close to the experience of the pupils.

The N and F group was not part of the original plan. It was added by the Hansard Society, with the approval of this Programme, but did not have to report to our Working Party, and was funded directly by the Schools Council as one of the feasibility studies. Yet we include their report, drafted by Alex Porter, because it shows very clearly that the political literacy approach can be made into a syllabus even for relatively conventional examination purposes. Even if the GCE examinations are still unreformed by the twenty-first century, our proposals could well be pirated or cannibalised to form a relatively conventional A level. If so, they would show that preparation for higher education and general education in the sixth form are, in one case at least, far from incompatible. No study has yet been made of what, if anything, university and polytechnic departments hope for in seemingly relevant GCE syllabuses; but the strong subjective impression is that they do not and would not (even if they thought about it) specify content, or a definite measure of attainment. Rather – one often hears said, vaguely but from the heart – that what is wanted is 'a sense of politics'. We may have been able to show that this is not necessarily so vague at all, and while the social need for political literacy is, indeed, for 'all our nation's children' not just the sixth form (so this report has otherwise ignored examination work in politics); yet we have become impressed in the course of the field work that unless a subject (or whatever we call it) has a firm base in specialised appointments in the fifth and sixth forms, it is not likely to have much influence lower down the school.

English and Political Literacy by Maureen Whitebrook will tell its own tale of difficulty in creating a group and keeping it alive, but again produces very useful materials as well as sensible guidelines. It is hard to draw clear conclusions from the report. Possibilities for cooperation are tantalisingly rich, both in the highly political content of many works of literature commonly found in syllabuses and in the growing use made by practical teachers of English of highly charged political and social materials in the context of 'Use of English' or 'Communication Skills' – when formal literature is, alas, often too difficult or remote to provide motivation for basic literacy. But there are some signs that teachers of English tend to polarise into the academic or traditional, defending literature against allcomers, intolerant of its 'use' for non-literary purposes; and the radical teacher of English who sees politics, indeed, everywhere but primarily as commitment or stirring-up. We cannot generalise from one failure to get a group going, nor be elated at the possibilities that these materials demonstrate, but it could be the case that teaching politics through literature or through 'Use of English' is a strategy more relevant to teachers lower down the school, than it appears to fifth or sixth form English teachers. However, it may well be that our general arguments, presented in their most intellectual form and in the right places, could have more eventual effect on teachers of English than any immediate provision of suitable and relevant teaching materials and curricula which they will probably refuse to touch if not coming from themselves.

The Further Education group certainly worked as a group in that it developed a mind and, to some extent, a methodology of its own. Linda Dove and Geoffrey Stanton have argued that 'situations', typically involving problems about the allocation or resources (supposing that there are not enough chairs to go round in the classroom, etc.) are closer to the experience of their pupils than many so-called political issues. Through situations, they argue, including games and simulations, students can gain political skills and some grasp in use, as it were, of basic political concepts. This is an interesting alternative approach. They emphasise, however, 'that feedback to us from teachers in the field was less than we hoped'. Indeed, they offer several suggestions from lecturers to explain why, apparently, 'students may use their freedom to opt out'. A difficulty with the situation approach, particularly with young adults rather than the 'desert island' games or 'classroom elections' often used with eleven to fourteen year-olds, is that the issues may simply seem trivial, or at least not real, red-blooded enough. We simply do not know. Robert Stradling's new group (working directly from the Hansard Society and funded by the Anglo-German Foundation for the Study of Industrial Society) is attempting to provide detailed classroom materials for young further education classes more directly based on salient political issues. So there may soon be a possibility of comparison. We may doubt whether all the materials that our further education group has provided are best used by further education students; but there is no doubt that many of their suggestions will be very useful to teachers 'lower down the school'. Certainly their formal lack of either academic or politically substantive content is of some advantage and exemplifies very well the sharp distinction that the Programme has tried to draw, right from the beginning, between the objectives of political literacy and the discipline of political science. It is not that the matter is any simpler: 'feedback on these lessons has revealed the complex range of skills needed for political literacy'. We conclude that any such modules will reveal gaps in these skills (as well as obviously in politically relevant knowledge) that then call for remedial action. There is a sense in which a very few such hours of teaching towards political literacy act as a diagnostic device rather than secure attainment of a skill. But will the remedial time be provided later and by who?

The Teacher Training group, convened by Tom Brennan, acted very much as a real group in that they decided that their given terms of reference to produce a model Politics module for teacher training were mistaken, since the chances of any one taking it up at this time were so small; so instead they concentrated on trying to discover what goes on already. The ideas behind their change of objective are (i) that policy decisions need to be made by governing bodies, so it is no use offering nice presents to overworked and often quite hostile teacher trainers – so governing bodies may be impressed by the lack of provision; and (ii) but that, nonetheless, it is better to build up slowly on what does exist already – and we simply did not know that, politics being either absent in teacher training or completely subsumed (sometimes smothered) in other disciplines. Their findings are alarming. Few teachers in training received anything that can be remotely said to relate to politics, political literacy or civics, either as an academic study (the substance) or as a professional study (the method). We are far from convinced that only graduates in politics or B.Ed.s with politics as a major component can teach effectively for political literacy. But we endorse very strongly the recommendations of the teacher training group that every LEA should offer in-service training in politics, as well as the need for departments or colleges of education to develop this area. Tom Brennan's group point out something obvious and very important, often neglected in our considerations, that many teachers do not attempt or are insecure in teaching civics not just through lack of courses of the 'teaching methods for political literacy' type, but lack of both basic and refresher courses on the content of politics. Here university and polytechnic political science departments could be far more helpful than all but two or three (and three extra-mural departments) have shown any signs of being. At the suggestion of the chairman of this Programme, a joint letter was circulated to heads of departments in universities and polytechnics by the chairmen of the Political Studies Association, and of the Politics Association, making such suggestions. The letter was circulated in the Autumn of 1975. In the spring of 1976 about eighty people attended a session on the work of this Programme at the Political Studies Association annual conference. Only six had heard of the circular. It is hard to avoid the conclusion that most heads of departments see school links as too much trouble except for recruitment. There is need for short courses, on an evening or half-day release basis, for school and further education teachers particularly on British politics and institutions but also on political ideas and issues. This is quite apart from the need for similar training courses that LEA teachers' centres, colleges, departments and institutes of education could provide.

We should have tackled Geography or Local Studies, since many teachers of these subjects now consider problems of local planning and environmental control which either involve them in learning about local politics and political institutions, or need to. Again a rather belated attempt was made but not pressed hard enough, with all our other involvements, partly because of confidence that at least one influential centre is working in this field on remarkable parallel lines to our own; information has been exchanged, meetings taken place and they stand ready to help if there is any attempt at diffusing our guidelines and findings. (See Appendix C.)

We should have tackled, given a far bigger programme, economics and also social studies. Economics, however, is rarely interested in anything other than sixth forms and GCE examination programmes. Social studies has an internal tension between those who see it as something very specific (usually schools of sociology) and therefore, in theory at least, very open to inter-disciplinary cooperation, and those who see it as very wide, a comprehensive social science, so wide indeed that like the jaws of the Lady of Riga's tiger it tends to swallow rather than relate to those subjects, like economics and politics, which it regards as its own sub-categories. However, most readers will probably feel, whatever the quality of our reports and whatever the omissions, that there are enough of them (a) to give teachers some immediate help and (b) to make some definite general points for a wider public. What points?

1.7 Findings based on the observed teaching programmes

Alex Porter's observations on four schools or colleges, together with Geoffrey Petter's report on one school, speak for themselves and contain their own conclusions (see Section 4). This section also includes an appendix explaining the methods used which includes important qualifications and a warning about the dangers of subjectivity with only one observer involved in each case. Though they followed broadly the same method of observation, yet the two observers plainly did not always look at things in quite the same way. What sounds like much the same kind of teaching situation in two different schools is described by Geoffrey Petter as a truly 'Socratic exchange' between the master and the boys but by Alex Porter as an example of 'closed-ended' predetermined question-and-answer routine incompatible with the political literacy objectives of this Programme. Perhaps, as Max Beerbohm once remarked, 'the Socratic method is not a game that two can play'. A situation of wide-ranging and open-ended discussion, dominated by the class, is described by Alex Porter as 'democratic', whereas Geoffrey Petter would approach a similar situation more sceptically as showing 'a relaxed informality'. Nonetheless, certain important general conclusions seem to emerge which influence our final recommendations.

'The teaching programmes which were most successful were those which were devised after the project had made its initial recommendations rather than those which were adapted to the project.' Alex Porter argues from his observations that the difficulties are greater than we first imagined of infusing political literacy indirectly, as some time on the side of, or a way of rendering more interesting, a conventional (say) History syllabus; or for that matter, a conventional A level course in British Government. If the two sets of objectives conflict, it will always be the political literacy objectives that suffer. Partly this is a subject restraint, but also an examination restraint. Pupils as well as teachers are trapped and grow impatient, in examination classes, of anything not likely to be bang on a possible question. The answer may be, of course (certainly for 'British Government'), reform of the syllabuses rather than any implication (which we do not make) that external examinations as such would necessarily hinder the flexibility and appeals to local experience inherent in the political literacy objective. But, nonetheless, despite obvious advantages, History and British Government as vehicles for political literacy showed some signs of, at the worst, crushing the hitch-hiker beyond recognition or, at the best, of simply taking him somewhere else, certainly compared to even a few hours' journey in a vehicle, however small, deliberately set aside for courses designed to enhance political literacy. Yet realistically the only opportunity for political education in many schools may be its infusion through the cognate established subjects of the curriculum.

Within such courses it seemed to emerge that 'The more successful ... were planned to focus on one or two issues and to explore them in depth. Those programmes which touched on several issues per lesson or which were not planned but rather were opportunistic, exploiting issues as they arose incidentally in the lesson, were markedly less successful'. This observation supports the view taken in documents 2.2 and 2.5 that the exploration of even a single issue in considerable depth, to involve all of the operations we would seek to assess in the 'literacy tree', will do more for general political literacy, will create a disposition and a skill that is readily transferable to other issues by the pupil himself, than any attempt to cover in a short time 'the main issues of modern British politics' and, of course, some World Affairs also (for we are not insular, are we?). This insistence of ours has puzzled some teachers. The point to be made is that 'political literacy' is not a subject like 'Current Affairs', indeed is specifically not current affairs. It is more a disposition and a skill. It is less 'knowing what all the issues are' than knowing how to handle any issue. To say that, however, is not to deny that it needs some hours on its own; or, for that matter, is not to be fussy what these hours are called: politics, civics, social studies, current affairs, world affairs or part of a general studies course. 'What's in a name?', indeed; but the rose by whatever name does seem to need some soil of her own in which to grow her roots, though when once even modestly established, her shoots can intertwine with several other plants to mutual benefit and support.

Within such a small sample we can learn nothing directly about what effect the organisation and style of management of a school as a whole can have on political literacy. Alex Porter reports: 'All the schools were similar in their characters – very friendly, relaxed and welcoming. Students were happy and cooperative. They were not the sort of places where, for example, one would expect truancy and discipline to be a problem.' But if his comments had somewhere indicated a lack of welcome, strained relationships and disciplinary problems, it would be surprising that these particular visits had been allowed or made. Schools are well used to receiving visitors; but a school whose characteristics appeared to be the reverse of those described by Alex Porter would have been unlikely to provide a fruitful experience for this project. Such a school would probably be unable to provide anything like a political literacy programme demanding at least some 'relaxed informality' in discussion between teachers and classes, presuming also that teachers are confident enough of their relationship with students to let a class have its own head not merely in discussion but in decision-making processes about what topics to discuss. We are not suggesting that a 'good school' includes some form of political education and that a 'bad school' does not. But we believe that a school which does include a political literacy component is unlikely to be a 'bad school' – i.e. one with indiscipline, rejection of learning, and/or grimly authoritarian. We do not believe that relaxed and informal discussion in class is a prescription for the undermining of authority. There is the famous story of George Endicott Peabody, High Master of Grotton Academy in Massachusetts, who was, in his relations with his colleagues and pupils, 'determined to be liberal if it killed him'; and it did. Nowhere do we argue against authority in schools: on the contrary, a legitimate authority can allow itself to be questioned, perhaps even thrives on questioning. Political literacy need not begin with discussing the school itself as a system of political authority: but it may be the mark of a 'good school' that this can be done without fear.

From limited observations, it is only possible to make conjectures about the character of the school as a whole. Alex Porter nevertheless implies that it may be possible to make generalisations based on observations of the atmosphere in a classroom and data from discussions with staff and students. Hence, in situations where teachers tended, by comparison with some others, to be less arbitrary and authoritarian and to allow more choice of what topics to study, not merely were the Programme's specifications of political literacy better met, but, in the context of those specifications, the atmosphere in the school might generally be regarded as more 'democratic' (using that term in its most commonsensical and least ideological sense).

A small but important finding was that: 'in the coeducational schools the girls generally appeared less willing to answer or to initiate questions. Question and answer being, after all, a basic and primary form of participation, this [finding] could prove significant'. But as no single sex girls' school was involved in the study, we cannot tell whether girls on their own would talk politics more or whether they regard it as an inherently male matter or muddle, certainly in the way it is commonly presented. This is a problem that would repay further study and which we regret not spotting earlier. Some contentious political issues that concern women particularly are not hard to identify.

'Without doubt, the most important feature was the extent to which, and the way in which, teachers enabled their students to participate in the teaching programme.' Some apparently lively discussion turned out to be simply rigid question and answer stuff: the teacher, well prepared, asking questions only as a cue for a correct factual answer or a conventional response from a narrow range of options and opinions. Such 'closed-reasoning' surely has little to do with, indeed could actually harm, political literacy or competence of any kind. And some analogies were used in teaching about topical issues, but analogies not of a homely kind, arising from the pupil's experience and enabling him better to join in a discussion, but all too often, on the contrary, analogies to historical events, scarcely known, totally undiscussable, only another hurdle not a help. One teacher had prepared a lesson closely based on our political literacy diagram and showed the viewpoints and groups involved in an issue, how they affected each other, how they might affect the students, alternatives, etc., the lot; but all this as a sprightly lecture to an inert and uninvolved class. 'This close correlation', Alex Porter claims 'between student participation and the success of the programme, arises not simply because some of the project recommendations depend on such participation, but also because it seems likely that the teaching and learning of concepts and procedural values in particular is better undertaken in this way than by the formal stance of lecturing.'

His general conclusions bear repetition and certainly could modify to some extent one of our original hypotheses: 'Thus, from this limited evidence [detailed in the commentaries which follow] the circumstances most conducive for a successful teaching programme appear to ideally be as follows. The style of teaching and general atmosphere of the school should be versatile, open and reasonably "democratic". That is to say the relationships between teachers and students should be relaxed and informal and there should be considerable give and take in the expression of opinions, the choosing of what to discuss and so on. There should be considerable student participation in as many aspects of the programme as possible. If the students are not actually involved in the preparation of the programme and the selection of subject matter, the means to those objectives should be made explicit to them and they should have a chance of criticising them. The course should be taught by a group of staff and the procedure in lessons should depend as much as possible on student contributions and actuations. It should have been devised with predominantly moral, social and political education objectives rather than adapted from, or to, a course with other competing or overriding objectives. The political literacy objectives are best conveyed through a programme and lessons which consider a limited range of issues supported by "packaged" presentations of background information. The "successful" programme is one which has been constructed in accordance with these factors and is considered by the staff to be a crucial part of the school's curriculum.'

In short, the evidence from our field work suggests that political literacy teaching is most successful where it is done through courses which have been constructed with exclusive political literacy objectives. However, we acknowledge that these objectives are not always either attainable or appropriate to local conditions, and that our evidence is very limited; therefore schools also need to explore the possibility of political literacy objectives being successfully infused or integrated into courses designed to meet other objectives. Indeed, some of the materials in section 3 show ways in which this can be done.

1.8 Recommendations for the improvement of political education in England and Wales

We assert our conviction that it is the need and the right of every pupil in school and young adult in further education to receive a balanced and realistic political education. We see this education primarily in terms of developing the knowledge, skill and disposition that we have called ' political literacy'. With political literacy, a pupil, student or young citizen should then be able to cope better with the political issues and problems whether in industrial or in everyday life that come to him or her either directly or through the newspaper and broadcasting media.

Moreover, what is good for Scotland should be good for the United Kingdom: we note that the Munn Report of the Scottish Education Office has just recommended as part of a study of the whole curriculum that all pupils in the third and fourth years of Scottish secondary school 'should undertake the study of certain units of work which deal with the political, economic, industrial and environmental aspects of life in modern society'.

We are convinced that the work of this Programme having specified what is basically entailed in political literacy, has provided ample evidence that it is capable of being implemented in a sufficiently wide variety of contexts. The teachers participating in the project have clearly demonstrated that, with a minimum of guidance, they can translate the theoretical precepts of political literacy into realistic classroom practice.

Therefore –

(i) We strongly recommend to all those working at every level in education that there should be a basic provision of political education in the common curriculum of all secondary schools and as an open option in all non-compulsory schools and colleges of further education.

(ii) We appreciate that the expansion of political education can only be gradual, so great is the shortage of teachers with relevant training. Nevertheless, this expansion must be a deliberate matter of public policy. We have been convinced that it can be done from within existing resources if college principals and headteachers accept their responsibility in this matter, and if certain outside support is forthcoming.

(iii) We support the recommendation of the Politics Association (see Appendix A) that the Department of Education and Science should take steps to encourage local education authorities to provide resources and support to schools and colleges which seek to include political literacy in their curricula.

These steps should include:

a. The appointment of an HMI with special responsibility for political education.

b. The holding of a national conference on political education in the training of teachers in England and Wales.

c. The provision of in-service training courses for teachers and head-teachers either run directly by DES as can be done or by assisting the Politics Association to do so.

d. A national survey of provision for political education which, if possible, should include Scotland and Northern Ireland.

(iv) We welcome the recent paper on 'Political Competence' produced by two HMIs and its recent publication as an authoritative and moderate statement of needs, aims and methods (see Appendix B).

(v) We believe that for *every* teacher in training some small core of general politics, primarily about British issues and institutions and related international affairs, should form a distinct part of his or her general education; and that political education should be far more widely on offer as an optional subject.

(vi) LEAs, colleges, departments or institutes should provide regular in-service courses since most existing teachers have not been trained in political education and since any expansion must come initially from existing teachers. These need to be courses both of an introductory and of a refresher kind; and most courses should contain both content and method, both political studies and political education.

(vii) Universities and polytechnics should agree to offer as part of their public responsibility short refresher courses (vacation, evening or half-day release) in the content of their subjects to teachers – which is an important and low-cost activity.

(viii) To further the necessary curriculum development and innovation in political education and to advise those who will be offering in-service or short courses, we see a case for some growth of and concentration of resources on the two centres that have shown interest in the field already: the Political Education Research Unit of the Department of Education at York University and the Centre for Political Education at the Institute of Education at London University.

(ix) We see the importance of increasing the number of sixth form and other schools' conferences at which politicians, balanced by party over time, talk to schools and colleges about their policies, in other words to implement on a wide scale the 'Joint Agreement on Sixth-Form Conferences' of 1973 agreed to by the three main parties by the arbitration of the Hansard Society. The Hansard Society and the Politics Association should seek support for this work. But we stress, as did the 'Joint Agreement', that these meetings need careful preparation in the school, need following up and are no substitute for ordinary classes, only an important supplement.

(x) We endorse the recommendations of Geoffrey Petter in his report to the Schools Council (see Appendix C) that it is time that the Schools Council should be more active in this field, particularly to help those LEAs who do stand ready to set up teachers' groups to produce detailed curricula within the guidelines of this programme.

(xi) Our object was not to provide materials. But we have come across many difficulties in teaching through issues in relation to obtaining quickly and cheaply enough a wide range ('balanced' in that sense) of controversial materials. We see the need for the trial of some kind of low-cost weekly or fortnightly magazine for schools which contains such topical documentation drawn from the Press, parties and pressure groups. We think this could be economically viable if the media could waive normal copyright restrictions for such a purpose.

2

The programme's working papers

2.1 An explanatory paper

OBJECTIVE AND ASSUMPTIONS OF THE PROGRAMME

1. Forgive the length of this document but we think it important to share with any one interested all the details we have about this programme at the present time, as well as to state its broad intentions. We do this because we need the criticisms of people in the field at this early stage, particularly suggestions from teachers themselves about how we can best develop our programme to help them. Most of this is informative, but the last paragraph sets out specifically what help is needed in this mutual attempt to raise the standards and relevance of political education.

2. Political education has, in the past, been a somewhat neglected concern of schools, and often handled in a rather *ad hoc* and amateurish way. Now there is both public and educational need to attend to political and civic education – particularly of the mass of school leavers, not simply children of high ability. So a Working Party of educationalists and practising teachers in politics and allied fields has been set up to produce a programme which seeks to establish the basic requisites and minimum political content for education in secondary schools, colleges of education and non-degree work in further education. It aims to produce such a programme together with detailed syllabuses for certain key levels and contexts, arrange for them to be tried out in the classroom and monitored, and will itself appraise existing materials and produce new types for testing. Bernard Crick, Professor of Politics and head of the postgraduate department of Politics and Sociology at Birkbeck College is chairman of the Working Party; Mr Ian Lister, Senior Lecturer in Education at the University of York is head of a small research unit based at York which will identify and assess over a three year period the effectiveness of some typical patterns of teaching politics and of on-going innovations as well as those emanating from the Working Party: and will also produce case studies of good teaching practice. The Working Party [see page 2].... While the Working Party is independent and completely unofficial, it has the advantage of the informal advice of a senior member of the Inspectorate, as well as of experts in various related fields.

3. The Hansard Society has recently obtained a grant from the Leverhulme Trust to make a survey of political knowledge and ignorance among school leavers. The planning of this is to be closely coordinated with the Programme for Political Education.

4. The Working Party will construct and recommend a generalised programme or outline of curriculum development for local adaptation, rather than single precise and detailed national scheme (as in the Nuffield Science projects), both because the contexts in which politics is taught vary so greatly (i.e. it is more often taught as part of history, economics, sociology, social studies or geography than on its own) and because there is a range of legitimate differences as to both the objects and methods of political education. This range is not infinite; one of the objects of the programme is to establish what the range of difference is and what methods are consistent with different purposes.

5. No approaches to political education will be ruled completely out of court except those which are so inflexible as to rule out other approaches, or those which in practice diminish knowledge of politics, potential and skills for participation or encourage attitudes harmful to free political institutions. It would, however, be both intellectually and morally wrong to assume that there is a 'consensus' in our society about political values, (even though there may be a consensus about procedures), to the extent that a single model curriculum could or should be instituted and taught. Therefore we speak only of a general programme or an outline of the minimal prerequisites of 'political literacy', and will only offer fully worked out curricula for particular areas as examples of what can be done.

POLITICAL LITERACY

6. By 'political literacy' we mean the knowledge, skills and attitudes that are necessary to make a man or woman both politically literate and able to apply this literacy. Knowledge alone is insufficient, for instance a person could be stuffed full of knowledge in an A level 'British Constitution' syllabus, could do well in an examination and score well in independent objective tests of information, but might nonetheless be incapable of or uninterested in expressing himself politically. Skills are sometimes developed in general education projects by gaming, simulation studies, project work or simply by debating and possibly by participation in democratic structures within the school. But participation without knowledge of how the real national institutions of the country work and can be influenced can be self-defeating. If good teaching begins from the experience of the class, yet it must extend their knowledge and skills beyond their immediate environment. Attitudes are relevant, but the kind of values to be encouraged are rules for civilised procedures, freedom, toleration, fairness, respect for truth and for reasoning, rather than substantive doctrines such as the parties in part embody. We do not fully share the hopes of the 'Humanities Project' to achieve a 'value-free' teaching of social problems. We hope to make the teacher more skilful in conveying the plausibility of differing value-

systems and what is entailed by different interpretations of concepts like democracy or equality rather than be too worried about suppressing his own values. We see political literacy as more concerned with recognising accurately and accepting the existence of real political conflicts than with developing knowledge of the details of constitutional machinery. Problems are prior to the institutions which try to resolve or contain them.

7. 'Political Literacy' must imply the ability to use knowledge to effect in politics. Minimal and formal involvement in politics or citizenship is voting, but political activity is also influencing people in almost any kind of group situation. 'Literacy' is then knowing something about what the issues are which are relevant to the decision to be taken, and being able to give some reasoned justification of why one did what one did. More specifically political literacy implies some knowledge of current affairs: perhaps the minimal task of developing political literacy is to get pupils to recall radio, television and newspaper items, and to help them look at them more systematically and critically. This is obviously much more important than formal knowledge of, for example, parliamentary procedure or the powers of Local Authorities. To illustrate our usage, we could imagine a student getting high marks on several A level examinations in this field, but being of low political literacy.

8. To enhance political literacy is to help the pupil develop a language in which to talk about politics that has some explanatory, not simply inflammatory or stimulative power – however simple an explanation it is. And an understanding of politics must be to some degree, at least, systematic. Perhaps almost any consistent cluster of concepts which people have used in political thought or in political activity is more helpful than none in developing political literacy. This is analogous to literacy in general. There may be no rules of correctness beyond usage, but usage needs constant attention to make it as consistent, clear and precise as possible. We stress the importance of some systematic conceptual language, however primitive. It is possible to imagine a student in general studies being brilliantly introduced to one burning and controversial social issue after another, even fired towards actual political participation, but still – in our sense – of low political literacy; or at least much less literate than when the 'problems approach' is informed by some systematic view of politics, especially if the burning issues are chosen simply for their assumed political importance and not as illustrative of points of political understanding.

9. So 'political literacy' must combine skills, attitudes and knowledge. The most important attitude is probably tolerance, not in a weak sense of indifference which can be developed in schools or permissiveness, but in the more traditional strong sense of having a definite point of view, indeed a definite and expressed disapproval of other points of view, but of limiting one's disapproval – limiting it, for instance, to argument, rather than blows; reasoning rather than abuse; ballots rather than bullets. To be able to be tolerant amid a strong

clash of opinions, demands, psychologically, considerable empathy, and cognitively, considerable knowledge of the other people's viewpoints. So here tolerance and empathy link directly with knowledge, and with a specific kind of knowledge: the knowledge of the main political viewpoints.

10. A politically literate person will then know what the main political disputes are about; what beliefs the main contestants have of them; how they are likely to affect him, and he will have a predisposition to try to do something about it in a manner at once effective and respectful of the sincerity of others. Put another way, the teaching should help to develop empathy about other political viewpoints and to give people a knowledge of the actual political conflicts of the day; some language or system of concepts with which to express themselves critically about these problems, and neither to expect too much or too little from their own action.

THE GENERAL PROGRAMME
11. The Working Party identifies three different objects of political education which are often seen as political alternatives, and as mutually exclusive.

a. The purely and properly conserving level of knowing how our present system of government works, and knowing the beliefs that are thought to be part of it.
b. The liberal or participatory level of development of the knowledge, attitudes and skills necessary for an active citizenship.
c. Beyond both of these there lies the more contentious area of considering possible changes of direction of government or of alternative systems.

The last is a proper area of educational concern, capable of treatment without bias, but only if it is reached after considering the previous two. We doubt very much the alleged stimulating effect of starting the teaching of politics by introducing extreme or minority viewpoints – as some fashionable educationalists have argued. This can too easily open the door to indoctrination. The true educational value of reaching this third level, is that whereas the second level simply habituates the pupil to conflicts of values, the third level must habituate the pupil to the critical use of partisan sources, whether revolutionary, racialist, nationalist or whatever, such as he will meet in the real world.

12. Thus these three different objects can better be seen as a sequence of stages or levels through which a full programme for political education in secondary schools would move. Common sense would suggest that where only a small number of hours for 'political teaching' are likely to be available, or where political questions are only some small part of another subject, that (a) and (b) above will form the best criteria for development of suggested curricular modules. If we strongly advise 'not dealing with (c) without also dealing with (a) and (b),' we also advise say 'not (a) without (b) and (c).' Indoctrination, in the sense of teaching a moral viewpoint without regard to showing what

33

the evidence is and to the need to develop a critical ability, is found both in Left and Ring wing forms.

13. The programme does aim to produce, however, a general model of such a triadic progression as above – even if not as detailed in terms of curricular materials as the modules.

14. The Working Party will begin by producing and circulating widely a series of papers for discussions, of increasing complexity and elaboration in each reissue, after it has been agreed what will constitute the most simple specification of a curriculum for political literacy for a very limited number of hours for classes of low ability and motivation in the final secondary school year and in, a somewhat different problem, further education day release. Preliminary discussions and papers published in the journal *Teaching Politics* show that we want to get away from the idea of a 'politics syllabus' which is a progressive simplification of a university discipline. Rather we plan to build from the bottom up by examining early perceptions of politics in non-academic contexts and streams, and to elaborate a growing process of political literacy through whatever discipline (in most of which the influence of 'political science' on the teacher is obviously only a very small factor).

15. The general programme will be set out early in the life of the project in a generalised and tentative form, circulated for criticism to all those expressing interest in the project, and several times revised and recirculated during the life of the project. It would be progressively revised and enriched from criticism of individuals and of consultative panels of teachers, from experience in producing specific curricula for different levels and circumstances, and from the results of monitoring actual teaching programmes. The final report will consist of an account of the work undertaken with recommendations for the reform and extension of civic education, together with the final form of the general programme; the particular and detailed curricula produced, reports on their effectiveness; and case studies of other innovations and examples of good teaching practice. It will be published by the Hansard Society for the Politics Association.

SPECIFIC PROJECTS
16. We would see the main groupings with which we would be concerned as

a. 13–16 year-olds in schools
b. 16–19 year-olds in full time education, either in schools or colleges of further education.
c. 16–19 year-olds (and possibly beyond) in part-time education.

Within these groupings there would be those whose courses were terminal in nature and those who were going on to seek further qualifications; there would be those who were in examination courses and those who were not; there would be those for whom politics were a full-time course within their curriculum and there would be those for whom it formed an ingredient within courses in other subject areas.

To meet these very varied needs there will be the production of specific and fully articulated curricula for a sizeable number of hours per week which could be fitted into the existing examination provision at 16 and 18 +; small politics modules for use within existing general, liberal or social studies courses etc., both examined and unexamined; and exemplars of how political literacy might be enhanced within the teaching of other subjects; for example, History, English, Geography, Social Studies, Sociology and Economics.

This production will arise both directly from the Working Party working through bodies such as the Politics Association, through groups of schools and colleges and through individual teachers; and also from suggestions made by teachers in schools and colleges either in the form of ideas which they would like to see developed, or in the form of existing developments which could be written up as case studies and used as a means of stimulating further work. Precisely which areas we tackle and what subjects we involve will depend in substantial measure upon the responses to this paper.

RESEARCH AND MONITORING

17. The research or 'monitoring and assessment' team is headed by Ian Lister of the Department of Education at the University of York. Their role is to assess over a two or three year period the effectiveness of innovations of some typical patterns of teaching politics, coming both from local initiatives and from the Working Party itself; and they will also identify and provide case studies of good teaching practice. The research team will help other teachers by suggesting procedures of self-assessment for programmes or developments which might not easily fit in the general pattern. The Director of Research shares in the work of the Working Party. The research team will work with the Working Party in making the concept of political literacy more explicit and hence testable; and would test levels of political literacy among pupils, correlate them with relevant variables, and especially test whether the Working Party's own programmes lead to gains in literacy ratings or not, compared to other types of existing programmes.

18. Thus the research team has an independent role which has been lacking in so many projects. Its job is not to implement or 'sell' the new curricula, but to see whether they work: thus by monitoring the particular projects, to monitor the whole programme itself.

19. Methods of monitoring programmes will vary according to the nature of the project. Questionnaires, depth-interviews, classroom observation, and analysis of tape and video recordings will all be used on occasion. We do not envisage elaborate and expensive longitudinal studies with control groups: that would be possible in theory, but because of the multiplicity both of situations and of objects, only a very few examples could be tackled that way; and we believe that results likely to have more immediate effect on actual

teaching practices would be achieved, even if less scientifically conclusive, the more teachers themselves are involved in self-assessment. Teachers in the Politics Association and associations in allied subjects and local branches would be helped and advised by the research team to set up criteria and procedures for assessment, but they themselves would do most of the work of assessment. What is lost in scientific precision would, we hope, be gained by being able to cover far more ground, and we would teach people procedures that they can continue themselves to use long after the project is over. Most so-called 'educational experiments' have been simply innovations, not experiments at all in the sense of having built-in procedures for verification of falsification of clearly stated objectives. Three different categories of schools must be looked at by the research team:

a. those with formal programmes of political education but not using our project materials;
b. those without any formal programmes of political education but using our project materials;
c. those using or adapting curricula programmes developed by the Working Party.

THE HELP THAT IS NEEDED

20. We have just under £40,000 for three years work, which is little compared to some of the Schools Council Curriculum Development Projects of the recent past. But we think we can do an important, useful and practical job within these limits if we can involve as many teachers in the work as possible. We can only do something for teachers if we do it with teachers. We want to hear from people who think that they have either an interesting on-going programme that they would like studied, or the opportunity within the next two school years to implement one. We will also want panels of teachers to help in the assessment of some of the projects, both in their formulation stage and in their stage of being monitored. Write to either Ian Lister at York or to the Developments Officer at the Hansard Society in this early stage if you think that we have anything that could help you, or you anything that could help us. (July 1974)

2.2 Political literacy
Bernard Crick and Ian Lister

THE CENTRALITY OF THE CONCEPT

1. Document 2.1, 'An Explanatory Paper' on the aims and methods of our whole project, has a section on 'Political Literacy' (paras. 6–10) in which we specified the concept in very general terms. It is clearly a concept central to our project. In this paper we want to be more specific. But in being more specific, we must make clear that the concept then appears as a cultural ideal. For most people it is a goal to be achieved, not a summary of experience. In many respects, it will follow from our specification that many people are not politically literate, perhaps we should not say 'politically illiterate'. Some may be politically *effective*, but that is not quite the same thing: unconscious habits can sometimes make one politically effective, as may in other circumstances fanatical intensity. Or a passive and deferential population, who think of themselves as good subjects and not active citizens, or who do not think of politics at all, may for some purposes pose few problems to the carrying on of government. But 'political literacy' involves both some conscious understanding of what one is about in a given situation and some capacity for action.

2. The reader might begin by rereading those paragraphs in Document 2.1. However, we could summarise them like this. Political literacy must be a compound of knowledge, skills and attitudes, to be developed together, each conditioning the other. Knowledge alone was rejected as an object of political education, but so was an unreflective and uninformed participation. A politically literate person must be able to use his knowledge, or at least see how it could be used and have a proclivity for using it; but equally his or her desire to participate must be informed by as much knowledge of what he is going into and of what consequences are likely to follow from his actions as is needed to make participation effective and justifiable. All actions affect others, so he must be aware of what effects his actions are likely to have, and then also be able to justify them. Some consistency, both in explaining possible consequences and in justifications, must be assumed. Hence to that extent, but to that extent alone, a politically literate person will show some consistency and subtlety in the use of political concepts. But the concepts are likely to be drawn from everyday life and language: a politically literate person may be quite innocent of the more technical vocabulary of the social sciences. We can certainly conceive, as it were, an 'advanced literacy' derived from the social sciences, which would put far more stress on genuine explanation rather than on practical understanding; but this is not our primary concern, for it is not relevant to the needs of the majority of young people in education.

3. A politically literate person will know what the main issues are in contemporary politics as he himself is affected, and will know how to set about informing himself further about the main arguments employed and how to criticise the relevance or worth of the evidence on which they are based; and he will need as much, but no more, knowledge of institutional structure as he

needs to understand the issues and the plausibility of rival policies. 'A politically literate person will then know what the main political disputes are about; what beliefs the main contestants have of them; how they are likely to affect him, and he will have a predisposition to try to do something about it in a manner at once effective and respectful of the sincerity of others.' (Document 2.1, para. 10.)

SOURCES OF THE POLITICAL

4. Before going further, however, we must pause to reiterate that underlying any theory of political education and any ideal of political literacy, there must be a theory of politics. Our theory of politics is much broader than many conventional view of politics – broader in two ways:

a. it stresses that politics is inevitably concerned with conflicts of interests and ideals, so an understanding of politics must begin with an understanding of the conflicts that there are and of the reasons and interests of the contestants; it cannot be content with preconceptions of constitutional order or of a necessary consensus. A politically literate person will not hope to resolve all such differences, or difficulties at once; but he perceives their very existence as politics;
b. it stresses the differential distribution of power there is in any society and the differential access to resources. Hence we are concentrating on a whole dimension of human experience which we characterise as *political* (much as Graeme Moodie has said that a politically literate person would have 'the ability to recognise the political dimensions of any human situation').

5. Where do we find examples of the political? We find them (i) in the speeches and behaviour of professional politicians and political activists; (ii) in the writings and teaching of political scientists; and (iii) in observing and experiencing what we may call the politics of everyday life – in the family, the locality, educational institutions, clubs and societies, and in informal groups of all kinds.

6. For ordinary people only the third category necessarily involves them in participation. The first two categories involve extraordinarily few people. But one of the aims of political education in general (particularly of this project) is to open up access for majorities to the kinds of information and skills possessed by professional politicians and professional students of politics.

TYPES OF POLITICAL LITERACY

7. Our immediate problem is that we are now passing from the rhetorical stage, where we have asserted political literacy as an ideal, to the second stage, where we must specify it, see how to assess it, and discover educational strategies from promoting it. We have identified political literacy as the key element in the Programme for Political Education, not only because (as we use it) it is a much broader concept than, say, 'political competence' or 'political understanding',

but also because we believe that we will be able to assess it in ways which are meaningful to a lot of people; and we believe that, particularly in the areas of information and skills, it is teachable and learnable, that its further specification can provide a framework for developing better curricula at all levels.

8. Political literacy has the further advantage that, being a condition, there might be alternative ways of attaining it (just as there are alternative ways of learning a language and the social actions with which language is related). No two societies will have the same view of it. It is not an absolute condition (a political danger of 'assessing political literacy' is that simplifiers might label majorities 'politically illiterate' and unworthy of active participation in political life). Rather, political literacy has levels of understanding, minimal and advanced, basic and more sophisticated. Whether there are also critical thresholds, between the two levels, is something that we will need to investigate at a later stage.

9. So in speaking of a 'politically literate person' we are not postulating some universal role or model: different politically literate persons might have quite a lot of characteristics which vary one from another. However, it is the common elements which exemplify and typify politically literate persons that we are interested in. But before we go on to that, there is one caveat: certain kinds of knowledge might be attributes of a politically literate person (such as, they would know the name of the Prime Minister, or the President of the United States), but such knowledge alone would not be a sufficient condition of political literacy. In a similar fashion while the possession of such knowledge alone might not be an indicator of political literacy, the lack of such knowledge would be a likely predictor of a low level of political literacy. Thus, political information tests are often more useful to explore ignorance than knowledge.

WHAT KINDS OF KNOWLEDGE WOULD A POLITICALLY LITERATE PERSON POSSESS?
10. At the most general level a politically literate person would possess the basic information which is prerequisite to understanding the political dimensions of a given context. Thus, there is a sense in which the necessary knowledge is contextually related (if not narrowly contextually defined). For example, in each parliament, factory, school and family, active participants need to know some basic facts about it; something about the structure of power in the institution, where its money comes from, and something of the ways and means in which it works. A politically literate person would not only have a high level of understanding of a given context and situation, but would be able to operate efficiently within that context and situation. This would involve having notions of policy, of policy objectives, and an ability to recognise how well policy objectives had been achieved as well as being able to comprehend those of others. Political literacy is not simply an ability to pursue even an enlightened self-interest: it must comprehend the effects on others and their viewpoints, and respond to them morally.

11. A politically literate person would also know the kinds of knowledge that he or she needed, and did not possess, in a given situation, and how to find them out. Paradoxically, the politically literate person knows what he or she does not know.

12. A politically literate person would possess a knowledge of those concepts minimally necessary to construct simple conceptual and analytical frameworks. These need not necessarily be – indeed are unlikely to be – concepts drawn from 'the high language of politics' (i.e. the arcane language of professional political scientists), but rather from everyday life – yet used more systematically and precisely than is common.

13. Differential political literacy is possible. The professor of Political Science might be quite lost in the politics of Hull docks, or of a social club. Some clusters of concepts, adequate to understanding and even allowing an active participation in a local situation, might be restricted both in time and space. Only a highly politically literate person would have a command of both local and more universal concepts. A programme of political education should be aware of both and be able to relate both to each other; it is likely to on the more universal, though perhaps to draw its material and examples from the more local or immediate level.

WHAT ARE THE ATTITUDES OF A POLITICALLY LITERATE PERSON?
14. It would be wrong to define a politically literate person as someone who necessarily shares all values of Western European liberalism. That would be, indeed, a curious up-dating of the Whig interpretation of history into present day political education. Such views are to be learned as part of our tradition, but they must themselves be subject to criticism, some scepticism must be part of any citizen and of any worthwhile education; and they must not be universalised without the utmost self-awareness, self-criticism and thought for consequences. However, it is clear, at the least, that there are some kinds of political effectiveness which simply destroy the possibility of other kinds of political literacy. Some biases are compatible with a true knowledge of the motives, beliefs and behaviour of others, some not. Functional political literacy may well be imposed and narrowing. All values are not equal.

15. Attitudes cannot be ignored. We reject the assumptions of those whether of Left or Right, who would have only the correct attitudes taught (which narrows political literacy) and the theoretical assumption that all values and attitudes are equally 'socialised' – says one theory – or equally important parts of tradition – says another (and therefore beyond the reach of educational reason). Certainly all values should be interpreted in different social contexts, but some are more conditioned than others – to put the case at its weakest. If we value truth and freedom it is not possible to be free of values, and it is a poor example for a teacher to set to try to do the impossible in some over-elaborate manner.

16. We assume that the teacher should not seek to influence basic substantive values and that frontal assaults are, in any case, not likely to be successful; but that it is both proper and possible to try to nurture and strengthen certain procedural values. In para. 6 of document 2.1 we identified 'freedom, toleration, fairness, respect for truth and for reasoning' as such values. Anyone can see that in real life and politics there are many occasions in which those values may have to be modified, because they can conflict with each other, or with substantive values such as religion, ethical codes and political doctrines embody. Part of political education is to examine just such conflicts: but this does not affect the primacy of these procedural values within a genuine political education. The objection to them is, indeed, more likely to be that they are vague platitudes rather than indoctrinatory concepts. This we will try to resolve in document 2.3, 'Basic Political Concepts'.

WHAT SKILLS WOULD A POLITICALLY LITERATE PERSON POSSESS?

17. The real difficulties of political education are likely to lie not in areas of bias and indoctrination but in its encouragement of action. There are still some who appear to want 'good citizenship' without the trouble of having citizens. The great difference between literacy and political literacy is that literacy can involve only a solitary pursuit, but political literacy involves the action and interaction of groups. It is true that certain relevant skills (such as critical and evaluative skills) are 'intellectual' and, like reading, can be performed by the individual in solitude. However, this itself constitutes a very limited notion of political literacy which would preserve politics as a spectator sport for most people, or would reduce the politically literate person to the under-gardener role voluntarily adopted by so many English philosophers, that is dealing only in second-order activities. (As Sir Edward Boyle has put it: 'The major political differences in our national life are not so much between Government and Opposition as between the Government and everybody else. Governments "do", the rest of us talk'.)

18. The ultimate test of political literacy lies in creating a proclivity to action, not in achieving more theoretical analysis. The politically literate person would be capable of active participation (or positive refusal to participate) and should not be excluded from the opportunity to participate merely because of lack of the prerequisite knowledge and skills. The highly politically literate person should be able to do more than merely imagine alternatives. We are not trying to achieve a condition of ecumenical mutual exhaustion, rather a more vigorous kind of tolerance of real views and real behaviour. The politically literate person must be able to devise strategies for influence and for achieving change. He must see the right means to an end he can justify. And while action certainly does not imply any particular kind of change, it does imply effect on others or change of a sort.

SPECIFICATION OF POLITICAL LITERACY

19. Diagram A attempts to set out in some detail what is minimally involved

Diagram A Political literacy

Perception of issues

Perception of different responses, policies and conflicts

Self-interest and social responsibility

Relevant knowledge

Action skills

(Realistic political judgements)

(Political democracy)

(Effective political participation)

1

a Knowledge of who promotes what policies

b Scepticism about factual claims and knowledge of alternative sources

c Alternative ways of looking at things

2

a Knowledge of the institutional arena for the conflicts

b Knowledge of customary ways of settling disputes and institutional materials and constraints

c Knowledge of alternative ways of settling disputes and possibilities of institutional change

3

a Knowledge of different ways and means of influence in our present society

b Knowledge of the appropriate ways and means of influence for particular purposes

c Knowledge of alternative types of societies and of the ways and means associated with them

4

a Effect on oneself

b Ability to express one's own interests and principles

c Ability to offer justifications and reasons for pursuing one's own interests and ideals

5

a Effect on others

b Ability to perceive the interests and principles of others

c Ability to understand the justifications and reasons of others

6

a Experience of conflicts of values and interest in home and everyday life

b Experiences of participation, debate and decision-making in home, etc.

c Insistence on taking part and being heard in home, etc.

7

a Making real choices in school work generally and using independent study time, etc.

b Debates, games, simulations and projects of a political and social kind

c Making effective decisions in schools

Diagram B Political literacy
(Simplified diagram for classroom)

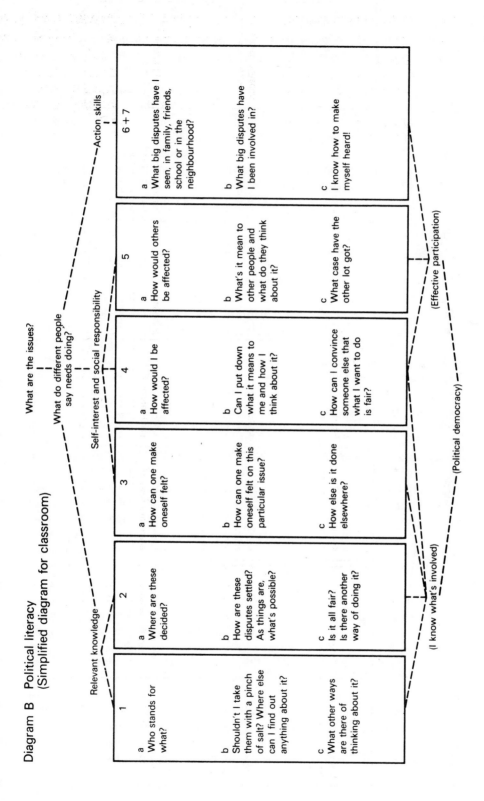

What are the issues?

What do different people
say needs doing?

Action skills

Self-interest and social responsibility

Relevant knowledge

	1	2	3	4	5	6 + 7
a	Who stands for what?	Where are these decided?	How can one make oneself felt?	How would I be affected?	How would others be affected?	What big disputes have I seen, in family, friends, school or in the neighbourhood?
b	Shouldn't I take them with a pinch of salt? Where else can I find out anything about it?	How are these disputes settled? As things are, what's possible?	How can one make oneself felt on this particular issue?	Can I put down what it means to me and how I think about it?	What's it mean to other people and what do they think about it?	What big disputes have I been involved in?
c	What other ways are there of thinking about it?	Is it all fair? Is there another way of doing it?	How else is it done elsewhere?	How can I convince someone else that what I want to do is fair?	What case have the other lot got?	I know how to make myself heard!

(I know what's involved)

(Political democracy)

(Effective participation)

in political literacy. Diagram B attempts to set out the same thing only in colloquial language of a kind that might reach the pupil directly or may serve as some guide to those preparing curricula.

20. The specifications may seem formidable, but we think that there is no flinching the fact that the number of relationships to be grasped in political literacy (of beyond a minimal kind) is quite large; that it is dangerous to over-simplify what politics is about; and that a major educational effort is needed. However, as will be clear later, the amount of knowledge demanded can be much smaller than is often thought. The media, not the school, inevitably supply much of the information about politics that a person needs: the role of the school is to help him handle this information in a critical way, to help him form his own opinions, to appreciate those of others, to give him the will and the means to participate effectively and responsibly.

21. Similarly, while we specify that the politically literate person must be able to give reasons and justifications for beliefs and actions and to understand those of others, it would be an advanced literacy indeed that could discuss the criteria for the validity of the judgements. That is political philosophy in a technical sense. The respect for reason we talk of only implies the giving and the demanding of reasons at all. The meaning and the implications of political beliefs, but not their validity, is all we hope to be generally examined in schools.

22. The fundamental point about our scheme is that the need for political literacy arises because people are in fact faced with issues and problems of a political nature. Civic need and educational theory go together. The teaching of politics and the learning about politics must arise from issues and experience. We reject the argument that a knowledge of institutions must come first. The politically literate person needs to know about institutions, but ònly as much as is relevant to knowing the context in which issues arise, can be affected and are resolved. There is, of course, a wider knowledge of institutions which those who work for them have to know. This may be a proper and interesting subject for A level, vocational and university study. But a glance at our diagram will show how easily a person with only that kind of knowledge could be politically illiterate.

23. We repeat, yet again, that political literacy is a compound of knowledge, skills and attitudes. We have laboured the point already as to how these attitudes may reasonably be defined. But we did not imply, as the diagram shows, that they should be taught directly. What is to be taught and learned directly relates only to skills and knowledge. Columns 1 and 2 are forms of knowledge directly teachable, teachable in the conventional way that, for instance, 'British constitution' or 'British institutions' have often been taught, except that Column 1 stipulates that such taught knowledge must include knowledge of alternative sources of information (otherwise it is indoctrination). Column 3 can also be taught directly, though it less often has been taught:

a knowledge of the tactics and strategies appropriate to particular political goals. Columns 4 and 5 are knowledge of a different kind, knowledge of effects and of responsibilities, of what kind of arguments one can put forward to justify some effects on others and of their kind of arguments. This is now commonly done in Moral Education curricula, oddly it has rarely been related to politics, though it is the heart of political life. Columns 6 and 7 relate to experience and activity, both real and simulated. Some participation in decision-making in school is essential. How much is needed, we recognise, is extremely debatable in theory, and is highly relative in practice. But schools with no such opportunities, or with derisory or token ones, plainly will at some stage in a child's development negate our idea of political literacy.

24. Read horizontally the diagrams represent stages, stages in a logical sense, that (a) must ordinarily precede (b), and (b) ordinarily precede (c) if (c) is to be effective, and responsible. These are also possible stages in curriculum development, though we see all this as ordinarily fitting into a very short compass of time. As we said in document 2.1, we think that knowledge of alternative forms of political and social organisation is a necessary part of a political education, but that it is not the best way to begin – only after conservative factors and participative opportunities have been explored should one begin to think about alternatives. (See document 2.1, paras. 11 and 12.) However minimal political literacy, however little time is available for political education, it must involve knowing what the main issues are thought to be. The kind of sources we will suggest (opinion polls, party manifestos and newspapers) are unlikely to come up with more than a half-dozen issues which dominate politics at any given time. But even these are too many to be pursued through the twelve or so operations we suggest. Only one or two would be followed in small modules of politics, but the skills and perceptions that could then be formed or strengthened would have, we suggest, a general applicability: a transferable skill would have been created.

25. An advanced political literacy may well be defined in terms of (i) an explicit and critical study of this model and its implications, (ii) extending it into consideration of alternative forms of political and social organisation, and (iii) criteria for judgement and justifications and for political obligation and disobedience, and (iv) knowing what Political Science has to say of relevance to these factors.

26. Perhaps there is no need to say that in asserting the very great social and educational importance of political literacy, we have tried to narrow the concept down to the specifically political so that it can be integrated with other subjects. Indeed, politics is not an end in itself, but a relationship between or within other things. For these reasons we have not specified what is obvious, that a politically literate person will have some general knowledge of the kind of society he lives in, its people, history and the broad economic and geographical factors that define and limit us. All this is part of a general education.

27. So what we offer in the diagrams has two direct purposes: (i) as criteria by which it may be possible to assess whether a person is politically literate or a curriculum likely to enhance it; and (ii) as a direct outline or general model of what should be involved in all political education.

28. For the moment we leave aside the important question of attitudes and values. Our view is clear, that some are to be taught and learned, but none can be taught directly. In the third of these general, introductory papers, that on 'Basic Concepts' which will follow, we will make clear which combination of factors in the diagram relate the most to particular basic 'procedural values' (freedom, toleration, fairness, respect for truth and for reasoning), and will suggest at what stage each of the suggested elements in a larger but minimal family of political concepts can best be introduced.[1]

(November 1974)

---

[1] And subsequently in papers 6, 7 and 8 also.

2.3 Basic concepts for political education
Bernard Crick

INTRODUCTION

1. In Working Paper No. 2 on 'Political Literacy' of the Programme for Political Education it was suggested that 'A politically literate person would possess, among other things, a knowledge of those concepts minimally necessary to construct simple conceptual and analytical frameworks. These need not necessarily be – indeed are unlikely to be – concepts drawn from 'the high language of politics' (i.e. the arcane language of professional political scientists), but rather from everyday life – yet employed more systematically and precisely than is usual'.

2. This paper simply attempts to suggest one possible set of basic concepts and to offer working definitions of them for the teacher to apply to whatever materials he or she is using. Since there is no possibility of final agreement either about which concepts are minimal and which are basic (that is, not a compound of others), this paper is inevitably more personal than some others in the Programme. The Working Party endorse it simply as a useful contribution to discussion rather than as a policy document or as carrying their agreement in every respect.

3. We perceive and we think in concepts. Concepts are, as it were, the building blocks with which we construct a picture of the external world, including imaginary or hoped-for worlds. So concepts are not true or false, they simply help us to perceive and to communicate. To quote an earlier article of mine which offers a fuller justification of this approach: 'I will argue for a conceptual approach, that is I believe that all education, whether in school or out of school, consists in increasing understanding of language and increasing ability to use it to adjust to external relationships and events, to extend one's range of choice within them and finally to influence them. At all times we have some general image of the world in which we live, some understanding, however tentative, primitive or even false and the slightest degree of education consists in forming explanations of these images or offering generalisations, however simple, about alternative images or modifications of early ones, with some argument, some appeal to evidence. The images are composed of concepts. Willy-nilly, we begin with concepts and we try to sharpen them, to extend their meanings, to see links between them and then to go on to invent or accept special sets of concepts for new problems'[1].

4. By a 'conceptual approach' I do not mean that concepts themselves should be taught directly. The approach is for the teacher, not necessarily the class; it is an underpinning of curricula, not an outline curriculum. A 'conceptual approach' only accentuates the positive, that we think and perceive in concepts,

[1] See my 'Basic Political Concepts and Curriculum Development', *Teaching Politics*, January 1974, p. 13.

and eliminates the negative, that we do not directly perceive 'institutions' or 'rules' – these are imposed upon us, taught to us or gradually become clear to us as patterns of behaviour, specific structurings of related concepts. The cluster of concepts I will suggest do not constitute the skeleton of a curriculum, unless for some advanced level indeed but rather something for the teacher to have in mind and to elaborate and explicate when occasion arises. The teacher will be better able to help the pupil order and relate the disparate problems and issues of the real political world if he or she has some sketchmap, at least, of basic concepts. Most of the concepts I will specify do in fact occur frequently in ordinary people's talk about politics, whether or not the same words are used. Concepts can be translated into many different language codes and conventions; but I do not believe that any would be genuinely political (meaningful in any way, for that matter), if they were not translatable. We do not need to go beyond the language of everyday life to understand and to participate in the politics of everyday life and all those things that affect it.

5. So to increase political literacy we need to work through everyday speech, sometimes tightening and sharpening it, sometimes unpacking its ambiguities. Political science as a discipline that aims at generalisation and explanation may, indeed, need a different and a more technical vocabulary. But for this reason it has no direct relevance to increasing the political literacy of the ordinary school child; and indeed I have some personal doubts if it has much to offer as a discipline in either teacher education or sixth form work. I am surprised to find sociologists trying to teach systematic sociology in schools, rather than – perhaps – using their skills for more relevant purposes. Political scientists should not follow suit, but consider the different game of political literacy.

6. My suggested concepts, or rather my explications of them, are drawn from the tradition of political philosophy far more than from political science or political sociology. Philosophers in talking about politics have usually used the ordinary language of actors in political events. (I am impressed that, for instance, John Rawls' recent account in his seminal book *Justice* of justice as 'fairness', very much confirms or parallels how children of about eight or eleven talk – about football, of course: not 'what's the rule?', i.e. law, but 'is it fair?', i.e., justice. Indeed they can have a valid concept of 'fairness' without ever having read the rules.) Political philosophy, however, is technical in so far as, of course, it goes beyond definition of usage and meaning and attempts to establish criteria for the truth of judgements. This is not for schools, at least in any systematic way, although perhaps it should be for teacher training. 'Political literacy' merely implies using concepts clearly and sensibly and recognising how others use them. It does *not* imply solving the problems, getting them right; it only implies understanding them and trying to have some effect. So a conceptual approach to political education does not imply knowing or doing any political philosophy. It is simply a specialised vocabulary within 'the use of English' or 'communication skills' – which is, however, the beginning of reflection, only the very beginning but the necessary beginning. So not to set the sights too high:

to improve the *usage* and *meaning* of concepts, not to judge the *truth* of propositions or assertions using them, should be our goal; and perhaps with the most able we can consider the validity of forms of political and moral argument but hardly their truth.

7. There is no reason why at an advanced level these concepts cannot be treated explicitly, perhaps as the basis for a syllabus.[2] But I cannot stress too strongly that I am not suggesting to teachers of the majority and of school-leavers of earlier age groups that they should teach these concepts explicitly or in any particular order. That is beyond my competence, and I doubt if it is desirable or possible in any systematic way. It lies in the nature of politics that there can be more plausible and sensible variations in approach than to almost any other topic (and possibly more unsensible ones too). Belief that a single method is best or that a single usage of a concept is correct, would come close to an imposed tyranny. All we can hope for is that a relatively greater conceptual awareness, clarity and consistency will improve teaching at every level; that the ability to conceptualise and distinguish concepts is a real persuasive, moral and political skill; and that concepts can be drawn from everyday speech.

8. A final and important reservation: the paper only suggests concepts which are genuinely *basic* or *primary*, that is only those from which others can be derived and on which theories, generalisations, explanations and moral judgements can be based; but they are not necessarily the most important or the most widely used politically. This reservation is important and must be understood. For example, 'democracy' is plainly one of the most important concepts used in political vocabulary. But it is plainly a compound of more basic concepts – such as liberty, welfare and representation, sometimes 'rights'; even 'justice' is built into the definition. 'Equality', on the one hand, and 'tradition' or 'custom', on the other, are similar compounds. Plainly it is not much use asking 'what is the definition of democracy or of equality, etc.?', for straight away one is faced with several different and plausible theories and doctrines about what should be done or how things should be done.[3] It is very important to ask such questions but they can only be discussed rationally, that is, with some agreement about meaning of terms and procedures of argument, if there is some prior general agreement about what the component basic concepts mean. Hence first things first. A politically literate person must be clear what he or she means by 'democracy' or 'equality', but in order to do so political education must provide a basic vocabulary. Perhaps with advanced level pupils it is possible to begin with complex, compound concepts like 'democracy' and to 'unpack them', to work backwards to their component basic elements; but with earlier ages and abilities it is surely better to begin at the beginning.

[2] These concepts are specified in a new London G.C.E. 'A level' syllabus in Political Studies which will replace the present British Government and Political System paper from June 1978 onwards. Presumably tests of their usage will be set, very much as in Use of English or English Language papers, not attempts to establish their truth.

[3] See my 'Democracy, a definition', *The World and the School*, January 1973, Atlantic Information Centre for Teachers, special number on 'Democracy'.

THE CONCEPTS IN GENERAL

9. Surely the simplest perception of politics is that it is about the relationship of rulers to ruled, the few to the many, 'them and us', government and its subjects or the state and its citizens. We may wish it not to be so, but it is so. It is about differential use of and access to power over others. We start from the *fact* of government. But government is not a madman sitting on a sandcastle giving commands to the waves; it is men and women commanding, controlling or persuading other men and women. Whether government is prior to consent (either in time or logic), or consent prior to government is perhaps a chicken and the egg problem. We want to know why such a question is asked before we try to answer it. What is clear is that all leaders need to be followed but equally clear that all large associations of people need and produce leaders. Societies without government may be a speculative possibility, but not the subject matter of ordinary politics. (One may say that the object of all politics should be the happiness of individuals. But accounts of 'politics' which begin with attempts to establish what are individual rights and how to get them tend to be notoriously unrealistic – the old civil liberties approach, which nowadays can be the potentially highly parochial 'community politics' approach.)

10. So we must start simultaneously with perceptions of what is done to us by government and external forces; and with perceptions of our human identity as people, what we think we are, what is due to us and what should not be done to us. And then we consider perceptions of all the different kinds of relationships there can be between rulers and ruled. Thus the very simplest and most fruitful model is:

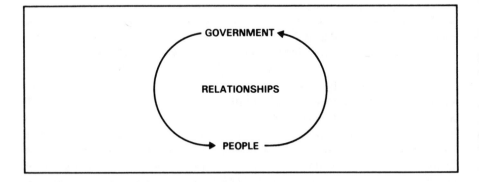

And right from the beginning the relationship must be seen as one of mutual dependence. Leaders must be followed (and pure coercion can rarely work for long, so immediately doctrines, ideologies and legitimation enter in) and people must have some reasonably settled organisation for their welfare and protection. The more a government seeks to do, the more agents and support it needs (particularly to wage war or to industrialise); the more people seek to do collectively even for their own good and protection, the more instruments of government they create.

11. I suggest that a more elaborate model, setting out basic concepts associated with these very generalised perceptions, could be of this kind (which differs slightly from my earlier suggestion in *Teaching Politics*, January 1974):

		GOVERNMENT		
Power	Force		Authority	Order
		RELATIONSHIPS		
Law	Justice		Representation	Pressure
		PEOPLE		
Natural Rights	Individuality		Freedom	Welfare

If this appears ridiculously simple, (i) there are some advantages in simplicity, (ii) not so when one begins to explicate different usages of these same terms and to show, for instance (as the political literacy diagram in document 2.2 suggests), how different social groups or political doctrines interpret them differently. But I do claim that an understanding of the usage and *working* of these concepts in politics could take one far and that other, more elaborate, concepts can easily be derived from them. And, once again, let us walk before we try to fly. We should try to fly, but we must learn to walk first.

12. Two examples: what earthly relevance has this model to those who would say either that 'politics is all a matter of class structure' or that 'politics is all a matter of tradition'? Simply this, that 'class' is, anyway, a very complex and elaborate sociological concept. Its political relevance is as a perception of a form of **order** (there are other perceived forms), and it can also be seen as a form of **representation**, the main kind of **influence** and even in extreme cases as the definition or negation of **individuality**. It is a very complex concept indeed, not as simple as it seems. We could not understand it without using more primary concepts, let alone evaluate its truth as a theory seeking to explain political behaviour. If taught first (i.e. 'before you can understand anything at all, comrade kids, you must understand the concept of "class"'), it is simply imposed knowledge, the very kind of structured socialisation that radical teachers object to most. Similarly 'tradition' can be seen as a particular type of claim to **authority** (the experienced should/do rule), and as a form of

representation (history and our wise ancestors), even as a form of **welfare** (the well-being of a community is to be judged in terms of its historical continuity rather than the precise wealth or poverty of its members at any given time – otherwise, why shouldn't we sell out to the highest bidder?). It is a theory to be considered at a later stage, not a basic concept.

13. Let us now look at each of the terms in turn and some of their conceptual neighbours. What I cannot do is to suggest in detail what kinds of materials and what ability levels or what situations are best for illustrating which of these concepts. This can only be done by curricula development groups of actual teachers at the various levels and by monitoring actual teaching.

14. These 'definitions' are meant only to be useful, to furnish a starting point. 'Beware of definitions' sayeth truly Sir Karl Popper. Definitions are only proposals for usage or abbreviated accounts of usage. They cannot establish 'truth'. But I have tried to sum up a great deal of debate and to provide 'working definitions' for teacher and learner (and particularly learner–teacher) which are close to the centre of the clusters of meaning often revolving around these words. I am not deterred by the fact that any of my colleagues would come up with something different. It is about time that someone had a go, came off the high horse and said, 'From the tradition of political philosophy and public debate about politics, in my opinion these concepts are indispensable and have these basic cores of meaning.'

THE CONCEPTS SPECIFIED: (i) THE GOVERNING CONCEPTS
15. **Power** is, in the strongest sense, the ability to achieve a premeditated intention. Thus, to have power over people is to be able to affect them in definite and defined ways. Some have gone so far as to say that power 'is acting in concert' (Hannah Arendt)[4], that all political power is, in however narrow a sense, collective, needs to carry other people with it, whether by **force** or by false or true **authority** (of which persuasion is only one form). Even a Nero or Caligula needs to keep the Palace Guard sweet and even a nordic hero had to trust somebody while he slept. Bertrand Russell suggests that this strong sense of power as 'achieving an expressed intention' is often confused with a weak sense, that of (mere) 'unchallengeability'. It may be, for instance, that no one else can do it if the Prime Minister doesn't, but he may not be able to, e.g. prevent inflation. 'Power' as unchallengeability is often mistaken for 'power' in the broader sense. If more power is accumulated in fewer hands, it does not necessarily follow that intentions can be fulfilled. Armies may fight better and workers work harder, for instance, if power is devolved. Sometimes so, sometimes not. Power can be used for good or for ill, there can be too much or too little at any given time for our own good; but a society with no concept of or use of power is inconceivable. And sometimes 'power' requires '**force**', but sometimes the force is unusable or irrelevant.

[4] See Hannah Arendt, *On Violence*, Allen Lane, 1970, for a very clear set of distinctions in the power, force, coercion, violence cluster.

16. **Force** or *coercion* is when either physical pressure or weapons are actually used or when threat creates fear of use. Probably all government requires some capacity for or potentiality of 'force' or *violence* (a near synonym); but probably no government can maintain itself through time, as distinct from defence and attack at specific moments, without legitimating itself in some way, getting itself loved, respected; even just accepted as inevitable, otherwise it would need constant recourse to open violence – which is rarely the case. Again Arendt interestingly suggests that violence is at its maximum not in the concentration of political power but in its breakdown. When government breaks down, violence can thrive. Now 'force', as such, is a neutral thing; it is an instrument which is used for clear or unclear purposes, for good or evil purposes. A few evil men (Fascists or types of anarchists) have made a cult of violence but it is foolish or hypocritical to think that all violence is bad. The minority pacifist argument is to be considered and respected but a majority of people would agree that self-defence is justifiable, as is the use of violence in apprehending and containing criminals or in preventing greater violence. All power is not violence; all violence is not unjustifiable; and it is probably dangerous to believe that 'all power corrupts': such a nervous view goes oddly with those who want, for instance, more participation, i.e. more popular power, Max Weber did *not* define 'the State' (i.e. the modern State) as the monopolist of violence but as the monopolist of the 'legitimate means of violence (which some call **force**). He argued that the modern state at least ensures **law** and **order** by trying to abolish private means of violence. Besides, as Milton remarked:

'Who overcomes by force
Has overcome but half his foe.'

17. **Authority** is the respect and obedience given to someone in respect of fulfilling a function which is felt to be needed and in which he or she is agreed to have excellence. If this sounds complicated it is no more than to contrast 'he knows what he's talking about' – the exercise of a function – with 'he's throwing his weight about' – the assumption of status. Thus every government seeks not merely enough **force** to defend itself but sufficient authority to legitimate itself. As Rousseau said, 'the strongest is never strong enough unless he can turn power into consent, might into obligation'. Oppressive despotisms, even, do not rule primarily by naked force but by imposing on people beliefs, typically and historically through religion and education, that they alone can fulfil functions which are thought to be necessary (e.g. they embody the commands of the gods – who may not exist; they defend the country against barbarian hordes – who may be quite unwarlike; they ensure that harvests will be gathered and corn stored and that irrigation takes place – when the peasants might anyway do these things for them; or that they alone can preserve order – when other forms of order, both better and worse, are readily possible). Authority can be legitimate or illegitimate, false or true, depending on how free people are to question the alleged needs and functions of government, to recognise alternatives and to judge how well the functions are being fulfilled. Authority – is it needful to say? – is not necessarily *authoritarian*. All authority

is not bad, neither is it good *per se*: it is ordinarily thought of as legitimate authority when (i) its powers are derived from commonly accepted procedures; (ii) it does not suppress discussion of alternative ways both of defining and fulfilling needs; and (iii) does not seek to extend its functionally defined powers generally into any or every concern. For example, the authority I have as a university teacher is because students want to study and, in varying degrees, respect my competence; but that competence does not extend to laying down the law about their morals. The functions of a primary school teacher, on the other hand, are far more general and less specific: his or her authority is much more general, and more like that of a parent. Hence the greater difficulties. The limits of proper authority are then far harder to define. Or consider Dylan Thomas's old and blind Captain Catt in *Under Milk Wood*; 'Damn you, the mulatto woman, she's mine. Who's captain here?' And the implied answer is either that no one is captain among whores in a tropical seaport, or else that a different kind of functionally defined competence would be called for than that which gave him the unquestioned captaincy in keeping his dirty British coaster afloat in mad March gales, etc.

18. **Order** is the most general perception that rational expectations about political, social and economic relationships, almost whatever they are, will be fulfilled. *Disorder* is when one doesn't know what is going to happen next, or more strictly when uncertainties are so numerous as to make rational pre-meditation or calculation appear impossible. Faced with *disorder*, the radical philosopher Bentham said, 'mankind will choose any kind of "order", however unjust'. 'Order' is, in this sense, a prerequisite of any kind of government at all, good or bad. **Justice**, **rights**, **welfare**, all need 'order' and even **freedom** (as we will suggest) becomes trivial or simply ineffective if there is no reasonably settled context. But the concept is morally completely neutral. It is simply knowing where one stands, however bad and oppressive the system ('at least one knows where one stands' – which is no excuse, for the same could be true in a better system). Only a lunatic would attack **order** as such, or could possibly adjust to a complete breakdown of expectations; but those who justify 'order' as such, rather than simply point to its minimal necessity, are usually smuggling into the concept their own particular ideas of the best form that 'order' should take. And prophecies that 'all order will break down if something isn't done about it' – whatever it is, are notoriously rhetorical and alarmist. Concepts of *disorder* can best be elaborated as specific negations of 'order'. I mean that different types of disorder are best understood in terms of what they are challenging rather than as things in themselves; and nor should we necessarily assume that they are instruments to some other purpose, their main purpose may be to protest against the existing form of 'order'. I would suggest that these negations of 'order' could be seen as some kind of continuum from *public opinion, pressure, strike, boycott, parade, demo, rebellion, coup d'état, war of independence, civil war*, through to *revolution*. And that each of these concepts has specific and limiting characteristics; in other words, *violence* is rarely un-controlled and explosive, it is usually intended and specific. 'Ungovernable fury'

is usually fairly deliberate. Ideas of how much types of violence threaten 'order' are highly conventional and historically specific. Some people today fear 'a breakdown of law and order' from a degree of violence on the streets which was easily tolerable (if disliked) in the eighteenth century. And in some of the Arab kingdoms of the early Muslim era, civil war and fratricide were the recognised institutions for settling the succession to the throne.

THE CONCEPTS SPECIFIED: (ii) THE POPULAR CONCEPTS
(So far looking, as it were, down; but now looking up; and we all want government both to do things for us and to keep its distance.)

19. **Natural rights** (or basic rights) are what we claim as the minimum conditions for a proper human existence. 'Life, liberty and property', said John Locke, or 'life, liberty and the pursuit of happiness', said Thomas Jefferson. Thomas Hobbes was even more minimal: man only had two rights, which were absolute – 'by all means to defend himself' and 'to seek peace and preserve it', in other words life itself, our basic human individuality, is all we have by natural right. As with **order**, there is a great temptation to stuff into the concept everything one desires – the 'right to an eight-hour day and a five-day week', for instance; but clarity of discourse is likely to be greater the fewer basic assumptions we make. By all means demand an eight-hour day or eight-hour week, but such demands should be conceived as **welfare**, one possible thing that we wish for among others beyond our basic or natural rights.

Many of the things we call 'our rights' are, more correctly, seen as things the law allows us to enjoy (like free speech) or commands others to provide for us (like education); such legal rights are beyond number. And political rights are simply the minimum conditions needed for citizens (as defined by legal rights) to be politically effective – so these will vary vastly, depending on who are citizens and what the role of citizenship is thought to be. The Greeks of the fifth century B.C. valued political rights so much that they actually said that a man not fit to exercise them was not really, or properly a man – but a natural slave. But 'a man's a man for a' that', as Robert Burns (following Rousseau) sees better than Aristotle. The basic concept must refer to what we think all legal and political systems should allow, indeed enhance; to what are our rights simply as human beings. But, of course, man is a sociable animal, so some would argue that groups can have 'natural rights'. Religions and nations are the most usual claimants. Opinions differ greatly but I am sceptical of this; they can be or should be justified on other grounds, they appear to me to be historically specific rather than universal (if they are 'rights' then is there a right *not* to have a religion or *not* to be member of a nation, or to change either?). The family is sometimes considered by some to have rights that are prior to those of its individual members (but this may be confusing biological and cultural need with moral judgements – I cannot avoid having been in a family and obviously should have some special obligation to it; but haven't I also on certain conditions a right to break from it?).

20. **Individuality** as a concept is closely related to the concept of **natural rights** but it is what we perceive as unique to each man and possibly to mankind. The content of the concept varies greatly from society to society. Ours is 'individualistic' in a sense almost unknown to the medieval or ancient world to whom in many ways group loyalties were more significant than individuality. We commonly believe that the object of our political activity is the happiness of 'individuals' and sometimes we even believe that actions and opinions can be justified for no other reason than that they are authentic manifestations of individuality, sincere expressions of personality. Marxists teach that 'the individual' is in an imminent category and will only be truly free and individual in the classless society when all oppression ends; and liberals preach that actual individual self-interest is the only possible measure, in the here and now, of the goodness of public policies.

Conservatives tend to be more sceptical about 'man as the measure of all things' and to share with some socialists a sense that community is more important than individualism. But individualism ('thou shalt be as individual as thou can be') or the cult of 'personality' may simply be a caricature or un-necessary extension of individuality. It is hard to conceive of a community that was not composed of, in some sense, biological units exhibiting 'individuality'; but they will not necessarily believe in individualism.

'Individuality' is one of the most difficult concepts to get across in our present society, for an almost militant individualism is so much assumed as natural. We should somehow respect individual differences while being fully aware how much we tend to exaggerate them. (I find that to discuss 'the attempt to dress differently' is a good way to sharpen this perception: the paradox that it all ends up so much alike and that the new clothes don't ensure new or radically different personalities.) No species in nature differs less in physical attributes from member to member than man, yet can differ more in character or psychology.

21. **Freedom** in its weaker or negative sense is being free from arbitrary or unwanted control or intervention but in its stronger or more positive sense it is actually making choices and doing things in a self-willed and uncoerced way. Modern liberalism has tended to stress 'freedom from', as if being left alone as an individual is the best thing to hope for. But the classical idea of 'freedom' was tied to the concept of citizenship, indeed to political activity itself; a free man was someone who takes part in public life in an uncoerced way. Far from 'freedom' being 'the recognition of necessity', things that we must do can hardly be called free actions. 'Necessity, the tyrant's plea', said Milton. Some 'freedom' in a negative sense may exist in autocracies, between the gaps of the laws, the indifferences of the ruler or the inefficiency or corruption of the bureaucracy. In totalitarian societies 'freedom' is actually denounced as an illusion (or else praised to the skies as a great far future event), everything is held in theory to be determined by economic or racial factors. But genuine 'freedom' depends on some distinction and interplay between private and public life. We have

to believe that some things (though they will vary from society to society) are private, not of public concern, and that people are free to immerse themselves in private life; but 'freedom' is obviously endangered if most or many do not choose to participate in public life. In free societies participation is voluntary for each individual, but it is – in greatly varying degrees – encouraged and it is functionally necessary for such societies that 'freedom' is exercised in public affairs. 'Freedom', then, is neither isolation nor loneliness, it is the activity of private men who help to maintain public politics. Politics are the public actions of free men, free men are those who do, not merely can, live both publicly and privately. (My implication is that 'freedom' has to be practised, not just enjoyed, that we have a duty as human beings to make use of our rights; but, of course, when this actually occurs, it can be disturbing for all who govern, manage or teach.)

22. **Welfare** is the belief that the prosperity and happiness of communities and individuals beyond mere physical survival should be the concern of governments. The concept of *needs* is much the same perception and like **rights** both seem to express something which if minimal is almost self-evident, but when elaborated and detailed become infinitely arguable – all the desirable things that the State *could* do for us, at a cost (both of resources and liberty). The 'common good' (which Aquinas stipulated as an object of human government) is close to 'welfare' and as seemingly necessary but as specifically ambiguous. The provision of 'bread' (or whatever is the staple food) is almost universally agreed to be a legitimate demand by individuals upon governments. 'Health' is a very recent candidate – disease and pestilence were once seen as uncontrollable, certainly by governments, perhaps not by prayer or sacrifice. 'Employment' is very modern – only in the 1930s did people begin to believe that periodic cycles or spasms of unemployment were avoidable at all, and some are still not convinced. Education and minimal care of children are now hard to avoid; they are firmly seen, both by governments and governed, as parts of 'welfare'.

Everyone wants more 'welfare'. It seems a self-evident good. But there are two entailments of the concept which cause difficulties: (i) Whereas some 'rights' may be basic to all humanity, 'welfare' is always a package with differing contents. What goes into the package must be considered both economically and morally in terms of a price to be paid in terms of other concepts, values and goods: we live in a world of finite resources and potentially infinite demand. (ii) It is possible for governments to smother people in 'welfare' in order to keep them quiet and politically passive. A century and a half ago Alexis de Tocqueville imagined that despotisms in the future would not exploit their subjects so much as seek to satiate them or keep them full of well-being and entertainment, to do almost anything for them, except to let them govern themselves or enjoy **freedom**. ('Bread *and* circuses', as it were. Some see 'the consumer society' in this way.) Ernest Gellner has recently called our society a 'Danegeld State', and has earlier argued that the legitimacy of all governments in the modern world almost entirely depends upon their ability to increase the standard of living.[5] Of course 'welfare' and 'rights' must progress and go hand in hand; but as concepts they are distinct, and both distinct from 'individuality' and 'freedom' with which they must always be balanced, compromised, related, synthesised – use whatever word you think is best.

THE CONCEPTS SPECIFIED: (iii) THE RELATING CONCEPTS
(Each of these concepts covers a wide range of institutions and beliefs that relate governed to government, and each of which looks different when viewed from on top or from below.)

23. **Law** is the body of general rules, commands, prohibitions and entitlements made by or recognised by government, published and enforced by it and recognised as binding (even if not as **just**) by those whom they can apply to. This definition is complex, largely because I do not believe that people ordinarily regard 'law' simply as the particular command or will of a sovereign – this is a pseudo-realism ('law' must be general, published and recognised as binding, i.e. not 'Off with his head' but 'Be it enacted that all those playing croquet who hit the ball of the Queen of Hearts, whether by chance, accident, design or deliberate intent, either of themselves or of others, whether people or beasts, shall forthwith be beheaded, if it so pleaseth Her Majesty'). Yet the famous 'positive theory of law', that law is the command of the sovereign, is at least half-right; if people do not ordinarily confuse 'law' with mere command, yet they do not confuse it with 'justice' either. Laws can be seen as valid and yet unjust. 'Off with his head' is not law at all; but the 'Be it enacted . . .' as above is clearly a 'law', even if an unjust one.

Constitutional Law is a very complex concept, neither a basic concept nor an especially suitable beginning for an understanding of politics. And 'the Rule of Law' is either a truism, that there should be laws (but about what?) or else is a politically very tendentious assertion that we should ordinarily obey a law simply because it is the 'law'. Others would argue that we should always consider whether or not laws are just before we obey them. Somehow both positions seem extreme in practice.

Many people say that any civilised behaviour necessarily presupposes a belief in 'a rule of law', that is obedience to rules – so that even if the rules are unjust, we should only try to change them according to accepted rules. (Sometimes this is the *only* concept introduced into political education when taught – so incompletely – as 'British Constitution' or 'The Institutions of British Government'.) But two problems arise: (i) What if the rules are so constituted as to avoid change? (ii) Is it true that all complex activities presuppose legal rules? Consider again 'fairness' and the young footballer: he learns to play football by playing football, not by reading the rules (try learning to play croquet by learning the rules!) and his concept of what is fair (or just) does not in fact depend on knowing all the rules (only on observing behaviour and convention),

[5] See Ernest Gellner, 'The Social Contract in Search of an Idiom: the Demise of the Danegeld State', *Political Quarterly*, April–June 1975; and also his *Thought and Change*, Weidenfeld, 1965, chapter 3.

nor logically need it – for the rules could be unjust, ambiguous or self-contradictory. Anyway, 'rules of law', like 'democracy' (the one usually conservative, the other usually radical) is arguably anything but a primary or basic concept.

24. **Justice** or what is right is the most important and complex of concepts into which everyone intrudes their own values; but generally speaking what is just is what people accept as done fairly even if they are either ignorant of the outcome of the process or are even personally disadvantaged. 'Is this a *fair* way to decide?' usually means the same as 'is this a just way to decide?'. Analogies and comparisons are more often invoked than absolute standards or first principles. To deal with people justly or fairly is always to deal with them consistently relative to other cases and to changed circumstances. When absolute standards or first principles are invoked, they have to be applied to concrete problems; so inevitably the application will involve comparisons, relativities, calculations of the probable consequences, and – most important morally – consideration of other people's standards and principles. How easy it would be if 'idealism' were always confronted with 'naked self-interest'; but idealism is often confronted with idealism, morality with morality and 'naked self-interest' anyway usually wears fig leaves of many colours. 'To temper justice with mercy' is usually to confuse **law** with 'justice'. For 'law', as general rules, needs mercy, forgiveness or justifiable exceptions to be morally acceptable; but the concept of 'justice' ordinarily includes all these already. All political doctrines are concerned with social justice, or the proper distribution of goods, rewards and punishments of all kinds. Political doctrines are necessarily accounts of both what can or could be the case and of what should be the case. Hence nearly every relationship possible between ruler and ruled is perceived in some way as concerned with 'justice'.

25. **Representation** is the most general justification for why a few may rule many or for how the many try to control the few in terms of embodying some external attribute. But there are many more external attributes validating claims to represent than to represent 'the people'. Historically most governments claimed to represent the will of the gods or of God. Others have claimed **authority** because they are representative of a race or a caste, a tribe or a family, a class or a nation; or of reason or of either inherited or acquired skills; or of traditional areas, of property, interests, the 'general will', the Party, 'the People' or of individuals. And all of the claims can be put either in the form that representation is a mandated delegation, or else a responsible discretion. The matter is complicated but not infinitely so. If people have claimed that their **power** is representative for other reasons, then I have missed them. My point is simply that the concept is of far wider applicability than 'representative institutions' in parliamentary or electoral senses. A 'representative of the people' should also beware that he may be representing government to the people quite as much as he represents the people to the Government. 'Representative institutions', indeed, can both control and actually strengthen governments. It is

a two-way business. 'Representation' is not just to be seen then as a **right** of the people, it can also be a necessity of power. 'Because we wish to build the Federal pyramid to a great height', said one of the participants in the Philadelphia Convention, 'its roots must go deep.'

26. **Pressure** constitutes all those means by which government and people can influence each other politically for specified purposes, other than **force** or **law** directly. Force or Law may both be used as threats: if expressed public opinion, persuasion, example, economic, social or psychological influence fail or falter, then 'force' may 'have to' follow or the 'law' will 'have to' be changed. But public opinion, persuasion, example, economic, social and psychological influence are the normal forms of 'pressure'. To exert 'pressure', organisation is ordinarily called for, thus parties and pressure groups are the most important institutionalised forms of 'pressure'. But to stress institutions exclusively, as often happens in introductory teaching, is to make the same kind of mistake as when **representation** is remorselessly narrowed to electoral systems from the word go: both comprehension and imagination are limited. Certainly there is an element of unreality in assuming any longer that most political pressures in our society come from the parties, even perhaps from the obvious pressure groups. And pressure is not merely exercised through representative institutions, it is exercised through the press and the other media, indeed, books still count surprisingly: and it is exercised privately just by words and gestures. Types of disorder (see 'order' above) are also, when used as threats for limited and defined ends, types of 'pressure'. And there is not merely the stick but also the carrot; praise is a form of pressure as great as blame, criticism or threat. Almost any kind of 'pressure', like 'force', can be justified *in some circumstances*, provided that the object of the pressure is definable, specific and potentially realisable.

WHAT IS ALL THAT ABOUT?
27. Two words of warning. To understand concepts is not to understand a society, but only a preliminary step. To understand a society and its political system is to understand the *working* of its dominant concepts and their relationships.

28. To say again that I do not advocate the direct teaching or learning of concepts except perhaps at an advanced level (anyway definitions of concepts can be learned by rote quite as easily as constitutional rules and conventions). All I advocate is a far greater conceptual awareness in interpreting material in any study of politics from the simplest component of early secondary school Social Studies to Public Administration for DMA; that curriculum development should build-in issues, cases and problems that establish and sharpen some such concepts and distinctions as I have tried to make. A large part of political literacy will consist in exposing the conceptual presuppositions of assertions about institutions and needs which claim to be purely factual and descriptive (but having exposed them, of course, it does not follow that all repressions are bad,

as Marcuse once sweepingly assumed: some would do better for themselves if exposed to critical light, some not).[6]

29. A second paper will argue that there are five concepts which must be treated as 'procedural values', that is as preconditions of political literacy or necessary assumptions of any political education which is not simply indoctrination or imposed socialisation.[7]

---

[6] See the title essay in my *Political Theory and Practice*, Allen Lane, 1973.
[7] Since the first issue of this paper, a strong attack on the propriety of proceeding by 'political literacy' rather than by political philosophy has been made by John and Pat White, 'A Programme for Political Education: a critique' *Teaching Politics*, September 1976, and replied to by Bernard Crick in the May 1977 number of the same journal. [Editors]

Tabular summary

Government

Power
The ability to achieve an intended effect either by force or more usually by claims to authority

Force
Physical pressure or use of weapons to achieve an intended effect—latent in all government, constant in none

Authority
Respect and obedience given by virtue of an institution, group or person fulfilling a function agreed to be needed and in which he or it has superior knowledge or skill

Order
When expectations are fulfilled and calculations can be made without fear of all the circumstances and assumptions changing

Relationships

Law
The body of general rules made, published and enforced by governments and recognised as binding by the government even if not as just

Justice
What is due to people as the result of some process accepted as fair irrespective of the outcome

Representation
The claim for the few to represent the many because they embody some external attribute, of which popular consent is only one of many

Pressure
All the means by which government and people influence each other, other than by Law or by Force

People

Natural rights
The minimum conditions for proper human existence—prior even to legal and political rights

Individuality
What we perceive as unique to each man and to mankind—to be distinguished from individualism, a purely 19th-century doctrine

Freedom
The making of choices and doing things of public significance in a self-willed and uncoerced way

Welfare
The belief that the prosperity and happiness of individuals and communities is a concern of government, not merely mere survival

2.4 Procedural values in political education
Bernard Crick

1. This paper constitutes Working Paper No. 4 of the Programme for Political Education.[1] It follows from the last paper[2] which suggested a possible set of basic political concepts which could be useful to the teacher to apply to whatever materials or methods he or she is using, and from which all more complex political concepts and theories could be constructed. This table serves as a brief reminder.

GOVERNMENT			
Power	Force	Authority	Order
RELATIONSHIPS			
Law	Justice	Representation	Pressure
PEOPLE			
Natural Rights	Individuality	Freedom	Welfare

These are, in one sense, value-free, when considered simply as concepts or as definitions of usage. But when they are put to use in political life, they will always be value-charged. Every political doctrine will adopt a usage or offer a definition which is partial, one part of the cluster of meanings of the concept developed, bent, slanted, twisted or pointed in a particular direction. If the twisting goes so far, however, as to contradict the common core of meaning or associations of meaning in other partial definitions of the concept, we are entitled to say that a person is then talking nonsense, failing to communicate. or being as proud and silly as Humpty Dumpty who, we all remember, told Alice that words meant what he said they meant. For example, the ordinary conventions of language come near to breaking point when people say, however well-meaning they are, such things as 'In thy service, Lord, is the only perfect freedom' or 'Freedom is the recognition of necessity'. What in fact has happened is that something other than freedom is being talked about, perhaps something more important than freedom (the love of God or the laws of history, respectively); but then it is better said through the direct use of these other concepts; to drag in 'freedom' is both rhetorical and confusing. And in morals and politics it is very tempting, as Orwell was forever showing, to try to take over a prestigious

[1] Unlike documents 2.1 and 2.2, this and the Basic Concepts paper while issued by the Working Party do not necessarily represent their individual or collective viewpoints.
[2] See Bernard Crick, 'Basic Concepts for Political Education', *Teaching Politics*, September 1975, pp. 153–68.

but awkward word, rather than to argue either explicitly and rationally for its modification or that it is irrelevant. We are all for 'democracy'.

So whatever our objective, whether to understand political life or to participate in it effectively, or better still, both, some conceptual sophistication is needed wherever there is politics and political activity. Of course every society will have its special values and every society needs concepts more complex than those in my box. All I claimed in the previous paper was that all the complex concepts that we are likely to encounter can be built up from them, so that they are a more suitable beginning than complex concepts, however important.

2. But though concepts are value-free in themselves, high degrees of political literacy are, in fact, rare. Even in Western democracies much encouragement to participate is hot-air, or wills the end perhaps but rarely the means; there can be positive discouragement; and there is also a sheer lack of political education. In most other types of regime, political education is not allowed at all, only indoctrination; and so much of that that it gives political education a bad name. Even in regimes with political education, there is often more unconscious indoctrination than is supposed. We are socialized into many expectations even before we think about them; but, of course, to realise this is to be able to guard against it, to remedy or remove by critical thought some of the bad consequences (for surely not all socialisation is wrong or un-free; much is trivial and much is convenient). If there is a genuine political education, certain values are presupposed. I will call these procedural values, for they are not substantive values like various justifications of authority, like equality or types of justice, but rather presuppositions of any kind of genuine political education or free political activity. For one thing, the politically literate person cannot just accept one set of values as correct; he will see that the very nature of politics lies in there being a plurality of values and interests, of which he must have at least some minimal understanding.

3. In paragraph 6 of document 2.1 of the Programme for Political Education these procedural values were boldly and simply identified as 'freedom, toleration, fairness, respect for truth and respect for reasoning'. I claim that these are procedural values in that there cannot be any reasonable study or practice of politics, other than simple indoctrination, which does not presuppose such values. As we will see, they are not specifically 'liberal' – except in a very broad humanistic sense: they are compatible with many different doctrines and social systems. My omission of 'market values', indeed of economic concepts in general, is (*vide* Sir Keith Joseph's criticism[3]) deliberate. For they are too specific and their entailments, however justifiable, are too partial to be the basis of any possible genuine political education (although they are part of the subject matter which should be studied as doctrines, in the societies in which they arise or to which they might sensibly apply). We deal with conflicts of values. So we protest against any attempts. Marxist or liberal-capitalist, to build into the whole

---

[3] See Sir Keith Joseph, "Education, Politics and Society" *Teaching Politics*, January 1976, an interesting critique of some aspects of the Programme.

activity of political education the very assumptions that they wish through practice to universalise. It is strange that those who talk well about a 'critical sociology', a 'critical political economy', or 'critical politics', in fact seem to presume a far more complete social theory than I can easily imagine to be possible, let alone desirable to teach as if it was true; or they see 'a true perspective', a theory quite as comprehensive as the liberal theory of the capitalist market which they attack. This reduces criticism to a laboured, mechanical and uneducative account of the discrepancy between their model and what they claim all other people's models to be. Theory itself must be included in criticism. This is another reason why we are for beginning with issues, specifying 'political literacy, and working through basic concepts, rather than beginning with theories and doctrines. Only if the pupil, the student, the citizen finds for himself through dealing with issues that patterns of explanation and response emerge, will theory prove meaningful and useful. If it comes first, it is imposed – whether in the names of Burke, Adam Smith or Karl Marx.

4. I assume that a teacher should not ordinarily seek to influence the substantive values of pupils – and that frontal assaults are not likely, in any case, to be successful.[4] But I assume that it is proper and possible to nurture and strengthen these procedural values precisely because they are educational values, rational and public. Anyone can see that in real life and politics there are many occasions when these values may have to be modified, because they can conflict with each other or with substantive values such as religious, ethical and political doctrines embody. Part of political education is to examine just such conflicts. But this does not in any way affect the primacy of these procedural values within a genuine political education. The objection to them is, indeed, more likely to be that they are pie more than poison, nebulous platitudes more than harsh indoctrinatory concepts.

5. But has one any right, it will first be asked, to indoctrinate even the basic assumptions of a genuine political education in or for a political-democratic order? If we follow I. A. Snook's argument in his *Indoctrination and Education*, Routledge, 1972, indoctrination is teaching something to be believed as true regardless of evidence. This points to how indoctrination can be avoided even in the introduction of basic procedural concepts. But what is the 'evidence' for a concept, it will be argued? The 'evidence' for a concept is to discover a common core of meaning amid a variety of different political usages, to bring out the implications of using it in different ways and never to be categorical that there is one correct usage. But no more than with the basic concepts am I suggesting that these should be directly taught, still less taught first. Rather they should gradually be made more explicit, being already implied in whatever

---

[4] The more exclusive and vicious values may appear, for example that all Blacks, Papists, Prods and Green-haired men (and women) are despicable, the less open they are to influence or reason of the kind possible or proper in the classroom. But *how* these values are held and expressed can and should be influenced though schools alone can rarely change them.

is done – if it is education and not indoctrination. At the end of this paper, I set out a diagram specifying 'political literacy' and superimpose on it the points where these procedural concepts are most likely to be made explicit. Now to consider the values themselves.

6. **Freedom** Freedom is the making of choices and doing things of public significance or potentially public significance in a self-willed and uncoerced way. This is not merely a basic concept and a value, it is in a formal sense, a procedural value, for without freedom there can be neither knowledge of nor voluntary participation in politics. True, some regimes deny freedom and thus knowledge of politics is low, but even the secret writing or the samizdat is some sign of freedom, however minimal, of potential importance; but it is hard to imagine (even in Nineteen Eighty-Four) that there is not a functional necessity for some freedom of action for some agents of the oppressor. Even in science-fiction's despotisms, the computer and the robots need programming (and when they begin, as is customary, to get their own ideas, we are back where we started again with something like the dilemmas and delights, the uses and abuses of human freedom). But to conceive of a political education which did not seek to maximize freedom would be paradoxical.

I prefer to use the word 'freedom' to the word 'liberty' simply because it has a somewhat more positive connotation. It suggests not merely being at liberty from specified restraints and interventions, but being free actually to choose between alternatives. 'They are perfectly at liberty to complain', is usually a very qualified truth, whereas 'they are acting much too freely', may well be true, but it does imply action. Easier to restrain excess than to try to arouse habitual passivity. Liberty can be potential or on licence, but freedom is an activity. No value is an end in itself, however, or automatically overrides all other values. Freedom is to be encouraged, and tested by whether it is exercised; but it will be limited by other values. So if freedom is a component of political literacy, it carries an image of recurrent use about it, not simply learning how our glorious liberties were preserved for us by well-meaning gentlemen.

7. **Toleration** Toleration is the degree to which we accept things of which we disapprove. The need for toleration would not arise if there were not disapproval. It is inherently a two-dimensional concept, both disapproval and restraint or forbearance are involved. Thus to be tolerant is usually to express a disapproval, but to express it in a fair way and without forcing it on another. But absence of force does not at all imply absence of any attempt to persuade. What is fair by way of persuasion will be relative to the circumstance. (We surely, to make a small point in passing, expect to be exposed to different sorts of influence and information in the class room than in the party or union branch meeting.) It is very important for political education to grasp the difference between 'toleration', in our sense, and 'permissiveness' – an often futile debate. 'Permissiveness' may, indeed, imply not caring whether something is done or not. But from the fact of a person caring, it does not logically follow that he must be in favour of restraints: he may be in favour of toleration, for instance,

of allowing the behaviour but making his disapproval clear. Certainly toleration should not be encouraged as an end in itself; it is simply a response to living together amid conflicts of values. Neutrality is not to be encouraged: to be biased is human and to try to unbias people is to emasculate them. Bias as such is not to be condemned, only that gross bias which leads to inaccurate perceptions of the nature of other interests, groups and ideals.[5] Teachers, educational institutions and political regimes are not to be condemned for bias or for anything as natural and inevitable as attempting to maintain themselves; they are only, in terms of reason and education, to be condemned if they do so in an intolerant manner, in such a way as to repress deliberately or to distort unpleasant facts, contrary opinions, rival doctrines, challenging theories.

Two important inferences can be drawn from the concept: (i) someone who is politically literate will hold views of his own, but will hold them in such a way that he is tolerant of the views of others; and (ii) that as tolerance in part depends on knowledge of the behaviour and beliefs associated with other viewpoints, this knowledge should be taught and the pupil should be tested in his powers of empathy.[6] 'State the case for...', 'what would a conservative/liberal/ socialist want to do about this problem...' and 'Play the role of a Scottish Nationalist in this game...' – are all familiar devices which help strengthen an important component of political literacy.

Empathy is a skill to be developed quite as much as direct participation, indeed the one strengthens the other: toleration is neither simply an attitude nor knowledge, but is both together. Even in political life, empathy has great tactical value. The dogmatic activist all too often fails to understand his opponents, commonly hanging them all together as 'fascists' or 'Marxists', and therefore adopts wholly inappropriate tactics.

8. **Fairness** 'Fairness' may seem vague compared to 'justice', but it is the word of common usage. Also the most ambitious modern attempt to state a philosophical theory of justice, John Rawls' *A Theory of Justice* (Oxford, 1972), resolves the overly legalistic, traditional discussion of 'justice' into the more general considerations of what is thought to be fair and what is fair. Earlier, though certainly influenced by Rawls, W. G. Runciman's work on equality, *Relative Deprivation and Social Justice* (Routledge, 1966) showed empirically that working people judged other peoples' wages by whether the differences were 'fair' or not (some were thought to be fair, some not) and concluded that whereas equality cannot be stated precisely as a social goal or justified in general terms as an ideal, 'less unjustifiable inequalities' (or less unfairness) can. So it is reasonable to demand that all inequalities should justify themselves. (It

[5] See Bernard Crick, 'On Bias', *Teaching Politics*, May 1972 and Jonathan Brown, 'Bias' in his and Tom Brennan's (eds) *Teaching Politics: Problems and Perspective*, London BBC Publications, 1975, pp. 33–40.

[6] A third consequence would follow, that it is rarely sensible (even if justifiable) to try to influence 'prejudices' directly, however reprehensible they may be/seem, i.e. racial prejudices. Usually better to extend knowledge of the other group, and to try to identify and extend what areas of tolerance there are; not to show concern with the prejudice as such, but only with its perceptual accuracy and its mode of expression. See Bernard Crick and Sally Jenkinson, 'Good Intentions and Muddled Thinking', *Times Educational Supplement*, 6 November 1970, 20 and 55.

is fair, says Runciman, to respect all men equally, but unfair to praise them equally.)

Certainly 'fairness', however vague, is to be preferred to the misleading precision of 'rule of law' which many would make a prerequisite both for political-democratic order and for political education. 'What rules of law?' can be asked. If only there were, but that begs the question. Must we adhere to 'rules in general' so long as they have been legitimately made or derived whatever their content or outcome? Perhaps, but then have they been fairly made or derived? That may be the very question to ask; otherwise making 'rule of law' a basic value begs the question and usually smuggles into an argument about rules or procedures some highly substantive content. Surely, 'Are the rules fair?' is a prior question to 'Is it fair by the rules?' You may have accepted the Social Contract, but (i) I don't know what it is; (ii) I haven't. You must convince me that it is fair. A propensity to obey rules in general is surely good if the rules are good. Plato, after all, long ago distinguished between law and justice (by which he meant righteousness). Socrates was a good man – who broke the law; so did Jesus. We cannot hide behind such a vague formula; we have got to come out, in the classroom as well as (hopefully) our leaders on the platforms, and justify every instance that is challenged, defend it or abandon it, not claim that they all hang together and that the unjustifiable must be carried by the justifiable (which is often what people mean by the 'rule of law'). Besides, it simply is not true that we need to know what the rules are before we can effectively and responsibly participate in politics or, for instance, play football. Football, even played reasonably fairly, long preceded the existence of known or enforceable rules; and a precise knowledge of them would not be high in the list of relevant skills. Similarly a knowledge of constitutional rules is an odd beginning for a genuine political education.

The simplest version of Rawls would seem to be that we should accept an outcome as fair if we can imagine that we were party, along with all others likely to be affected, in a state of equality (or equality of influence) to establishing rules to settle disputes without prior knowledge of the outcome. In other words, 'fairness' follows from what in principle I would accept as a proper way of making decisions without knowing whether the outcome of the process will benefit or harm me.

This sounds very abstract. But the politically literate person will question whether the distribution of goods, rewards and praise is fair or not. And he will be satisfied (or not) that it is by being asked and asking the further question, 'Can you think of a better way of doing it that would be acceptable to others?'

Tripped in the penalty area, penalty given and the vital goal scored, there can be four reactions from the defenders. (i) 'Not fair to lose by a penalty', both invalid as an argument and immoral; (ii) 'That's the rule, what the Ref says is it', which implies a passive fear of the referee or a dangerous assumption that one may properly do anything if not seen or stopped; or (iii) a calm or even grudging 'Fair enough' – which is fair enough and the best we hope for. But if (iv) the defender improbably said, with happy civic virtue and self-righteousness, 'Well I declare, that's a good example of what happens if we break the rules' we might judge this man to be politically illiterate even if, of course, well-taught. Let us not ask for too much.

9. **Respect for truth** If relevant truths cannot be told about how government is conducted or what politics is about, then political education is impossible. Anything that is even potentially relevant to how government is conducted, how decisions are made, how the individual may perceive what his interests are and how he may defend them, must be capable of being stated publicly, if believed to be true on some evidence that is stateable; and stated at any level of education in which the questions arise, however simplified it has to be. If the full truth is too difficult to grasp, or is simply unknown, what are strictly speaking 'myths' should never be put forward, either for mistaken social or moral reasons or simply to have simpler models – i.e. the stork, the Queen as ruler, the British Constitution, the Prime Minister as above the battle, the cabinet as collective and dispassionate wisdom, the House of Commons as 635 members elected for and by constituents in the general interest (with no thought of Party), civil servants only carrying out orders not helping to make policy or that each social class has a clear mind of its own, etc. etc. Simplification must not involve falsification, however innocent the motives. When the teller of what lies is found out, it is he who has discredited legitimate authority.

A politically literate person will ask awkward questions early. Political literacy must involve knowing that the truth has to be faced, however embarrassing or difficult. The child is surely shocked by parents quarrelling openly with hysterical selfishness. If he has to be made aware why this can happen in the world, this does not imply habituating him to it. Individuals can only grow and societies improve amid the tension between knowing what the facts are and wishing to change them.

Formidable arguments based upon 'reason of state' were once made that there are some things only knowable by natural rulers and that there is some knowledge that must always be kept from the people if order is to be preserved. This might seem utterly discredited. But some modern concepts of 'ideology' are sophisticated versions of this old 'politic' argument, i.e. that those who really understand the ideology, the inner party, or the free-lance dialecticians, know that it is best for everyone if propaganda and indoctrination could replace the elitist, humanist practice of genuine critical education – for the moment, of course, until conditions are right for freedom and truth-speaking and non-censorship. Truth is what is useful to the cause. The 'ideologically correct' is what the truth will be tomorrow (if we can get our hands on you today), rather than what you miserable, supine load of brainwashed brothers happen to think it is right now. But as modern writers like Orwell and Koestler have argued, there is a simple sense in which a lie is still a lie, and a half-truth is a half-lie, whether told for country or party; and that regimes that depend upon systematic lies are neither worthy of support, nor likely to be stable without systematic coercive oppression. But if these opponents cannot make enough capital out of exposing the untruths of autocracy but invent their own counter-myths and ideologies, then this is a sure sign that they are trying to make too much capital too fast and before the shareholders wake up to see what is happening.

Put positively, one necessary condition of a free and just regime is/would be that the truth can be discovered and publicly told and taught about how all decisions of government are made. There are obvious practical limitations: security, anticipation of economic decisions, confidentiality and libel. There are occasions in which limitations on truth-telling, indeed on forms of expression in general, are justifiable. But the literate person must presume a right to know and that everything should be told unless there are compelling and generally acceptable reasons to the contrary. If there are occasions when for the safety of the state truth should not be told, in political education these must always be presented as extraordinarily exceptional, as calling for very special justifications and reasons. In hard times lying or just not telling the truth can be regarded as a test of party loyalty, but never of a political education.

10. **Respect for reasoning** It may seem pompously needless to include respect for reasoning as a precondition for political literacy. But it does need stressing that to be politically literate means a willingness to give reasons (however ill-formed or simple) why one holds a view and to give justifications for one's actions, and to demand them of others – simply because to do so goes against some other powerful cultural and educational tendencies of our times. Some hold, for instance, that if an opinion is sincerely held, it should not be questioned (a belief that all prejudices are equal), nor should justifications be pressed for in respect to actions that are held to be authentic expressions of personality (a belief that no feelings should be hurt by being questioned). Others regard reasons as unnecessary if actions can be certified as authentic or typical emanations of some group interest – 'working class solidarity' or 'middle class moderation', for instance. Some progressives, after having properly attacked Burkean ideas that prejudices drawn from experience and tradition are a sufficient guide to political conduct, have now made a cult of sincerity, authenticity or typicality. Sincerity, authenticity, spontaneity, typicality, etc. are values to be cultivated, but not as a cult or a one-crop moral economy; such values must grow alongside others. Since politics is so much concerned with consequences on others, that reasons shall always be given and justifications offered for effects unwelcome to some others, is of fundamental importance.

Another reason why this great part of our Western political tradition that came from the Greeks, that politics involved reasoning among ourselves, is not to be taken for granted is because such political education as there now is usually comes not from schools or media, but from waging of General Election campaigns by leading politicians. A young person could form the opinion that politics is (i) a residual claim to govern on the simple ground that the other side is inherently stupid and tells so many lies: (ii) simply the expression of social interests, and (iii) simply an auction of speculative benefits for probable support. So little reasoning and canvassing of principles enters into current electoral campaigning that politics may seem just a question of 'who gets what, when and how'.

Respect for reasoning comes from analogy and examples: in the polity, the home and the school. We are only discussing the latter, but the context is always there. The teacher himself must give reasons why things are done in certain ways, particularly when he meets a new class or when changes are made. It is beside the point to object that reasons given to young children may often not be understood; for the real point is that the habit of giving reasons and expecting them to be given is basic both to intellectual method (as distinct from memorizing) and to political democracy (as distinct from passive obedience). I do not understand why I should do some of the things the doctor tells me to do, but I do believe (usually rightly) that he could explain if I asked (and I get worried if he refuses even to try). Of course there is much more to it than this, for I know that there are other doctors: part of political literacy is knowing that there are both alternative means towards any end and alternative sources of information.

The giving of reasons, even the obligation to give reasons and to justify what one teaches and how, does not destroy legitimate authority – on the contrary, the refusal to give reasons encourages either passivity or rebellion. The indulgent, permissive view that all reasons are equally subjective simply enshrines sincerity, self-expression and authenticity as king, as against reason, truth and love; so that then all authority is seen as bad authority. As we have argued above, a basic part of political literacy is to be able to distinguish between power and authority. Few types of authority can subsist on coercion alone, but then some authority is justifiable and some not. In general authority has been seen by political philosophers as justifiable when it fulfils expertly or skilfully some function widely agreed to be needed. To exercise authority is not, as such, to be authoritarian: to be authoritarian is when 'an authority' seeks to exercise power beyond the admitted function. The most simple form of authoritarianism is the extension of legitimate authority into topics and areas in which it has no relevance and competence. Education, both in home and school, can be seen as a process of increasing differentiation of function; thus the authority of both the parent and the school are originally very wide and generalised, but then they become more and more specific. Within the accepted areas, the authority can actually be stronger. But such authority depends on the giving of relevant reasons.

Similarly it is not intolerant as such to disapprove of people's viewpoints and to express the disapproval, only if the disapproval (by 'authority', for instance) refuses to hear contradictions and suppresses opportunities for dissent. 'Taking advantage of one's position' is not wrong, indeed usually proper, often a duty – if, and only if, 'the others are given a fair chance'.

Obviously a respect for reasoning and for legitimate (i.e. specified) authority is part of all education, not specifically political education. The question how much political attitudes are conditioned by the general organisation of the school as distinct from particular teaching within the school is, we would argue, an empirical question – on which little reliable research has been done. But we are not impressed by the *a priori* argument that reforms of school organisation are the only way to get a better political education. The argument that the school is a good model of the general political system, to be studied as such, must seem of limited truth even in the United States where it is often heard; here it seems faintly ridiculous. But *a priori* we might suspect that important negative relations exist: the kind of presuppositions to political literacy that we are discussing could hardly be expected to flourish in those few schools, for instance, where children can still see a head teacher interrupt his colleagues without apology or warning, and know that nothing is ever discussed between those 'authorities' whom they know and respect, their teachers, and 'the authority', the one man of power, the head.

11. Lastly there follows the diagrammatic specification for political literacy from document 2.2, with the 'procedural values' imposed on it to show the kind of factors in an 'issues approach' which might best combine to illustrate the actual working of the concepts which I have been discussing. This is for the teacher's own benefit but perhaps could usefully be made explicit with students who have already done a good deal of work on social and political problems by use of the 'literacy tree'. Again I stress that I am not advocating the direct teaching of concepts, 'basic' or 'procedural'.

12. Another paper will suggest how to specify what are political issues and problems. That will conclude all I personally think useful to say about political education in principle, or that at any rate all that I feel competent to say, until we discover far more from teachers, students and surveys about what happens in practice and what works best. Much of this series of essays could be wrong or misguided. And no one account of how to decide what are issues is ever likely to be generally acceptable; others will follow. But one must begin somewhere.

(January 1976)

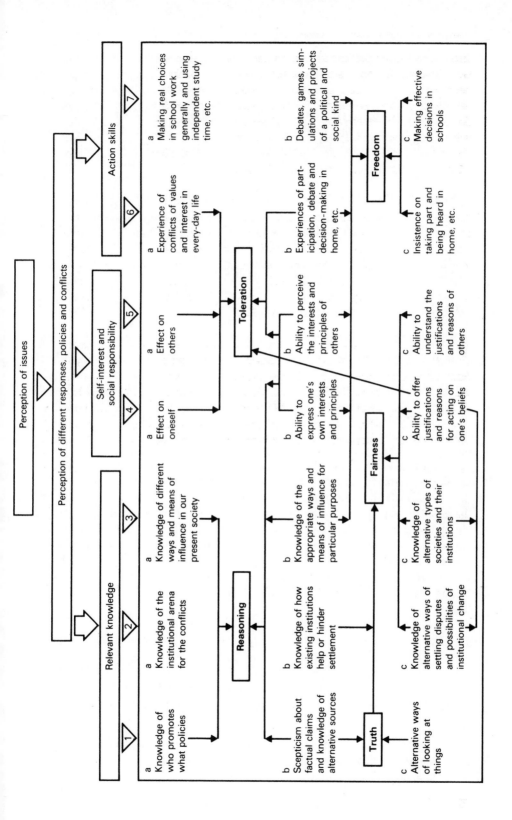

2.5 Issues and political problems
Robert Stradling and Alex Porter

WHAT IS AN ISSUE?

1. In previous working papers issued by the Programme for Political Education it has been suggested that one of the most appropriate ways to begin to develop political literacy is through a consideration of political problems and issues rather than through the study of political theories or institutions. But what are political issues and problems, what methods can we use to identify them, and how can they be treated in the classroom?

2. In document No. 2.2 on 'Political Literacy' it was stated that examples of 'the political' can be found in the speeches and behaviour of professional politicians and political activists, the writings of political scientists, and in 'the politics of everyday life'. This clearly implies a wider definition of politics than, say, the activities of the State, and throughout this paper we have used the term 'politics' to refer to the process through which conflicts of interests and values within a group are conciliated. Such conflicts generally arise over the way in which scarce resources are allocated, and by resources we mean not only material goods but also power, status, skills, time and space. This kind of conflict can occur in any group of two or more people (hence the reference to 'the politics of everyday life') but does not necessarily or always lead to political activity. Recourse to this process of conciliation is most likely to occur in those groups where there is some element of compulsion upon the members which makes secession from the group difficult, and therefore conciliation is necessary if the group is to continue to exist. The most obvious example of such a group is the State which, through its territorial monopoly of legitimate authority, is able to use such sanctions as the power over life and death, imprisonment and exile in attempting to enforce its decisions. Other groups may not have such weighty sanctions but are still characterised by some element of compulsory membership, e.g. the school. Political activity is not so frequent or so extensive in voluntary groups. The absence of compulsion means that when there is a serious conflict of interests or values the group may simply break up. There is, then, a qualitative difference between voluntary and involuntary groups which should be borne in mind when looking at the politics of everyday life.

3. Conflicts of interest and values only arise when the members of the group perceive that they are affected by some past, present or future decision and, furthermore, perceive those effects as injustices rather than as inevitabilities. In other words, the conflict arises because this particular decision is or will be a matter of dispute or issue within the group. By 'issue' we mean disagreements over:

> **goals** – where are we going? what purposes would a given action serve?
> **values** – in what way should we act or not act?
> **methods** – how should we do it?

74

results – was it the right outcome?
the fairest?   the best?
the one that was required?

Not all issues are necessarily political. Some may be purely technical, scientific, artistic or moral. An issue is political only if it creates the kind of conflict within the group which generates political activity.

4. This kind of conflict or political problem arises under the following conditions:

a. when there is a dispute amongst the members of the group concerning the allocation of resources or over values;
b. when the disputing members of the group demand a common decision to be taken which will be binding on the whole group;[1]
c. when this common decision has to be taken if the group is to continue.

PROCEDURES FOR SELECTING ISSUES
5. There are at least five ways in which teachers may set about selecting issues:

Objective Measures
a. They may turn to the opinion polls. Some half-dozen agencies publish findings based upon political research but only the two largest, National Opinion Polls, whose findings appear in the *Daily Mail*, and Gallup, whose findings appear in the *Daily Telegraph*, regularly publish public opinion on the key national issues. There are minor differences in the questions which these two agencies ask but basically they follow the same format of presenting people with a list of issues and asking them which one is the most important. Some academic surveys also provide useful guides to public opinion on issues (see, for example, Butler & Stokes, *Political Change in Britain*, London 1969.)
b. A second source is the media both at the national and local levels. Because of their role as a two-way intermediary between the government and the public, the media inevitably play an important part in determining whether an issue becomes salient for the local, national or even international communities.
c. They may also turn to the vast amount of material issued by the political parties in the form of manifestos, election addresses and party political broadcasts. Such political communications do not always, of course, provide the reader or viewer with lucid discussions of the issues of the day. Governments often seek to play down issues in the belief that their chances will be enhanced by a 'quiet election' or they emphasise their past record, while Opposition parties sometimes prefer to fight an election on the negative aspects of the Government's record or on the grounds that they have 'the better men for the job'.

---

[1] This does not necessarily mean that the decision will affect the whole group (in a large group most decisions will only directly affect a part of the group), nor does it necessarily mean that all members of the group will be in agreement about the decision. It means only that for the time being they are prepared to abide by it.

Nevertheless they are still a useful first step towards identifying what the politicians believe to be the national issues of the day, particularly if supplemented by reports of parliamentary debates on the key issues.

'Politics of Everyday Life'
d. While these first three approaches may be said to be empirical, an alternative is, of course, for the teacher to use his or her own judgement and select the issues situationally. We would suggest, however, that in adopting this approach the teacher should look at political or potentially political situations through the set of filtering criteria suggested in *Analysis of Political Issues* in this document.
e. Such questions link up with the fifth possibility, namely that of asking the pupils themselves to select the issues. There is a risk with this approach that it might simply reinforce the existing prejudices of the pupil and we therefore suggest that the teacher still uses the filtering criteria suggested below and, in the case of national issues, draw comparisons with the other sources outlined in a, b, and c above.

6. We make no attempt here to specify which issues are most suitable but the following guidelines should be kept in mind when choosing examples. Where possible select those issues: (i) which are appropriate to and manageable in a particular teaching context; (ii) on which there is sufficient resource material; and (iii) which are interesting to pupils, although, of course, we realise that this last suggestion is fraught with difficulties. Finally we should also stress that while the national importance of an issue is always a factor to be kept in mind it is not, by itself, necessarily the best indicator of suitability for teaching or developing political literacy.

7. The first three approaches outlined in paragraph 5 are useful, objective means of identifying national political issues, i.e. those public disputes which are perceived as having important consequences for the nation as a whole or about which a significant part of the nation is deeply concerned and seeks government action. However, there are both advantages and disadvantages in each approach and the latter should be briefly considered here. Opinion polls, for example, do not always find out which issues people think particularly relevant or salient. Their check lists tend only to find out which of the *listed* issues is thought to be the most important. The open-ended approach as adopted by Butler & Stokes, does not have the same disadvantage.[2] Also the check lists tend to use broad headings such as **housing** or **industrial relations** which may conceal a wider range of issues, but this is not always the case. Other issues on their lists such as **unemployment, cost of living** or **immigration** are much more clear-cut. In spite of disadvantages the polls do provide the teacher with a useful insight into what the public thinks are the main issues or, in some cases, the main problem areas on which the government should take action. The media also present some difficulties as sources, chief of which is their tendency to select the issues for

[2] David Butler and Donald Stokes, *Political Change in Britain*, (London 1969).

extensive coverage which make good copy and are newsworthy and, in the case of television, provide good television pictures and may, in consequence, not always give full coverage to issues thought to be important by the politicians or interested sections of the public. Because of this it is inadvisable to rely solely on the media as a means of identifying issues but they do usefully complement approaches 5a. and c. Some of the difficulties in using party literature have already been mentioned and, of course, it is often the case that the politicians do not always feel as strongly about some issues as the public, while some issues which do concern them may have little salience for most of the electorate. Nevertheless, as Macfarlane has shown, election addresses have tended to focus on the same issues as those which have ranked highly on public opinion polls.[3] This is not the place to examine whether this rough consensus between the public and the political parties on national issues is the result of the public's influence on the government or vice versa. We are suggesting only that the most appropriate and objective approach to identifying national issues is to *combine* all three ways (5a., b. and c.).

8. In contrast to the first three approaches, the last two (5d. and e.) are more appropriate for identifying political issues in everyday life. More is said in document 2.6 about the implications of these two approaches for developing political literacy, but at this point a brief comment about the use of the politics of everyday life in teaching is necessary. Firstly, because this area of politics is directly experienced by the pupil it is possible that he or she will find it more interesting (although we should point out that there is no evidence to show whether they are more interested. This is something which can only be established in the classroom itself). Secondly, for most people this is the only area of political life in which they can participate. The politics of everyday life may also serve as a useful heuristic device for understanding political concepts and political behaviour at wider levels but its usefulness as an analogy is limited. The state is not the family or the school on a larger scale, and so the analogy should not be stretched too far. For this reason, and also because there is some evidence that young people have a rather narrow conception of 'politics' and may therefore have difficulty in following the analogy, we have doubts about the wisdom and efficacy of constructing a teaching programme which implies some form of concentric model, i.e. starting with the politics of everyday life, then community politics, national politics, and finally the international level. We would suggest that it may be better to draw direct comparisons between the different levels from the outset.

ANALYSIS OF POLITICAL ISSUES

9. In paragraph 5d. we referred to a set of filtering criteria which teachers could employ in selecting issues. This would involve firstly examining the form or forms in which the dispute is expressed, i.e. 'that's not the way! ... not fair! ... not sensible! ... not right! ... not on! ... not what we want/need! ... not

[3] Leslie Macfarlane, *Issues in British Politics Since 1945*, (London 1975).

enough!' etc. If one begins by looking for the expression of these opinions – and they are likely to be expressed in one or other of these forms regardless of whether the disputes are national or arise within everyday groups such as the family or school – then it should be possible to trace them back to the source or sources of the political dispute, i.e. the conflicts of interest or values which are at the heart of the issue.

10. The forms in which disputes are expressed also provide both teachers and students with the basic information for analysing the nature of the dispute, i.e. is it over goals, values, methods or results, or a combination of these? (In some disputes one group or faction may support a certain position for practical reasons while another faction may support an opposing position on principle, and yet another faction may oppose such positions because of their perceived end results, and so on.) Statements such as 'It's not fair!', 'It's not right!', 'It's not enough!' etc., also provide the teacher and his class with indicators of who the parties to the dispute are and what they stand for; while the process of tracing opinions back to the source of the dispute and analysing its nature is also likely to reveal those groups and individuals who may not have expressed a viewpoint but are still affected by the dispute. From here it is then possible to analyse the situation and the behaviour of the groups and individuals within that situation to see what opportunities are open to them to influence the outcome of the dispute and the methods of influence which can be used or, in the case of historical examples, were used. Finally we should emphasise that we are not suggesting that the analysis of issues should be confined to an objective examination of the pronouncements and behaviour of those who are actually involved in and affected by the chosen issue. It is also important for the development of political literacy that the members of the class should also consider where they stand or would stand on this issue, what it means to them and what they would do to make their views felt.

SOME EXAMPLES OF THIS APPROACH

11. It is not our intention here to provide a comprehensive syllabus outline or teaching programme on political issues. The range of possibilities is too large for that. Our aim is simply to demonstrate how some political situations can be examined directly, as in the case of conflicts and issues arising in everyday life, or indirectly through source materials, as in the case of most national issues, in such a way that teachers and pupils can explore a series of questions which we believe to be central to the political literacy approach. It is worth reiterating these questions in a more explicit form. They are as follows: (i) In what form(s) is the dispute expressed? (ii) What are the sources of the dispute? (iii) What is the nature of the issue? (iv) Who are involved in the dispute, and which standpoints do they adopt? (v) What opportunities are open to them to influence the outcome of the dispute? and (vi) What methods of influence do they or can they use?

12. Our choice of situations or issues for discussion in this section is necessarily

a personal one, though we hope that readers will not find our selection too idiosyncratic. The school, for example, is a highly suitable source of political or potentially political issues. As an institution it exhibits many of the characteristics of a political system. That is to say, the membership is compulsory, rules and procedures are institutionalised within a defined authority structure, and there are formal decision-making processes for allocating resources. Given such characteristics it would be surprising if one did not find in most schools some evidence of strongly-held opinions of the kind referred to in paragraph 9 amongst pupils or teachers or between pupils and teachers regarding decisions which affect them, and in tracing these opinions back to their sources within the school one may come across such issues as: Should the official school leaving age be restored to fifteen? Should school uniforms be compulsory? Should corporal punishment be abolished/restored in the school? Should sixteen year-olds be allowed to leave school after their examinations? Should pupils have a say in the administration of the school through school councils, etc. and how much say should they have? and so on.

13. The nature of such issues will naturally vary with some being considerably more complex than others. The issue of the official school leaving age may be essentially a dispute over the results of the ROSLA decision, but the issue of pupil participation, on the other hand, may involve disagreements over goals, values, methods and results. Thus for some the issue may focus on the purpose served by introducing a school council. For others the issue may be whether or not the existing distribution of power within the school is a fair one or whether or not changes in that distribution would be sensible. Others may accept the need for pupil participation but disagree about the methods for implementing it. Where analysis goes from here will, of course, depend upon specific conditions within each school and upon how the pupils perceive the issues involved. Nevertheless it should be possible to go on to consider, if not find answers to, most of the other questions outlined in the previous paragraph for this and similar issues of everyday life.

14(a). Our second example is drawn from the area of contemporary national issues rather than everyday political life. Throughout most of this century and particularly since the 1944 Education Act, education has figured in the top rank of political issues dividing both the major political parties and the mass public. Education is, clearly, not so much an issue as a major problem area or compendium of issues, but the two fundamentally political issues in education have centred upon:

a. the priorities for allocating resources to different educational sectors (Which is the best investment for the nation? Which is the fairest distribution of resources? Where is the greatest need? etc.);
b. the abolition of selection at 11 + and the development of a universal system of comprehensive secondary education.

Finding out where people and groups stand on both issues should not prove much of a problem. Source materials are extensive. Since 1955, for example,

Labour Party manifestos have consistently propounded the case for Comprehensive schools, while Conservative manifestos have emphasised with equal vigour the case for the preservation of good grammar and direct-grant schools and the upholding of the parent's freedom of choice. And similarly on the issue of priorities for educational expenditure recent manifestos have revealed marked differences between the two main parties with Labour advocating an expansion of facilities for 16–18 year-olds and the Conservatives attaching special importance to primary school education.[4] Flesh can be put on the bare bones of the manifestos by also drawing upon Government publications and Parliamentary debates (the debate on the abolition of grammar and direct-grant schools (*Hansard*, 19 May 1975) for example, provides a useful overview of the range of political opinions on the Comprehensive school issue), and by canvassing national and local pressure groups such as the Campaign for Comprehensive Education, the Independent Schools Association, Teachers Associations and Unions, and so on, to determine their standpoints on these issues.

14(b). There is no reason why teachers and pupils should not be able to obtain sufficient information about the standpoints of those inside and outside Parliament who are involved in current educational disputes (and the same is true of most other national issues) but this information gathering exercise also has other important 'spin-offs' which can contribute to the development of political literacy. Whether the sources used are manifestos, polls, parliamentary debates or the media, or all four, this exercise provides a good opportunity for encouraging students to make distinctions between factual information, expert opinion, party ideology and all other kinds of value judgement. It also provides students with an opportunity to exercise some of the procedural values, such as respect for truth and reasoning and toleration; and finally it also introduces them to a number of political concepts as they are used in context by politicians and other interested parties. In the case of these two educational issues it introduces such concepts as social justice, social equality, rights of the individual, freedom, welfare and so on. With other national issues the concepts may be different but there are unlikely to be many issues where no basic political concepts are employed by the participants in the dispute in order to justify their case.

14(c). At this point in the analysis it is probably also a good time to get pupils to consider what they think and where they stand on the chosen issues and why, and to analyse their own perceptions in the same way as they have analysed the standpoints of political parties and pressure groups. And then to consider possible methods for influencing government policy (e.g. working through a particular political party, setting up or joining a pressure group, writing letters to newspapers or the local M.P., organising a petition, organising protest marches, demonstrations and sit-ins, etc.) comparing their choices with

[4] F. W. S. Craig's *British General Election Manifestos 1900–1974* (London 1975) is an invaluable source book here.

the methods actually employed at the national or local level by the people involved.

15. Broadly speaking it should be possible to adopt a roughly similar approach to that set out above for analysing any kind of national issue whether it be basically economic, such as inflation or unemployment, or moral, such as abortion. However, it should be emphasised that we are not necessarily assuming that national issues can only be taught in examination courses on British Government. A similar approach could be utilised for considering national political issues in previous eras (there is certainly ample source material available for the twentieth century) or History teachers could draw some interesting parallels between different periods. Economic issues might be particularly amenable to this approach. Interesting parallels, for example, might be drawn between unemployment or inflation as political issues in the 1920s and today.

16. But finally it should also be re-emphasised that we are not advocating that teaching through political issues must necessarily focus on national issues. An alternative approach is outlined in document 2.6.

(April 1976)

2.6 Constructing a programme and teaching through issues and political problems[1]

1. The work of the Programme for Political Education has been concerned with two distinct contexts for developing political literacy – through the teaching of the traditional subjects which are commonly found in the curriculum of most schools and colleges, History, English etc., as well as through general courses which could include an explicit political literacy module.

2. The syllabuses of traditional subjects are often prescribed by examination boards or delimited by the areas of teachers' expertise. The only choice a teacher may have would involve the selection and the ordering of issues within the subject such that the teaching will contribute to the development of political literacy. In selecting issues from the subject matter any of the five methods described in paragraph 5, document 2.5, may be appropriate. For example, knowing whether 'immigration' is a concern of the parties, the media and the public may justify its consideration in the context of history or literature.

3. There are, however, many issues which feature in syllabuses but do not feature in party manifestos or opinion polls. In such cases method 5d. of document 2.5, may be more useful. To illustrate this take the example of a history teacher intending to develop political literacy while teaching the French Revolution and wanting therefore to identify issues as defined in this paper (see section 3.2 of this report for a fuller treatment). Using the criteria in paragraph 9, the following may have been described by various groups or individuals *at the time* as 'not fair/sensible/right etc.'

> the social structure of Eighteenth Century France
> the form and procedures of the Constitutional Assembly
> the treatment of emigrés
> the position/treatment of the Monarchy
> the rights and status of citizens
> the treatment of dissenters and conspirators
> the status of the church and religion.

Which of these issues are more appropriate in a political literacy programme will depend on further criteria mentioned below (paragraph 5).

4. In the context of general courses again any of the methods in paragraph 5, document 2.5, may be used but with much greater scope and freedom. In this respect the basic advice given in paragraph 6 is particularly appropriate. It is advisable to take account of the pupils' age group, past experience, complementary studies etc. as well as the existing teaching expertise and available resources. Inevitably such courses will be devised with especial regard to the particular teaching situation. However, some general guidelines may be helpful (and are specified in more detail in section 3.1).

[1] This paper originally appeared as a Supplement to Discussion Document No. 5 (see 2.5). We are indebted to many of the teachers working with us in this project for their detailed comments on early drafts of this paper, which have been influential in this final version.

5. In the absence of other more obvious opportunities or constraints a political literacy programme should take account of two factors in particular: (i) of the pupils' immediate interests, and (ii) of those issues which are more frequently experienced by the pupils and through which therefore political literacy is likely to be operational and not merely speculative. Selection methods 5d. and 5e. are likely to be more useful in this respect.

To identify issues which the pupils regard as important or interesting they could be asked, within a carefully defined context, to complete such sentences as:

I feel sorry for people who...
It always annoys me that...
It isn't right that...
I don't really believe it when they say...
We would all be better off if ...
I would defend to the last my right to...
They should (not) have the power to...
They would be going too far if...
There should be a (new) law/rule about...
I don't think it is fair that...
I wish I had some say in...
I don't like it but I can't see what can be done about...[2]

6. A combination of methods 5d. and 5e. is more likely to indicate the material from which the teacher may make a selection, using other relevant criteria, for a course including or based upon the issues of 'everyday life'. It is likely also to fulfil the further consideration that many of the issues selected ought to be common to the whole teaching group. These will probably be family, school or peer group issues which provide, from all accounts, very useful starting points or material for analogy and illustration. This approach is not likely, however, to fulfil all the specifications of political literacy. Families, schools and peer groups are only political in strictly limited features of their behaviour. The essential value of this material lies in the provision of analogy and illustration and in the opportunity it provides to develop the skills and understanding of participation, which is not readily available with national political issues.

7. *The treatment of issues.* Here only the most general and tentative guidance can be suggested in response to such questions as 'What should be the objectives/sequence/process of the analysis?' and 'How should the teaching of each issue be organised?' A primary objective should be for teachers to enable pupils to understand that in the case of each problem:

a. Those who are affected will have certain **interests** and principles, and there will be reasons for their having these interests and principles.
b. Those who are affected may have the **opportunity** to make their views felt. The accepted procedures and opportunities will vary and the use which can be made of them will vary.

[2] The complete list of sentences has been devised to elicit material which should enable the teacher to cover all the political concepts and procedural values.

c. There will exist various **methods** of influence appropriate to particular circumstances, some, but not all, of which will be regarded as legitimate.

In the course of dealing with these points, an understanding of which is fundamental for the development of political literacy, it will be possible to consider the basic political concepts and the procedural values of political education.

8. A variety of approaches to the treatment of issues may be located in the following diagram B[3] listing questions which can be asked in connection with all issues and political problems. Teaching which gave consideration to the full list of questions would cover all aspects of political literacy as propounded in project document 2.2. Any sequence of questions which is implied by the diagram is merely one suggestion of the many which can be formed by regrouping the questions. The questions in diagram B are so arranged as to group together those which relate to particular political concepts (see diagram C) or procedural values as defined in project documents 2.3 and 2.4.

9. Issues may therefore be treated in a wide variety of ways. In most cases question 1 would be the more usual starting point (but see vi below). The rest of the sequence could be varied according to the circumstances. Some examples:

(i) An examination course in British Government may be concerned with the institutions of British Government and therefore with questions 4a and b. The teaching could begin with a selected issue, could cover questions 2, 3 and 5 before looking at 4, 6 and 7 and ending with the required institutional material.
(ii) A History course will concern itself with an understanding of the events in history and not with any of these questions exclusively but particular questions may become obvious starting points in certain circumstances. If 'Iskra' and 'Vpered' are deemed to be significant in the events of the Russian revolution, then question 6 and 6c in particular would lead to a consideration of many of the other questions – and perhaps of *Isvestia* and *Pravda* and the British Government's referendum literature.
(iii) If the teaching objective is to handle the concept of justice, questions could be selected to include 1c, 2d, 4d and 6 for example.[4]
   Alternatively, one could begin by introducing a concept, seeing that it is understood, then introducing the proposed issue and applying the concept to that issue. This analysis will create a need for further concepts and so a route through the questions will be determined (as has already been done successfully in a programme associated with the project).
(iv) If the teaching objective is to include the procedural value, respect for truth, then questions 5c and d should be applied in the analysis of the issue.
(v) A few questions could be selected and arranged to serve as a theme

---

[3] Diagram B has been adapted from the political literacy diagram in project document 2.2 in the context of which it may be better understood.
[4] For an account of teaching political concepts in a specific context see Alex Porter, 'Political Education below 14', *Teaching Politics*, Vol. 4, No. 4, September 1975.

throughout a whole course, each issue being treated in a similar way.

(vi) One question (almost any one) could be used as an alternative introductory theme to question 1. For example: 6a 'How are people generally persuaded to act or to change their minds?' Having thoroughly explored this question it could be applied to a variety of issues.

From these examples it can be seen that it is not regarded as necessary to subject each issue to a detailed scrutiny under each of the headings of each question on diagram B. In most cases this would not be feasible but it is certainly possible to devise teaching programmes which would involve issues being so thoroughly and systematically treated.

10. It will perhaps serve to clarify the intended use of these diagrams if sufficient time is taken to examine carefully how all the questions could be used to devise a programme which pursues any of the following issues and possible problems:

Should you be compelled to join a trade union?
Should the law governing obscene publications/abortion be relaxed/tightened?
Should there be a compulsory common core curriculum in all schools?
Should the local authority provide us with a new swimming pool/'bus service/nursery unit/home for discharged mental patients, etc.?
Should sixteen year-olds be allowed to leave school after their final examinations?
Should the 19th century Russian revolutionaries plan to encourage peasants to revolution or seize power themselves and effect reforms from above?

The sequence of the questions and the depth of analysis would therefore depend on or determine the particular teaching programme.

Diagram A (being a simplified guide to diagram B)

Political literacy involves

1. A perception of issues and political problems
   Regarding the allocation and present use of scarce 'resources',
   what disagreement is there about

a	b	c	d
What people say needs doing and what is likely to happen?	What the purposes and contexts of their actions should be?	How they should set about doing things?	How suitable the result of their actions is?

An understanding of ...

2. *Own responses:* How does it affect you?

3. *Others' responses:* How would others be affected?

4. *Procedures:* Where and how are disputes tackled?

5. *Policies:* Who stands for what?

6. *Means of influence:* How can people be persuaded?

7. *Effective participation:* How can you persuade?

Questions 5a b, 6a b and 4a b, in that order, have provided the basis of a treatment used successfully in a teaching programme associated with the project.

Question 4c has also been used as the basis of a successful teaching programme associated with the project. In this case, as well as in the above example, the treatment involves the extensive use of 'practical' exercises, gaming and simulation, and of the media as a resource.

Diagram B

Political literacy involves a

1. Perception of issues and political problems and an

a	b	c	d
Understanding of ...		Fairness	Alternatives

	a	b	c	d
2. *Own responses*	How does this matter affect you— your rights, freedom and welfare?	What are your interests? What are your opinions? What are your rights etc?	Can you justify your opinions?	
3. *Others' responses*	How would others be affected—their rights, freedom and welfare?	What are others' interests? What are others' opinions? What are their rights etc.?		How do others justify the opinions they hold?
4. *Procedures*	What are the circumstances in which the disputes occur?	How are they normally tackled? What are the rules?	What conditions help a successful solution to the problem? Are the rules fair/being applied fairly?	In what other ways could the problems be tackled? Could the rules be changed?
5. *Policies*	Who proclaims what policies? What right/authority do they have?	What are their interests and attitudes?	Where does information on these policies come from? How reliable are these sources?	Are there other sources? Are there other ways of looking at things?
6. *Influence*	How are people persuaded to act or change their minds?	Who has the ability to get things done?	Is this done fairly?	Are there other ways you can go about this?
7. *Effective participation*	How can you get your point of view across?	Will anyone else speak for you?	Are these methods fair?	Are there other ways you can go about it?

and, What issues have you seen at first hand?
What issues have you been involved in?
Are you experienced in getting your views across?

Diagram C

Treatment of issues with reference to concepts (see project document 2.3)

Using particular parts of diagram B should facilitate the consideration of certain concepts

The popular concepts	*some relating concepts*
Natural rights	Justice
Individuality	Representation
Freedom	
Welfare	

The governing concepts	
Power	
Force	
Authority	
Order	

The relating concepts	
Law	
Justice	
Representation	
Pressure	

2.7 Notes for a spiral curriculum for developing political literacy
Robert Stradling

1. Generally speaking; the five working documents of the Programme for Political Education have paid little attention to those two inter-related problems of curriculum and course design: organisation and sequence of content – that is to the implications of organising courses around central ideas and principles, topics, themes or problems, and deciding where to start and what should follow. Admittedly, document 2.3 focusses on basic concepts and document 2.5 on the issue-based approach but both papers are more concerned to set down guidelines and criteria for the teacher rather than to describe the content of a curriculum. As pointed out in document 2.3 paragraph 4: 'the approach is for the teacher, not necessarily the class; it is an underpinning of curricula, not an outline curriculum.'

2. For sound educational and 'political' reasons the Programme has deliberately adopted the strategy of infusing the political literacy approach into existing curricula and subject disciplines such as History, English, Local and General Studies and because of this it was possible to regard course organisation and sequence as given. Nevertheless there will be teachers who seek to design a complete course around the political literacy approach; perhaps a Civics course for 13–16 year-olds or a Mode 3 CSE. With this in mind the Programme has produced a model outline of a Civics course, and document 2.8 offers some tentative suggestions on the design of a developing or spiral curriculum for Politics. My intention here is not to be prescriptive about content. Nor am I proposing the spiral curriculum as a panacea for the deficiencies – real or imagined – of current teaching practice. What I have attempted to do is to outline one of several conceivable conceptual frameworks for developing a Politics course, and to raise some of the problems which could arise in attempting to implement such an approach. As such it should be regarded as a discussion paper. Ultimately a suitable spiral curriculum will only emerge through a process of trial and error in the classroom.

3. In recent years interest in the potential of the spiral curriculum has developed on both sides of the Atlantic amongst those educationalists and teachers who have become increasingly concerned about the failure of some of the traditional curricula to provide students with the conceptual frameworks and cognitive apparatus for making sense of their world, coping with the information explosion and the consequent rapid and constant changes in the stock of knowledge, and interpreting new experiences.

4. One of the most influential writers in this field has been Jerome Bruner. He argues that the curriculum designer needs to:

a. isolate the *fundamental ideas and principles* of a specific mode of thought or discipline and present them in some concrete form which enables the child to relate them to his or her own experiences;

b. adopt a form of presentation through which the understanding of a concept or principle which the child acquires in a particular situation or problem is transferable on to other situations and problems;

c. adopt a sequence of presentation which enables the child to apply the same fundamental ideas and concepts to increasingly complex and sophisticated situations and problems, and to understand the more complex and sophisticated concepts which can be *derived* from these first principles.

Thus a curriculum as it develops should revisit continually the central organising ideas and concepts, firstly in simple, concrete and familiar contexts and then 'spiralling' outwards to a wider framework, and building upon these ideas until the student has grasped the structure of a given mode of thought or discipline.

5. To the best of my knowledge no attempt has been made as yet to develop a spiral curriculum specifically for Politics and, indeed, we have very few models from other disciplines to guide us. The best known are: *Man: A Course of Study* designed by Bruner and his colleagues, and the *Social Studies Curriculum* designed by Taba. During the last decade there have also been a number of interesting attempts to develop a spiral curriculum for Economics (see, e.g., articles by Senesh, Bach and Dunning), and more recently the Schools Council project *Time, Place and Society 8–13* has suggested the possibility of a syllabus founded on key concepts in the social sciences. It may well be that there is less agreement amongst political scientists and philosophers regarding the fundamental principles of their discipline than one might find amongst economists, for example, but nevertheless there seems no obvious impediment, exclusive to the study of Politics, which prevents us from at least attempting to adopt the spiral approach to the teaching of Politics.

FUNDAMENTAL POLITICAL IDEAS AND CONCEPTS

6. To quote one widely accepted definition, concepts are 'general ideas representing classes or groups of people, things, actions and relationships which share certain characteristics'. The question which concepts and ideas are fundamental to an understanding of politics is an open one and depends to some degree on one's definition of politics. Derek Heater, in analysing the subject matter of Politics takes as his starting point six concepts: Political Ideas, Administration, Leadership and Decision-Making, Role of the Individual, Techniques of Change, and Conflict. From each of these concepts, he argues, may be derived clusters of lower order concepts until 'all political material can be incorporated'.

7. Clearly the source for both these basic and derived concepts is the technical language of political science and political sociology. The Programme for Political Education, on the other hand, argues that the purposes of political education in schools should be to produce politically literate (politically aware and competent) individuals rather than introduce them to a subject discipline. The

starting point in document 2.3 on concepts is therefore the concepts which frequently occur in the language of everyday life and which are central to understanding and participating in the politics of everyday life. Is this emphasis on political literacy rather than the discipline of political science incompatible with Bruner's ideas? At first sight it appears to be; but, in fact, political literacy, as described in the Programme's documents, does constitute a structured mode of thought and action and, as such, meets Bruner's criteria of facilitating the retention of knowledge and the transferability of learning. Furthermore, although the Programme advocates starting with the everyday language of politics, this is not to say that this language is necessarily divorced from the language employed by students of politics. The twelve concepts selected by Bernard Crick in documents 2.3 (Power, Force, Authority, Order, Law, Justice, Representation, Pressure, Natural Rights, Individuality, Freedom and Welfare) and the concepts discussed in this paper are all founded in everyday speech and yet also fundamental to political philosophy.

8. While endorsing the Programme's approach, I would take issue with some of the concepts selected as basic in document 2.3. In order for concepts to be basic I would argue that they must:

a. exhibit a high degree of generality from which other concepts can be directly or indirectly derived;
b. are central to the understanding of theories, generalisations, explanations and behaviour;

and in order to be central to the development of political literacy they must:

c. relate to the everyday language of politics and everyday political experiences.

I think it essential that we include all three criteria in the definition. If we restrict ourselves to b. alone then we would probably select concepts like **democracy** as basic, but as Bernard Crick observes, such concepts tend to be compounds and derived from other concepts which we probably would not have chosen or defined if b. had been our sole criterion. On the other hand, if we restrict ourselves to a. then there would be good grounds for selecting some concepts as basic which either are not commonly recognised as 'political' or are central to all the social sciences, e.g. **action** or **group**. Such concepts do exhibit a high degree of generality and clearly some political concepts are derived from them but they could not be said to be specifically 'political' in the sense of b. or c. There may, of course, be some ambiguities here such as concepts like **conflict** but there will inevitably be some degree of overlap between the social sciences.

9. On these terms not all of the concepts in document 2.3 would seem to be equally basic. Power, for example is a highly generalised concept and so are force, authority and pressure whereas concepts such as law, natural rights, representation and welfare are considerably more specific. The latter concepts are fundamental to a particular view of politics – as a special activity to be

found only in particular contexts usually associated with Government. This would appear to be at variance with the idea of the politics of everyday life which permeates the Programme's working papers, i.e. that there is a political dimension to all human behaviour rather than a special kind of behaviour called 'politics'. This wider notion of politics is apparent in document 2.5 on Issues and political problems. Here politics is defined as 'the process through which conflicts of interests and values within a group are conciliated'. Political activity is said to occur when there is a dispute amongst the members of a group (any group but most probably those where there is some element of compulsory membership binding the group) over values or the allocation of resources or tasks; when the disputing members of the group demand a common decision to be taken which will be binding on the whole group; and when this common decision has to be taken if the group is to continue to exist.

10. On this basis it would seem reasonable to argue that all kinds of groups including the school and the trade union are sometimes faced with problems which on a smaller scale are similar to problems facing the State, e.g. what alternative means are available to decision-makers to ensure that the whole group abides by their decisions? What if there is a dissenting minority? How is power most effectively exercised under given conditions? and so on. These are all problems which have long exercised the minds of political philosophers and politicians but they are also problems which exercise the minds, ingenuity (and patience) of most parents, teachers, trade union officials and employers. Likewise there are political problems which face most members of groups whether they are subjects, citizens, employees, trade unionists or children, e.g. what means are available for influencing the decision makers? Which are the most appropriate channels of influence under given conditions? etc.

11. It is my contention that through the study of political problems in these terms, both within their own environment and outside it, children should be able to discover the relevance of certain fundamental political concepts and ideas:

a. the distinction between community and association, i.e. everyone belongs to groups; some they are born into e.g. nations, families, religions; others they join usually to pursue certain aims, goals or activities, e.g. trade unions, schools, youth clubs, etc. Membership in some of these groups will be more compulsory than others and because of this are more likely to require political activity to keep the groups functioning than non-compulsory groups where the effects of disintegration of the group or disorder within it may be less serious for members, e.g. a football team compared with a school or trade union.

b. Not always, but usually, there will be conflicts of interests or beliefs between members of a group about how scarce resources should be allocated (Who gets what, when, how and why?); how tasks should be allocated (Who does what, when, how and why?); and about the principles which should govern the actions of the group (e.g. freedom, rights, individuality, justice, equality, welfare and security).

c. Out of self-interest or principles members of the group will attempt to direct the group towards making a decision which will favour their own interests or values rather than the interests or principles of other members of the group. In order to do this they will seek to exercise **power** – i.e. their ability to achieve intended results. Depending on the circumstances power may be exercised through:

              force – using or threatening to use physical sanctions;

    manipulation – controlling the information available to other group members possibly through telling lies or half truths, *Propaganda*, or deliberately failing to explain all the options open to the group (the power of 'non-decision making');

       authority – getting others to support you and/or agree with you because they respect you or because they believe you have superior knowledge or because they believe you have the right to make decisions for them;

        influence – persuading or putting pressure on others to make a decision in your favour;

            reason – arguing the case for a decision in your favour.

d. Under these circumstances if a group is to survive it will have to act in common. Common action may have to be enforced (**compliance**) or members may agree to act in common (**consent**). If agreement cannot be reached on this particular decision (**dissent**) it may lead to the disintegration of the group but not necessarily. In many groups people may 'agree to differ' on this one issue and not seek to break up the group (a broad *consensus* over the importance of the group, the 'rules of the game', etc.) e.g. the typical situation in parliamentary political systems for the opposition parties but it could equally apply to non-parliamentary groups.

e. As the group survives, decision-making will tend to follow regular and predictable patterns (**order**) through the development of **rules**. The smaller the group the more likely it is (though not necessarily so) that the majority of members will be actively involved in making decisions (**participation**) but this will depend on the nature of the group and the personalities of the people concerned – more a hypothesis to test than an accepted truth. The larger the group the more likely it is that a minority will decide for the group as a whole. In some circumstances their position as decision-makers may be determined by virtue of their superior force but in other circumstances they will seek to justify their position (**representation**) e.g. 'Divine Right', 'Will of the People', 'elected', etc.

f. Regular and predictable patterns of decision-making within the group may be labelled:

autocratic
oligarchic
democratic

but in a state of **disorder** the pattern may be **anarchic**. The choice of labels here is inevitably a bit arbitrary. For one thing, there is bound to be some overlap. Autocracy can be oligarchic and so can a Democracy. Other labels may be equally applicable. I do not think it would matter very much at this stage in the line of development. What is important is that the child understands that the forms of power exercised within the group will tend to become 'institutionalised' into predictable patterns if the group survives over time.

g. In many groups, particularly the larger ones, the experience of making and responding to decisions will lead to the setting down of **rules** for the conduct of members.

h. The specific pattern of decision-making within the group will probably depend on the value-preferences of some or all of the members. For example, when priority is given to the **security** of the group they may adopt a different pattern of decision-making to those in a group where **freedom** of the individual is most highly valued, and so on. Other values which will affect the pattern of decision-making include **rights**, **individuality**, **justice**, **equality** and **welfare**.

12. The line of development underpinning the above approach has been traced in the following diagrams. The basic or fundamental concepts are written **bold** as in the text.

13. The first diagram looks in detail at the basic political problem as outlined above while the second diagram (B) illustrates the relationship between the concepts which are basic to this view of politics and the second order concepts which can be derived from them.

14. It could be argued that some of these concepts are more basic than others. I would be inclined to draw a cut-off point after **rules**; i.e. the concepts from **conflict** to **rules** are primary while the others are secondary and derived from and/or dependent on the primary ones.

15. Before moving on to consider the sequence of presentation a number of points need to be made about the above approach;

a. that it is not particularly important if children do not use the correct label for each concept so long as they understand the ideas behind the concept;

b. there can never be complete and final agreement about which concepts are basic or primary and which are secondary and tertiary. The above discussion is intended to be a stimulus for further discussion or a starting point rather than an *ex cathedra* statement;

c. developing an understanding of these concepts through moving from the simple to the more complex is central to the spiral approach but care should be taken to avoid over-simplification. Nothing should be taught which might have to be untaught later.

Diagram A

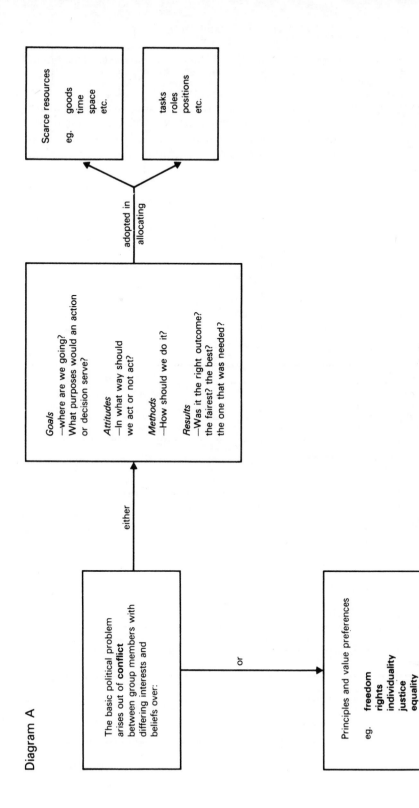

Scarce resources

eg. goods
     time
     space
     etc.

tasks
roles
positions
etc.

adopted in allocating

Goals
—where are we going?
What purposes would an action
or decision serve?

Attitudes
—In what way should
we act or not act?

Methods
—How should we do it?

Results
—Was it the right outcome?
the fairest? the best?
the one that was needed?

either

The basic political problem
arises out of **conflict**
between group members with
differing interests and
beliefs over:

or

Principles and value preferences

eg. **freedom**
     rights
     individuality
     justice
     equality
     welfare
     security

Diagram B A developmental approach to political thinking

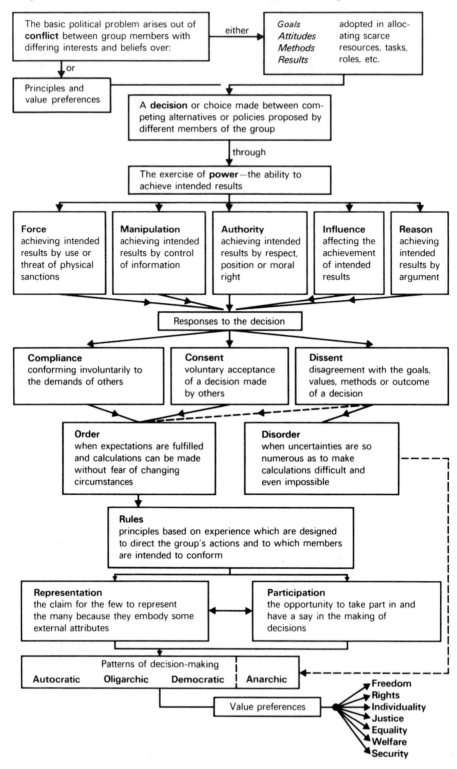

The basic political problem arises out of **conflict** between group members with differing interests and beliefs over:

either

Goals adopted in alloc-
Attitudes ating scarce
Methods resources, tasks,
Results roles, etc.

or

Principles and value preferences

A **decision** or choice made between competing alternatives or policies proposed by different members of the group

through

The exercise of **power**—the ability to achieve intended results

Force
achieving intended results by use or threat of physical sanctions

Manipulation
achieving intended results by control of information

Authority
achieving intended results by respect, position or moral right

Influence
affecting the achievement of intended results

Reason
achieving intended results by argument

Responses to the decision

Compliance
conforming involuntarily to the demands of others

Consent
voluntary acceptance of a decision made by others

Dissent
disagreement with the goals, values, methods or outcome of a decision

Order
when expectations are fulfilled and calculations can be made without fear of changing circumstances

Disorder
when uncertainties are so numerous as to make calculations difficult and even impossible

Rules
principles based on experience which are designed to direct the group's actions and to which members are intended to conform

Representation
the claim for the few to represent the many because they embody some external attributes

Participation
the opportunity to take part in and have a say in the making of decisions

Patterns of decision-making

Autocratic   **Oligarchic**   **Democratic**   **Anarchic**

Value preferences

Freedom
Rights
Individuality
Justice
Equality
Welfare
Security

SEQUENCE OF PRESENTATION

16. The spiral curricula referred to in the introduction have generally taken as their starting point the relevance of basic concepts to the understanding of simple and concrete contexts which are familiar to the child such as the family and the local community and then 'spiralled' outwards to wider and more remote contexts including the historical, national and supra-national.

17. The assumption underlying this is that initially children will more readily understand and be more readily motivated to understand the basic ideas of a discipline or mode of thought if they are presented to them in the form of concrete manifestations of their everyday lives. I would regard this view as a hypothesis which needs to be tested rather than a self-evident truth but if we accept it as a starting point then I hope that the preceding discussion will have demonstrated that the stuff of politics is manifest in the direct experiences of most school children. They see **power**, for example, exercised in its various forms in the home, the school, the group and the local community. Diagram C illustrates one possible spiral sequence for developing the concept of power (through the use of force, manipulation, authority, influence or reason) in this way. The concept is analysed firstly in contexts which are directly experienced by the

Diagram C The spiral development of the concept of power

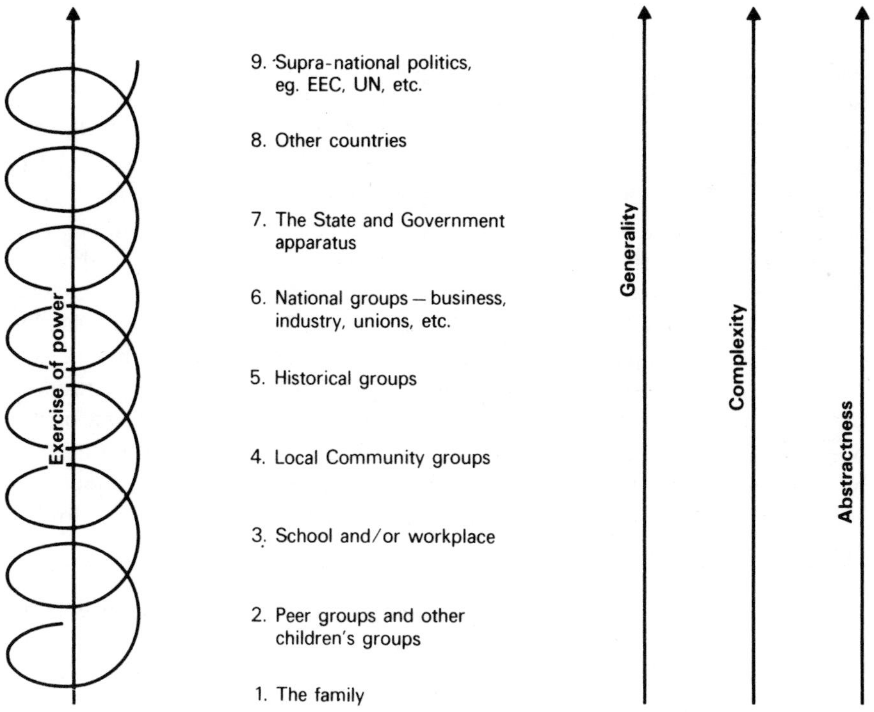
9. Supra-national politics, eg. EEC, UN, etc.
8. Other countries
7. The State and Government apparatus
6. National groups – business, industry, unions, etc.
5. Historical groups
4. Local Community groups
3. School and/or workplace
2. Peer groups and other children's groups
1. The family
Exercise of power
Generality
Complexity
Abstractness

child then spirals upwards through local, historical and national contexts to the international level. In so doing the generality, complexity and abstractness of the concept are developed and revealed.

18. There are alternatives to this approach and, again, I must stress that we are not yet in a position to assess the relative advantages and disadvantages. It could be argued, for example, that spiralling outwards from the simple to the complex is not necessarily the same as developing from the immediate environment to the remote. It may be that we can find relatively simple examples of, for instance, the use of force by those with power to cow the rest into submission at all of the levels described in diagram C. Political activity at the level of the State is not always or necessarily more complex than political activity at the level of the school even if in most instances it probably is (and even if there are differences in scale). Similarly, political activity at the level of community groups is not always less complex than national politics.

19. It could also be argued that the immediate environment is not always the most appropriate one for initially motivating the child. We should not ignore the child's capacity for imagination and entering vicariously into the experiences of others through novels, films, and role play.

FUNDAMENTAL CONCEPTS AND CHILD DEVELOPMENT

20. Bruner's oft-quoted assertion that it is possible to teach the fundamental concepts and ideas of any discipline to children at any age seems to run counter to stage theories of cognitive development and to the opinions of many teachers. Some disciples of Piaget, for example, appear to assume that an understanding of these concepts is dependent upon a grasp of abstract thinking and that this will only develop in mid-adolescence (a view which is frequently endorsed by teachers). It is only fairly recently that the epistemological basis of Piaget's work has begun to arouse interest amongst educationalists and they have begun to stress not so much the relationship between age norms and Piaget's stages of development but rather the notion that the stages define a *necessary* sequence through which the learner must pass when approaching a structured discipline or mode of thought, regardless of age. Thus, for example, as someone who is almost totally ignorant about atomic physics it is likely that my thinking on this subject will exhibit many of the characteristics of Piaget's first or preoperational stage of development. On other subject matter my thinking may be characteristic of the second or concrete-operational stage while, hopefully, in my own field of study my thinking will display the characteristics of formal-operational thought.

21. In each of these stages the learner is capable of using certain concepts but the *way* in which he or she uses them will be limited by the stage of development which governs his or her mode of thought. If this is the case, and if Bruner is right in arguing that the basic ideas that lie at the heart of all subjects are as simple as they are powerful then there is no reason why teachers should

not introduce children below the age of thirteen to basic political concepts in the manner outlined above, provided that due consideration is given to the child's level of cognitive development. We should not reject the possibility out of hand purely on the basis of the age norms established by research in cognitive psychology. As Lawrence Stenhouse has observed, education should serve to change these norms rather than reinforce them.

Bibliography

Bach, G. L. 'What Economics should we teach?' in E. Fenton, *Teaching the New Social Studies in Secondary Schools*, (London 1966)

Bruner, J. S. *The Process of Education* (Cambridge, Mass. 1963)

Bruner, J. S. *Towards a Theory of Instruction*, (Cambridge, Mass. 1966)

Crick, Bernard, *Basic Political Concepts*, Document 3 of the Programme for Political Education (1975)

Crick, Bernard & Ian Lister, *Political Literacy*, Document 2 of the programme for Political Education (1974)

Dunning, K. 'What Economics should we teach?' *Economics* (1970)

Elliott, Gordon, *Teaching for Concepts*, (Schools Council project: Place, Time & Society 8–13 (1976)

Heater, Derek, *History Teaching and Political Education* (Politics Association 1974)

Peel, E. A., *The Pupil's Thinking*, (London 1960)

Piaget, Jean, *Logic & Psychology* (Manchester 1953)

Senesh, L., 'The Organic Curriculum', *The Councillor*, (1960)

Stradling, Robert & Alex Porter, *Issues & Political Problems*, Document 5 of the Programme for Political Education (1976)

Taba, H., *et al.*, *A Teacher's Handbook to Elementary Social Studies: An Inductive Approach*, (New York 1971).

2.8 Outline of a civics syllabus
Political literacy as part of general studies for 4th and 5th years
Alex Porter

The following outline for a course is set out as a model for a two-year programme intended for 14–16 year-olds requiring approximately two hours per week times forty plus thirty weeks (approximately one tenth of available school time).

It is based on project documents 2.1 to 2.6, in particular documents 2.5 and 2.6, and also the notes written by Robert Stradling on 'The spiral curriculum'. It is therefore intended to be understood and taught as a spiral model in which concepts and political literacy themes are encountered and re-encountered in a sequence of issues.

The course would consist of four units each of which could be taught as a self-contained module within a broader general studies course. The units could be modified, to adapt them to the contexts and levels of other courses, by varying the number of issues considered and/or the extent of the questions covered in the recommended treatment in paragraph 5 below.

1. **Title:** 'Understanding Poltics'.

2. **Aims:** to provide guidelines for schools and colleges to devise courses adapted to local needs and conditions which will provide pupils with; (i) an understanding of different responses, policies and conflicts within political groups; (ii) knowledge and skills relevant to understanding and dealing with various political issues.

3. **Objectives:** in the context of the various issues specified pupils should be expected; (i) to understand the nature of disputes – whether they are about goals, values, methods and/or results; (ii) to understand how these disputes affect them or could affect them, and the groups to which they belong; to be able to state their own views and to justify holding these views; (iii) to understand how the disputes affect other people and the groups to which they belong; to be able to understand the views of others who are affected and their reasons for holding such views; (iv) to know the circumstances in which the disputes arise and how they are normally tackled; to know how disputes can be settled and what alternative procedures may be possible; (v) to know who promotes what policies, what authority each has and what their interests are; to know how to approach any given information critically and to be aware of alternative sources of information; (vi) to know about different methods of influence, how people may be persuaded or exhorted to act or change their minds and who is influenced, and by whom; (vii) to understand how they could be effective in matters which concern them; (viii) to have an outline knowledge of British politics and British political parties, their organisation and their policies, and of contemporary political ideas; (ix) to develop an understanding of basic political concepts and an awareness of procedural values (as expressed in the Programme documents).

4. Syllabus:

Unit 1 – Personal, school and local issues: This unit would serve as an intro-duction to issues and conflicts and should rehearse the analytical framework. It is to be concerned with issues which would normally be within the experience of the particular pupils in the particular school. Therefore the issues can only be described here in general terms (they must be specified or chosen by the teacher to suit the particular context). A dramatised, contrived or possibly a 'pencil and paper' issue such as leadership and consent in small groups and/or the distribution of scarce resources. A personal issue involving children's rights and freedom. An issue arising from some democratisation in the school. A local issue concerning the provision of a local amenity.

Unit 2 – Issues of party conflict: This unit would concern the political issues which have generally divided the main political parties: education, housing, industrial relations, unemployment, etc.

Unit 3 – Issues of institutions: This unit would deal with the constitutional issues relating to the rules, procedures and structures of politics. Devolution and nationalism, electoral reform, the referendum, selection of party candidates, 'democratisation' of the EEC, would all be suitable.

Unit 4 – Issues of personal politics and ethics: This unit should consider issues of conscience, moral judgement or personal stands on matters of principle which tend to be cross-party or even anti-party. Abortion, crime and violence, industrial democracy (including the 'closed shop'), 'Government by the best', are among many obvious examples.

There is no reason why pupils should not be invited to decide what issues are analysed within this general structure.

5. **Treatment:** The following treatment of political issues is presented as a guide to what a systematic course towards political literacy should involve. It is merely one of several treatments which may be derived from the work and the basic documents of our Programme. This treatment is derived largely from the suggestions in documents 2.5 and 2.6. It is arranged so that the full-range of considerations upon which political literacy is based may be covered system-atically.

The treatment is set out as a series of questions intended to be the basis of classroom analysis and discussion. The role of the teacher would be to see that the relevant knowledge and appropriate circumstances are provided such that students can arrive at a thorough understanding of those questions which are being considered and of the possible answers to those questions.

The form of these questions (and therefore the possible answers) is intended to evoke a sequence of basic political ideas and concepts. When the more fundamental ideas and concepts have been dealt with adequately the related questions can be given less attention. The range of questions, and therefore concepts, to be considered in lessons can then be gradually extended.

(The questions have been elaborated to provide a wide range of ideas and possible approaches for the teacher. It is *not* argued that all must be covered while dealing with each basic question – 'political literacy' must be flexible, not mechanical or rigid.)

In general:
What are (political) problems? What leads to **conflicts** and disputes? What sorts of things do people disagree about? What do we mean by 'scarce resources' and 'choice'? Why are certain disputes regarded as being political? What other sorts of dispute have similar features and what are the essential differences?

Stressing knowledge relevant to particular decisions or policies:
What's it all about? Is the problem political? If not then what features are like/unlike problems which are regarded as political? What exactly is the dispute about? What circumstances have led to this problem? In what respects are these circumstances unusual or typical for most disputes? What is the prevailing or proposed **decision** in this matter?
Who can get things done? How can people be persuaded to accept the policy? How can decisions be carried out? Who has the **power** to do this? How is this power exercised? Are these methods fair? What other ways are there of going about it?
How can things be changed? How can people set about changing the policy or stopping decisions being carried out? How can people be persuaded to change their minds? Who has the power to do this? How is this power exercised? Are these methods fair? What other ways are there?
Who stands for what? Who **consents** to the policy and who disputes it? What alternative policies are proposed? What are the interests of the various people involved? How accurate are there claims? Are there other sources of information available and other ways of looking at the problem? How reliable are the sources?
What's the outcome? Who appears to now accept the decision and who does not? To what extent does any refusal to accept the decision create uncertainty about future circumstances? What is the likelihood of **disorder**?
How are problems normally tackled? What conditions help or hinder a solution to the problem? What are the **rules**? Are there special institutions and special machinery for tackling the problems? Is the way of making decisions fair? Who decides that a problem has been 'solved'? Who can be **represented** in the procedure and who can actually **participate**? What ways are there of making decisions and what political values do alternative patterns reflect?

Stressing personal involvement and social responsibility:
What's your opinion? Does this affect you? Just imagine you are affected by it, how do/would you feel about it? What rights do you think you have? What do you think should be done? Anything at all? Where would the resources come from to do what you suggest?
What will others think? How would your proposals affect other people? Are there people who hold different views to you? What are their views? Why do you think they hold them?
What can you do about it? How can you get your viewpoint across to others?

Do you think anyone will support you? How can you convince them to support you? Do you have any experience of trying to influence decisions in similar/ different situations? How effective were the methods you used?

3

GROUP AND INDIVIDUAL PROPOSALS

3.1 A POLITICS SYLLABUS FOR THE PROPOSED NEW N AND F LEVEL
    MATRICULATION EXAMINATIONS

(This paper was commissioned by a Schools Council study group as part of
their feasibility studies in connection with considering whether to recommend replacing the present A level with a new 18+ examination at two
levels (N as normal and F as further) in five subjects, thus a wider
examination with the needs of the new, one year sixth form in mind as
well as preparation and selection for higher education; but each
subject would cover less work than the present A level - three-quarters
in the case of F and a half in the case of N. We were asked to undertake this - and the extra costs of a working group of teachers were
separately met by the Schools Council - specifically to see whether the
Hansard political literacy approach could be extended to sixth form
examination work, even though the concentration and priority of the Programme itself was with lower streams in the school and general studies.
It began work in August 1975 and reported in November 1976. It was well
received and specifically commended by the Schools Council study group.
Perhaps it is fair to say that though this group was not part of the
original Programme, it met most often and was thus able to provide, however debatable, the most clear-cut set of proposals consistent with the
Programme's objectives. This may well be because the group had a clear
and limited objective, official sponsorship and accountability and its
own budget for travel and meetings. Other groups were under much
greater constraint.)

B.R.C.   A.E.P.

Contents

3.1 A politics syllabus for the proposed new N and F level

3.1.1 Schools Council 18+ Research Programme
Studies based on the N and F proposals

Report of the Commissioned Politics Group based on
the Hansard Society 'Programme for Political Education'

Introduction

The brief was for teachers associated with the Programme for Political
Education to apply its early thinking to the preparation of syllabuses at
N and F levels. This approach was outlined in the first two project
documents and elaborated in a further four documents in the course of the
commissioned group's work.   The general aim was to produce syllabuses
which would help curriculum development in political education aimed at
enhancing 'political literacy'. The model stipulated was one which
involved an N syllabus as a core for the F syllabus.

 The teachers approached to serve on the group were personally known by,
or recommended to, the chairman as being experienced teachers with an
interest in curriculum development in political education. All were
members of the Politics Association and all lived within convenient
travelling distance to the centre of London. All but two were serving
teachers concerned with the subject at A level. One was a university
teacher and a chief examiner of the subject at A level. The other was a
former secondary school student of two members of the group who was then
sitting her finals for a degree in politics, sociology and philosophy.

 The interpretation of the brief presented some difficulties in
practice. The recommendations of Schools Council Working Paper 46 "16-
19: Growth and Response. 2. Examination Structure" is not without
ambiguity. To be asked to construct two syllabuses so that "... the
first can usually be included within that for the second", or, in the
words of the brief "... involving an N level syllabus as the core for
F...", can be interpreted in a significantly wide range of ways. The
form of relationship produced by the group may not be entirely clear from
a reading of the syllabus. There are three way in which the N level is a
core study to the F level options. Whereas the N syllabus makes no
stipulations about study in the subject before embarking on the course,
the F syllabus assumes that at least 70 per cent of the N syllabus will
have been covered. The examination of F level includes the examination
at N level. The N level is seen as a general objectives based syllabus
employing a flexible subject matter with which to develop cognitive
skills. The F level employs those skills to study specific topics in
depth partly to prepare for the actual substance of degree-level work but
more to indicate the suitability of the candidate to begin degree-level
work. It is contended that the F level could not be pursued without the
prior study of the N level (or another course with similar objectives).

 This relationship produced a number od difficulties. The group was
concerned with such questions as 'at which level would it be appropriate
to introduce a consideration of political concepts, or political theory?'
'How could a substantive content be clearly expressed without having the
effect of obscuring an objectives based syllabus?' 'How could F level
reflect the full scope of the academic discipline yet within a smaller
proportion of the curriculum than A level?' The answers to these and
similar questions, which may be discovered in the syllabuses, gradually
evolved in the course of discussion and compromise.

 The form of examination represents some sort of compromise between two
principles. In its more radical moments the group wanted to stress
forms of examination closely bound up with course work and the teaching

process. The basis of this was the conviction, held by several members of the group that the agreed objectives required an active personal involvement in learning through course work and that the assessment of such work ought to form part of the examination. It is intended that if the proposal is implemented teachers should be provided with notes for guidance on the supervision and assessment of course work. This led to difficulties in connection with moderation (which have not been fully resolved) and a concern that the form of examination should be widely accepted as valid. Objective questions were ruled out, not by the process of such compromise but because they were regarded as being inconsistent with the examination objectives.

In the group's deliberations we found it impossible to consider objectives, syllabus or assessment in isolation from each other. In preparing this report we have agreed upon and presented the objectives first.

Specimen answers have not been included in this report for two reasons. With the given limitations on space it was considered more important to include a full account of the syllabus and all supporting material. The group do not intend that a detailed mark scheme should be constructed with separate marks scored against itemised facts. At N level the short answer questions relate to specific learning objectives. Whether the candidate has adequately fulfilled the objectives will be determined by the examiners. At F level the essays will be marked according to the notes for guidance to assistant examiners giving broad specifications for the kind of answer that should warrant a particular grade, but with instructions always to mark the paper as a whole in the light of prescriptive criteria as to what a grade should mean. (As mentioned above difficulties regarding the assessment and moderation of course work were not fully resolved.)

3.1.2 <u>Proposal for new syllabuses at normal and further levels to be called 'politics' to replace the present syllabuses at advanced level</u>
(Unless otherwise stated all statements should be understood to apply to both N and F level.)

i. *The aims of the syllabus*

The aims of the syllabus are to enable centres to devise courses which through N level should provide the basis of both a broad political literacy and of a good general education in political and social problems, and through F level should provide an indication of the aptitude of a candidate to study politics as an academic discipline.

In particular the courses devised should provide both a perception of different responses, policies and conflicts within a political system, and knowledge and skills relevant to understanding and dealing with political issues.

ii. *The objectives of assessment*

To these ends candidates will be expected
(a) to show a knowledge of who promotes what policies, to have a critical approach to given information and a knowledge of alternative sources of information, and to have an understanding of different attitudes;
(b) to understand the effect of politics on themselves as individuals and on the groups to which they belong, to have ability to express their

Some general factors affecting political and voting behaviour (e.g. political culture, communication and elections).

Some general factors affecting the structure, recruitment to, and behaviour of political parties (e.g. parties' programmes and ideologies, pressure groups etc).

The role of central government and parliament (e.g. of cabinet, civil service, commissions and enquiries etc).

The role of local government and regional bodies.

The examiners will also expect a critical knowledge of and reference to current ideas and events such as can be gained by reading serious newspapers, weeklies and current policy documents.

At F level there is additional opportunity for the study of institutions and procedures in a disciplinary context.

iv. *Further level*

In addition to the basic N level core syllabus, candidates studying to F level will be required to study one of the options from the list below which will be varied from time to time.

a. Electoral sociology The conduct of elections in the United Kingdom and what general factors of class, age, sex, ideology, party allegiance, tradition, doctrines and institutions condition the outcome. To assess from the required reading what effect these factors have on voting and also what importance the readings attach to or assume in voting in the whole democratic process.

Required reading:

Peter G. Pulzer, *Political Representation and Elections in Britain* (Allen and Unwin, 3rd or subsequent edition)

F. Teer and J.D. Spence, *Political Opinion Polls* (Hutchinson University Library)

David Butler and Donald Stokes, *Political Change in Britain* (Pelican Books)

Richard Rose, *Politics in England Today* (Faber and Faber)

Some possible background reading:

D.E. Butler, *et al.*, *The British General Election of* ... (the current volumes in this series covering the last three elections)

Richard Rose, *Influencing Voters* (Faber and Faber)

D.E. Butler, *The Electoral System in Britain since 1918* (OUP 2nd edition)

Barry Hindess, *The Decline of Working Class Politics* (MacGibbon and Kee)

b. Political philosophy (set text) To consider the main ideas, meaning, structure and internal coherence of one of the following recommended books treated as literary texts. Questions will not be asked on historical background or social context, so for that reason specific commentaries from the many available are not recommended here and neither will questions be set on critics nor on schools of interpretation.

Machiavelli, *The Discourses*, ed. B. Crick (Pelican Books)

Hobbs, *The Leviathan*, ed. and abridged by J. Plamenatz (Fontana)

Rousseau, *The Social Contract*, any edition

de Tocqueville, *Democracy in America* (Fontana edition)

J.S. Mill, *On Politics and Society*, selected and edited by Geraint Williams (Fontana)

c. Concepts of democracy To consider some modern writings on the concept of democracy, what is meant by democratic behaviour and by democratic regimes? How far is rule of the majority compatible with individual liberties? How far do democratic regimes require or simply permit popular participation in politics?

Required readings:
Carol Pateman, *Participation and Democratic Theory* (CUP)
C.B. Macpherson, *The World of Democracy* (OUP)
J.S. Mill, *Essay on Liberty* (any edition)
Alexis de Tocqueville, *Democracy in America* Vol. I, ch. 14-17; Vol. II, Bk. 44
Some possible background reading:
Jack Lively, *Democracry* (Blackwells)
D.F. Thompson, *The Democratic Citizen*
A.D. Lindsay, *The Modern Democratic State*
d. Theories of the British Constitution The general nature of the British Constitution and how its rules and conventions affect the conduct of contemporary politics and rights of the individual. Separation of powers and so sovereignty of Parliament. The royal prerogative. The constitutional position of the Prime Minister, the Cabinet, judges and of the civil service. Relations of Northern Ireland and of Scotland to the Crown and Parliament.
(Plus required and background reading.)
e. The American party system The interests, ideas and policies of the main national political parties in the United States today. The paper will presume some knowledge of elections and events in the last ten years, and of the kind of view of topical issues that can be gained by regular, current reading of the American section of *The Economist*, but only of the general background which constitutes the tradition of belief and behaviour of these parties. Obviously some broad understanding of national political institutions will be needed to characterise the interests, ideas and policies of the parties; but questions will be asked specifically on institutions and context.
(Plus required and background reading.)
f. The party system of another foreign government To encourage collateral studies and the use of foreign language, centres may apply to the Chief Examiner for syllabus e. above to be used or adapted for any other country whose main language is actually being studied or has been studied for GCE by a candidate, provided that it is not his or her native language. Such examinations will be in English, except that the question papers may contain quotations in the appropriate language; but centres should submit for approval a short list of 'Required Reading' which may include books of either or both languages.

3.1.3 Notes for guidance

1. The educational objectives which underpin these syllabuses are those which were developed by 'The Programme for Political Education' ...

2. For N level no assumptions are made about any study of politics before the commencement of the course. A knowledge of the institutions and procedures of British politics should be acquired over the duration of the course. The reference to institutions and procedures in section 3.1.2 (iii)b. is in outline form to stress that the course is not a catalogue of the British Constitution. A knowledge of institutions and procedures is required only in so far as it supports an understanding (elaborated under aims and objectives) of the issues of modern politics. The depth of study of the issues will be largely determined by the coverage of these issues in the press and in the publications of parties, government and interest groups.

3. For F level it is assumed that the students, in common with N level

own purposes, interests and principles, and to have the ability to offer
justifications and reasons for pursuing their own interests and ideals;
(c) to understand the effect of politics on others and on the groups to
which they belong, to have the ability to perceive others' purposes,
interests and principles, and to have the ability to understand the
justifications and reasons underlying their attitudes and actions;
(d) to show a knowledge of the institutional arena for the conflicts, to
have a knowledge of customary ways of tackling disputes and of institutional constraints, and to show a knowledge of alternative ways of
dealing with disputes and of possibilities of institutional changes;
(e) to show a knowledge of different methods of influence in our present
society, and of their relevance for particular purposes, and to have
some knowledge of relevant methods of influence associated with other
types of society;
(f) to provide examples of conflicts of values and interests in everyday
life.

   In general therefore the aim of the normal level is to develop the
above knowledge and skills in relation to the materials associated with
political problems (newspapers, pamphlets, manifestos and popular polemic
writing) which the candidates should be able to evaluate critically as
citizens; and to introduce the candidates to theories and concepts
which will facilitate an understanding of modern politics.

   The aim of the further level is to introduce the candidates to literature of the discipline which puts such problems of modern politics into
an intellectual framework. This is to be done by taking relatively small
and concrete topics in which specified books can be examined in depth
which have the status of works of authority in the discipline. Thus F
level is intended to furnish a clear indication of a candidate's ability
to work at a higher level, but to do this by building on the basis of a
general political literacy, not by anticipating disciplinary subjects.
Many options have been offered at F level deliberately to mirror the
diversity of the discipline and to avoid prescribing an assumed core of
Political Science before degree-level work begins.

iii. *Normal level*

a. The issues (in the context of which the above will be examined) The
list which follows covers a wide range of possible areas of study and of
assessment. The examiners will vary the list from time to time. Only
those four which are marked with an asterisk will feature in the examin-
ation of the year for which this edition of the syllabus is applicable.
Those which will be examined will also be varied from time to time.
   Inflation and the management of wage and price levels
   Housing
   Industrial relations
   The level of unemployment
* Education
   Health and personal welfare services
   Environmental planning (including traffic and transportation)
* 'Law and order' (including civil rights and civil disobedience)
* Nationalism, regionalism and devolution
* Government intervention in industry
b. Institutions and procedures The examination will be concerned with
the candidate's ability to understand, analyse and interpret (as
detailed in document 2.2 paragraph 2) modern politics in the context of
the issues indicated in a. above. At N level some outline knowledge of
the institutions and procedures referred to below will be found useful.

students, will have completed about 70 per cent of the N level course
before commencement of their optional studies. The options require the
study of ideas and topics in depth, mirroring the diversity of the discipline but still favouring a broad political education, not miniaturised
political science, as the most appropriate preparation for degree-level
work. The options have been formulated so precisely on the assumption
that students are likely to achieve the level expected if they are given
substantial opportunity to study independently of fellow students (who
may well have chosen different options) under the general guidance of the
teacher, a necessary preparation for degree-level work in the social
sciences.

3.1.4 Schemes of assessment

1. At normal level candidates will be examined with:
one 3-hour written paper (56 per cent)
a folder of course work (44 per cent) which will be marked by the course
teacher(s) and moderated by procedures arranged by the Board.
    Candidates will be required to achieve a pass grade in both parts of the
examination. The results of the examination in both parts will be published together with the overall pass grade.
a. The written paper will be divided into two parts:
Section A, (28 per cent) (time recommended to candidates $1\frac{1}{2}$ hours) will
consist of four questions each based on one of the four issues marked in
section 3.1.2 (iii)a. Each question will have several parts which
require short answers. Candidates will be required to answer two
complete questions. All four questions carry equal marks. An additional
15 minutes will be given at the beginning of this section for candidates
to read and understand the paper.
Section B, (28 per cent) (time recommended to candidates $1\frac{1}{2}$ hours) will
consist of eight questions requiring answers in essay form. Candidates
will be required to answer two questions. All eight questions carry
equal marks. Candidates are at liberty to make use of material from
Section A in their answers to Section B.
b. The folder of course work should consist of four pieces of work prepared during the final year of study. The four pieces should be presented
in a different format as follows:
An essay, not exceeding 2000 words, on a subject of the candidate's own
choice.
The remaining three formats should not exceed 1000 words each.
A review of a recently published paper, pamphlet or article;
an analysis of a national and remote problem derived from newspapers and
other secondary sources;
an analysis of a local and more immediate problem derived in part from
first-hand evidence.
    These last three formats may be based on any three of the ten issues
which are listed in section 3.1.2 (iii) a. whereas the essay should not
be confined to any single issue but should broadly cover the aims and
objectives specified in section 3.1.2 (i) and (ii).

2. At further level candidates will be examined with two 3-hour written
papers (72 per cent)
a folder of course work (28 per cent) which will be marked by the course
teacher(s) and moderated by procedures arranged by the Board.
    Candidates will be required to achieve a pass grade in all three parts of
the examination. The results of the examination in all three parts will
be published together with the overall pass grade.

110

a. Paper I (36 per cent). This will be the same as the N level written paper. Section A will be allocated 18 per cent and Section B 18 per cent.
    Paper II (36 per cent). This will comprise six sections, one on each of the optional studies. Candidates will be required to answer questions from only one section. Each section will contain eight questions and candidates will be required to answer three questions. All questions carry equal marks.
b. The folder of course work should consist of four essays selected from those prepared over the full period of study. Two of the essays should relate to the N level core syllabus and the other two essays to the F level optional study selected by the candidate for Paper II. The folder must be submitted to the examiners together with the scripts of Paper II on the occasion of that examination paper.

3.1.5 Specimen question papers

Politics
'Normal level' and 'further level' Paper I
Total time allowed: 3 hours

An additional fifteen minutes reading time will be allowed at the beginning of the examination.
    Section A and B each carry half the marks of the total awarded to this written paper.
    You are advised to divide the time available equally between each of the two sections.

Section A

Answer ONLY TWO of the questions in this section. Read any extracts or other material carefully and answer all of the parts to both the questions of your choice.
    N.B. The material is intended simply to stimulate you into thinking about the issues generally. Do not confine yourself in your answers to discussing only those points mentioned in the material quoted but consider the questions generally in the light of the whole syllabus as it relates to the particular topic under consideration.
    (Question 1 would have covered 'Education', question 2 would have covered 'Law and order', and an example of question 4, 'Nationalism, regionalism and devolution', is in the original Schools Council paper.)

Question 3. Government Intervention in Industry

"Senior ministers, faced with challenges on two fronts, nationalization and the economy, are expected to decide this morning to remove temporarily from the firing line the Aircraft and Shipbuilding Industries Bill, which is due to be debated on two days this week.
    The decision is by no means cut and dried. There are those, including Mr. Varley, Secretary of State for Industry, who believe the Conservative challenge should be met and their resolve to stop the passage of the Bill tested at least once more before the Government attempts some form of accommodation.
    However, the majority view among ministers appears to be that the Government would be wise to postpone further progress with the Bill to allow tempers to cool and avoid the possibility of more unruly scenes in the Commons. The Government is also anxious to find a means of re-

opening the 'usual channels' with the Opposition.

It was recognised that the Opposition had a legitimate grievance over the voting dispute when the Conservatives accused the Government of breaking pairing arrangements. The Government has no intention of abandoning the Bill and it remains to be seen whether it can effect some kind of compromise with the Opposition in order to clear the blockage in the 'usual channels', which means there are no pairing arrangements, both sides have ordered their members to be on duty today.

One suggestion being canvassed in ministerial quarters yesterday is that the Government should leave it until after June 24, when the Rotherham by-election is expected to be held. The writ may be moved this week, and as Rotherham is a Labour stronghold, the Government would be given an extra vote in the division lobbies.

Such a delay, however, would increase the virtual certainty that the Government will have to bring in a guillotine motion on the Bill if it is to reach the statute book this session. Apart from Opposition amendments the Government has tabled 200 of its own. Any timetable motion, to curtail debate on the amendments, is bound to cause another furore." (*The Times* May 1976)

a. Distinguish between nationalisation and a workers cooperative.
b. Define one other form of public ownership.
c. Define what is meant by the corporate state.
d. Why should the government want to attempt 'some form of accommodation'?
e. Why might the government find it difficult to form such an accommodation?
f. Why do the Opposition oppose this measure?
g. Explain the viewpoint of the Liberal Party on this.
h. How will increased government intervention in industry affect you personally?
Give your opinions on this from the point of view of:
i. a member of the Stock Exchange, and
j. a worker in the aircraft industry.

Section B

Answer ONLY TWO of the questions in this section.

1. How far should Parliament express what the people want?
2. 'Political parties exist to perpetuate problems, not to solve them.' Discuss.
3. Is 'extra-parliamentary' politics necessarily 'anti-parliamentary' politics?
4. Can an ordinary individual ever hope to have any effect on getting a new law made or a bad law changed? Discuss this in the context of one issue that interests you.
5. If you felt that you were being unfairly treated by someone in authority, would you do better to go to the Press or to a Member of Parliament?
6. 'The answer to every social problem is the same: spend more money'. Discuss.
7. Should the power of any Government be limited by any forces outside Parliament other than the electorate?
8. If there was to be more popular participation in Great Britain in the business of government, do you know of any foreign institution which could or should be usefully introduced?

Politics
'Further level': Paper II
Total time allowed: 3 hours

There are six sections on this paper, A, B, C, D, E, & F. You should attempt ONLY THREE questions. All three questions selected should be from only ONE of the six sections.

Section A Electoral Sociology

1. It has been said that the Nuffield Studies are more concerned with prediction of election results than with explanation of political behaviour. Explain this assertion and assess what they really are about or should be about.
2. Is there any ground for disquiet either about how political opinion polls are derived or how they are used? Could more use be made of them and could they be made better?
3. What evidence is there about the effect of campaigning and of propaganda upon voting? Is there any need for change in the laws to deal with any of the factors involved?
4. Does Butler and Stokes book, *Political Change in Britain*, really establish what long-term trends are developing?
5. Does 'the working class Conservative voter' need explaining in sociological terms, rather than as someone who in thinking about it just happens to reach a different conclusion?
6. Is it possible or sensible to think of different doctrines of political representation apart from different theories of social class?
7. etc...

Section B Political Philosophy

Question 1. Machiavelli Answer ANY THREE of the eight parts of this question.

a. Why did Machiavelli attribute a greater stability to a Republic than to any other form of government?
b. Why did Machiavelli think that 'conflict' had a positive advantage in Rome?
c. Show the relationships of Machiavelli's 'Fortune', 'Necessita' and 'Virtu' to each other.
d. Is there a contradiction between his republicanism and his advocacy of doing anything that is needed to preserve the State?
e. What assumptions does Machiavelli make in *The Discourses* about popular power?
f. Comment on the construction or form of *The Discourses*. Does its structure throw any light on whether Machiavelli is writing for the moment or for the ages?
g. etc...

3.1.6 Trials and dissemination

General details of the work of the group were made available to teachers and others in the course of the regular communications of the Programme for Political Education.

On many occasions copies of the proposal in its successive draft forms were given to teachers for comment.

Without exception all reaction to the proposal was not merely favourable but was enthusiastic about the objectives in general and about the schemes of examination in particular.

During the summer term 1976 a collation of all the examination questions which had been suggested in the course of discussion was sent to about ten teachers for comment. Four teachers gave detailed comments and in some cases returned the essays and answers to questions written by their A level students. This work, although in no sense constituting a representative sample, indicated that the 'level' of questioning was comparable to that of A level. It also suggested that, in the case of short answer questions, the style of questioning despite being more demanding in many respects was at the same time more interesting and stimulating. The answers appeared to reveal an interest and involvement not often expressed in conventional essay answers.

3.1.7 Members of the commissioned group

Miss Yvonne Baglin	Kingsway-Princeton College, London
Mr. Christopher Cannon	Beauchamps School, Wickford, Essex (now in Australia)
Professor Bernard Crick	Birkbeck College, London
Mrs. Janice Derry	City University, London (now of Holborn Tutors)
Mr. Alex Porter	Solihull Sixth Form College (now of The Institute of Education, London)
Mr. Geoffrey Prout	Dartford Grammar School, Kent
Mr. Michael Strange	St. Albans College of Further Education

Professor Crick took the chair at the first meeting to discuss the broad strategy (and remained with the group throughout), but subsequently Mr. Alex Porter took the chair and acted as rapporteur. Nicola Evans, of Hatfield Girls Grammar School, Herts, worked with the group for most of the Autumn term 1975 and Mr. Rob Shepherd of Cambridge Tutors (now of Conservative Central office) attended the first meeting. Both felt unable to continue due to pressure of work.

3.2   HISTORY AND POLITICAL LITERACY

The Report of the History Working Group chaired by Derek Heater

Membership

The group consisted of Mr. Derek Heater as convener (Brighton Poly-
technic), Mr. Jerry Adams (Seaford Comprehensive School), Mr. Bill
Coxall* (Eastbourne College of Education), Mrs. Joyce Giles (Brighton
College of Education), Mr. John Hodgson (Whitehawk Secondary School,
Brighton), Mr. David Lambourne* (Bexhill Down Secondary Modern School)
and Mr. Richard Tames (School of Oriental and African Studies) who
attended meetings; and of Mr. Christopher Kemp* (Lancing College),
Mr. Geoffrey Stevenson* (Lady Spencer Churchill College of Education) and
Mr. Keith West* (Matthew Humberstone School, Cleethorpes) who were
corresponding members. Those who produced the material for the final
report are asterisked.

3.2.1 Mode of operation

Five meetings were held at Brighton and Eastbourne. Initially working
papers and ideas for discussion were presented and then refined by Derek
Heater to produce an overall framework. Having established such a framework, individuals worked on their own chosen syllabus. There were
difficulties. Some members lacked time or stamina to continue the meetings so detailed discussion of the individual proposals had to be
abandoned. We wanted to develop sixteen syllabuses, i.e. one example for
each box on the matrix (see 3.2.4 below) to show the flexibility and
range of the approach. But not enough people were available and several
people failed to produce papers. For instance, the lack of anything on
Local History from the original working group led to Mr. Stevenson being
approached as a corresponding member.

3.2.2 Using history

Although history has traditionally been used as a vehicle for political
education, we believe that this function has been eroded (a) because of
the aridity of much former teaching of political history; and (b) because of the (rightful) claims of other facets of history - e.g. social
and economic.
    We believe the civic function of history should be revived by history
teachers for the following reasons: (a) the potential interest of biography and narrative; (b) the heightened understanding that derives from
comparison and contrast; (c) the understanding of the relative nature of
political responses to social problems - different societies have produced different answers, there are no 'right' answers.
    We are nonetheless aware that some history teachers might well be sus-
picious of what we are trying to do. We are overtly recommending the
use of the study of the past in order the better to understand the present - by identifying comparisons or tracing developments. Purists may
reject the first technique by arguing that history does not repeat itself
and the second by condemning it as 'Whig' history. We believe that by
careful selection of the topics for teaching and by alerting the teachers
to these dangers, little violence will be done to the purity of history.

3.2.3 The problem of history and the concept of political literacy

The concept of political literacy poses certain difficulties for the teacher of history. Four major problems may be identified. Firstly, the concept is essentially focussed upon the task of enabling the individual to operate effectively in his own present-day society. History consequently can provide only perspective and comparison – no mean contributions but nevertheless not the totality. Secondly, the concept presupposes a society in which personal engagement in the political process is at least possible and, probably, desirable. But some politics that are commonly taught in school provide for no really meaningful participation by the mass of the people – e.g. Ancient Egypt. Thirdly some historical topics, especially in the fields of foreign policy, did not in fact capture the interest of the citizenry or the electorate even when one existed – e.g. the Seven Years War. Fourthly, if the chosen syllabus-structure is a chronological outline (e.g. Tudors and Stuarts), line of development (e.g. the monarchy) or comparative (e.g. revolutions) the pupils will be handling a <u>changing</u> situation. (And, after all, the concept of change, it could be argued, is central to the history teacher's task). However, the study of the components of political literacy in a static situation is probably as much as most pupils can manage: anything more complex would require considerable sophistication in the handling of multiple variables.

The style of history teaching most convenient for the transmission of political literacy is, therefore, the 'patch' or 'era' approach – i.e. th technique of studying a comparatively narrow period in depth so that the pupil can 'relive' that particular situation. The technique of imaginative reconstruction is a vitally important function of history teaching. Moreover, in its cultivation of <u>empathy</u> it finds itself in harmony with a crucial function of political education. However, in so far as an historical patch of time will be remote from the child's own age and experience, history will probably always be a more powerful tool for developing knowledge and attitudes than action skills.

An example

This is an attempt to translate Diagram B of document 2.2 into historical terms. The figures and letters relate to the boxes in the original. I have provided labels for each box and rewritten the questions. It is envisaged that the history teacher would invite the class to imagine that they lived in a certain social position in the society being studied and thereby to investigate the political opportunities and frustrations they would encounter. For the present example I have taken an artisan in Paris during the French Revolution.

   i. Policies and how to find out about them
a. What was the range of political principles generally held at the time? Arguments for constitutional monarchy and the growth of republicanism. The factions struggles of the Montagnards, Brissotins, Dantonists, Hebertists. Anticlericalism. Counter-revolution and Terror.
b. If I had lived then, what opportunities would I have had to become critically informed?
Pamphleteering in 1789 – e.g. Sieyes. Growth of journalism – e.g. Mallet du Pan's *Mercure, Moniteur*. Political clubs.
b. Looking back on the period now, can we perceive alternative ways of viewing the political situation to those available at the time? Arousal of passions tended to polarise opinion. The sans-culottes believed in

the revolutionary ideal - and yet their lot was little changed by the
Revolution.

ii. Institutions
a. What political institutions existed at that time?
The Paris municipality and Sections. The Assembly (Constituent, Legislative, Convention). Committee of Public Safety. Revolutionary
Tribunal. Political Clubs (Jacobins, Cordeliers).
b. How were political disputes settled then?
Debates in the Assembly and clubs. Mobilisation of the sans-culottes
(e.g. 14th July, 10th August). Purging of factions (e.g. fall of the
"Girondins").
c. What was unfair or inefficient in the ways then used for settling
disputes?
Dominant position of Paris - weakness of politicians who did not enjoy
a Parisian power-base - subordination of the interests of the provinces
to Paris. Use of force to resolve issues/impose will.

iii. Tactics
a. & b. If I had lived then, how could I have exerted any influence?
Become a member of a club or Section committee. Demonstrate during a
journee. Voting for Assembly (but N.B. indirect elections).
c. How did these opportunities compare with (i) opportunities in other
countries at that time, (ii) Britain today?
(i) Compare franchise in Britain and USA. Existence of radical/revolu-
tionary movements in most countries of the western world (Palmer/Godechot
thesis). (ii) Universal suffrage. Existence and power of TUs - illegal
in revolutionary France (Loi le Chapelier).

iv. Self-Interest
a. & b. If I had lived then, how would I have been affected by governmental or other political action?
Inflation - because of general shortage of food and abuse of assignats.
Maximum laws. Levee en masse - condition of total war. Terror.
c. Imagine you belonged to a particular group. How would you have justified your interests and ideals?
Practical and idealistic value of Liberty, Equality and Fraternity.
Defence of political rights and economic standards justified by these
criteria enshrined in the Declaration of Rights.

v. Responsibility
a. & b. Would government or other political action have affected other
groups in different ways from the ways it would have affected me?
Peasantry less affected by fluctuations in food supplies/price levels
than towns - also, less affected by faction-fights. Counter-
revolutionary activity and its suppression would have affected people of
the Vendee more than Paris. Priests - struggle with consciences over
Civil Constitution. Flight of emigres.
c. How easy would it have been to appreciate the points of view of other
groups?
Probably difficult - because of polarisation of opinion and attitudes and
limited communications (low level of literacy, no TV compared with
present-day Britain).

vi. vii. Action Skills
a. & b. How much say do you have at home and school compared with
what you would have had at that time?
c. Generally - subordinate position of children.

3.2.4 The translation of basic concepts into historical situations

Political concepts are easier than 'political literacy' to handle through the medium of history: indeed, the tendency of the historian in comparison with the political scientist to work in concrete/particular rather than abstract/general terms may well make the teaching of basic concepts by historical exemplification the most palatable and comprehensive method. And yet, one must expect the coverage of the range of concepts to vary according to the topic under review. The history teacher who is firmly committed to the task of political education will consequently need to select topics for study over a period of time that, in combination, embrace the full range.

The relevance of documents 2.3 and 2.4 to the history teacher is not perhaps immediately obvious. There follow therefore illustrations of the ways in which they might be applied. Because political literacy is concerned with the ability of the pupil to understand and operate the system in which he lives, the most useful aspect of history for this purpose may well be a patch of recent British History. However, because the study of more distant areas is both more useful for history and yet more difficult to apply to 'political literacy', the examples used here have been deliberately selected from societies somewhat removed in time and place from twentieth-century Britain.

An example - (by Christopher Kemp)

Topic: A comparative study of the French, Russian and Chinese revolutions.

i. Government
Power: The claims to legitimacy (especially dubious in the case of China) and the practical means (eroding) available to the ancien regime governments.
Force: Links with power in looking at the practical means available to governments and the very much increased means available once the revolutionary process is over - e.g. the Napoleonic police and the NKVD.
Authority: Should be seen functioning under the ancien regime governments (e.g. in Louis XIV's time in France), eroding (Bloody Sunday in Russia), and then functioning again under new governments (the rallying of some former supporters of the ancien regime under Napoleon).
Order: The collapse of the concept of order during the revolutionary periods and the return to a more ordered situation after a lapse of time, a return which in itself enhances the authority of the new government (the Chinese Mandate of Heaven) and reinforces perhaps an element of continuity underlying events (De Tocqueville's centralisation in France).

ii. Relationships
Law: The lack of an accepted body of such general rules (no common law code in France) in spite of efforts at reform (e.g. in Russia) and the filling of this gap (e.g. the Code Napoleon).
Justice: An examination of the extent to which a feeling that justice is a feature of the state is lacking under the ancien regime governments; an examination of the extent to which this situation has been rectified by the revolutionary process.
Representation: The lack of representational claims of ancien regime governments, the attempts of the new regimes to remedy this state of affairs and their measure of success (difficulties of elected assemblies in France, fate of the constituent in Russia).

Pressure: Lack of means for people to bring pressure on ancien regime governments other than by force. The corresponding governmental pressures on people and the way in which these may intensify after revolutions. The war situation and responses to it.

iii. People
Natural rights: Of especial relevance in the case of the French Revolution (the influence of 18th century thinkers on the work of the revolutionaries). Can a similar pattern be discerned in Russia and in China, or are attitudes here different? Ditto perhaps individuality.
Individuality: Are we investigating here a totally different political tradition from the Western European ones?
Freedom: Revolutions as an expression of a desire for freedom, or more freedom - the politicizing process par excellence. The limitations of any success in this field; greater perhaps in Russia and in China than in France (reference back to Natural Rights and Individuality).
Welfare: Development of this idea during the French Revolution - land and education issues. Further developments and extension in 20th century Russia and China.

3.2.5 The organisation of exemplars

There is no universally accepted or even recommended way of selecting the content of a history syllabus. We have therefore tried to build in as much flexibility to our approach as possible so that few teachers will be able to say, 'This is not my kind of history'. We allowed for four different geographical contexts, viz. Local; National (British); Foreign; International. Also, we allowed for four different modes of syllabus construction, viz. the traditional chronological approach; line of development (i.e. the study of one topic over an extended period of time); comparative (i.e. separate examples of one particular historical phenomenon); patch (i.e. a depth study of a society or situation over a limited period of time).

The arrangement may be presented in the form of a matrix:

	Chronological	Line of development	Comparative	Patch
Local				
National (British)				
Foreign				
International				

The plan to provide sixteen syllabus-documents unfortunately proved too ambitious. A number of colleagues started valuable work, but had to withdraw from the project because of the pressure of other work. We thank them, as we thank those who were able to see their work through to its conclusion in this report. The sample syllabuses we completed, only three of which are reproduced here, illustrate the following approaches:

I. *Local Patch* - 'Popular involvement in Banbury politics, 1830-80'

II.   *National (British) Patch* - 'The Radical Movement in Britain 1815-32'
III. *National (British) Comparative* - 'Trade Unions'*
IV.   *Foreign Patch* - 'The French Revolution'*
V.   *Foreign/International Comparative* - 'Empires'

The syllabus documents are organised into the following sections:

a.   Introduction: Stimulus material.
b.   Main events: Basic factual learning.
c.   Recapitulation with concepts: This is the crucial stage - where the political learning becomes explicit. We believe that much history teaching fails in its function as civic education because the style is weak or absent altogether. The approach recommended is to ask what basic political questions can be quite naturally extracted from the historical material under discussion.
d.   Balance sheets: The importance and impact of the events at the time.
e.   Legacy: Significance for the present-day and present-day parallels.
f.   Resources.

References

G. Connell-Smith and H.A. Lloyd, *The Relevance of History* (Heinemann, 1974)
D. Heater, 'Contexts for Political Education: History' in T. Brennan and J.F. Brown (eds.), *Teaching Politics: Problems and Perspectives* (BBC, 1975)
D. Heater 'History and Teaching Political Education' in B.R. Crick and D. Heater, *Essays on Political Education* (Falmer Press, 1977)

*Purely to save space and cost, these two sample syllabuses have not been reprinted here, but any one wanting either or both can obtain a photocopy from The Hansard Society, 12 Gower Street, London W.C.1. and will be invoiced for the cost of copying and postage. (Editors).

3.2.6 <u>Specimen syllabus</u>: <u>Popular involvement in Banbury Politics</u>
<u>1830-80</u>

1. Introduction: points of departure
<u>Banbury</u>: its location, history and economic function (as a market town,
and important route centre in the coach, canal and railway age, and as
an industrial centre, first in agricultural machinery, latterly in light
industry); its political importance (defensive site with castle,
strong-hold of Puritanism, centre of reforming radicalism – the last two
relating directly to its right to send an MP to the House of Commons,
1554 to 1885).

Its independent political power (a vigorous press, an MP, a Corporation
1554-1974, control of its schools, 1902-44) its decline, and its relationship to the national pattern.

Thus deserving study <u>in its own right</u> and as particular example of
wider trends (viz. the Stacey studies on its C20 development).

Politics

Possession of an MP was thought to be an important factor: why? Were
these periodic 'votes' an effective way of influencing laws in Parliament? How did MPs behave towards their constituents?

Popular involvement

Who voted? What proportion is this of the population of Banbury? Was
it fair that a restricted number of the people should vote? Were those
who had the vote keen to use it? Were those who did not keen to get it?

What 'model' of political behaviour fits the pattern of voting? What
is the relevance of party labels, local pride, and particular grievances?
Did the activity of voting in itself confer an experience of choice and
participation? How far were voters creatures of habit, deferential or
corruptible? Did it make any difference to have a vote in secret?

Do voters participate today in the same way as in the Reform age? By
active political discussion? By reading newspapers full of political
comments? By keen partisanship of one political party – even active
membership? By voting when the chance occurs?

2. Main events
Knowledge is required, firstly of the local situation, and a series of
support materials (e.g. Banbury election results, detail on the borough
franchise in the nineteenth century, biography of the MPs with full
information on their activities (or lack of) in national politics) is
required to support the range of possible activities and approaches by
the pupils.

Knowledge is required, secondly of the political structure of Britain
in the period (biographies of national leaders, a synopsis of political
events, a summary of social, economic and cultural change, an explanation
of contemporary notions of party and government) and of the place of that
situation in the development of Britain's institutions. Much of this
information is generally available in secondary material for pupils of
this age-range, and listed.

The electoral system in Banbury
i. Until 1832, Parliament was elected in a way which had not changed
for centuries. From 1554 to 1832 Banbury was one of five boroughs which
elected one MP (all the others elected two: in case one went missing!)

121

and the voting was for most of that time in the hands of the 18 aldermen and chief burgesses of the borough corporation. There was no list of electors, and in 80 years before 1832, only three elections were contested.

ii. The First Reform Act (1832) suppressed the right of small boroughs to send MPs to the House of Commons, but Banbury was not affected. Now, a Register of Electors was created, and revised each year by a barrister, and in all boroughs the right to vote was made uniform:

'Occupiers either as owners or tenants of any house, warehouse, or counting house, shop, or other building, either with or without land, of the clear yearly value of £10 within the borough, provided they had been in possession 12 calendar months prior to the last day of July in the year of the claim and had paid before 20th July all the poor-rates and assessed taxes payable from them in respect of the premises previous to the April preceding'.

Party agents attended the revising barristers' sessions, in order to prevent their known opponents from getting onto the lists. An elector had to pay a fee to register his name on the list (the lists for 1836-1850 and 1864-6 are in Banbury Public Library).

Voting was in public, so that local printers (Potts and Rusher) were able to publish how people had voted. As they produced pollbooks for every contested election from 1832 to 1868 (Tancred was returned without a contest in the General Elections of 1832 and 1852), they must have sold enough copies to make it worthwhile, and this is material evidence of public interest.

iii. The Second Reform Act (1867) extended the right to vote in boroughs to all householders with a one-year residential qualification, and to lodgers who had occupied lodgings worth £10 a year also for a year. In Banbury the electorate rose from 581 to 1529.

iv. The Ballot Act (1872) introduced secret voting, and thus brought an end to the publication of pollbooks. We can see whether the change made a dramatic difference to voting habits by comparing Banbury's result in 1874 and 1880 with those in the 1850s and 1860s.

v. The Third Reform Act (1884) did not change the right of Banbury people to vote, but the Redistribution Act (1885) ended its right to elect a separate MP.

vi. Further stages in electoral reform have been the granting of the vote to all males over 21 (1918), to all women over 21 (1928), to all persons over 18 (1970); in 1948 all votes resting on business interests such as 'counting-houses, warehouses, etc.' were ended.

Note:
The sources for this information are 1. Hanham H.J. (1968), *The Reformed Electoral System in Great Britain 1832-1914*; and 2. *Victoria County History of Oxfordshire* Vol. X pp 89-94.

<u>Elections for Banbury's M.P.</u>

Date	Winners		Losers		Electors
1806	W. Praed	10	D. North	6	18
1808	D. North	5	W. Praed	3	18
1831	J. Easthope (Whig).	6	H. Hutchinson (Tory)	2	18

————————————————————————————————Reform Bill (see ii.)

Date	Winners		Losers		Electors
1835	H. Tancred (Whig)..	203	E. Williams (Tory)	43	368
1837	H. Tancred (Whig)..	181	H. Tawney (Tory).	75	
1841	H. Tancred (Whit)..	124	H. Holbech (Tory)	100	491
			H. Vincent (Chartist)	51	
1847	H. Tancred (Lib)...	226	J. McGregor (Tory)	164	
1857	H. Tancred (Lib)...	216	E. Yates (Tory)..	58	
1859 Feb	B. Samuelson (Lib).	177	J. Hardy (Tory)..	176	535
			E. Miall (Lib)...	118	
1859 Apr	Sir C. Douglas (Lib)	235	B. Samuelson (Lib)	199	
1865	B. Samuelson (Lib).	206	C. Bell (Tory)...	165	581
			Sir C. Douglas (Lib)	160	

————————————————————————Reform Bill (see iii.)

Date	Winners		Losers		Electors
1868	B. Samuelson (Lib).	772	G. Stratton (Tory)	397	1529

————————————————————————Ballot Act (see iv.)

Date	Winners		Losers		Electors
1874	B. Samuelson (Lib).	760	J. Wilkinson (Tory)	676	1952
1880	B. Samuelson (Lib).	1018	T.G. Bowles (Tory)	583	

————————————————————————Reform Act (see v.)

Notes:

i. The confusion over party 'labels' (none in 1806, and 1808; two Liberals in 1859 and 1865) tells us that the electors did not think of voting as we do (in 1974 the party of each candidate was printed on the ballot form).

ii. Dudley North was the only member of his family (settled at Wroxton Abbey) to lose a contest in Banbury: from 1770-82 Banbury's MP, Lord North, was George III's Prime Minister.

iii. Except for Samuelson (1885-1895) and another Liberal (1906-1910) the North Oxfordshire seat had been Conservative-held since 1885.

iv. Labour candidates did not stand for North Oxfordshire until after 1918, How far was the Chartist candidate a forerunner of modern Socialist thinking?

v. See the separate paper for an explanation of the technical details of voting: this will show why there could not be any more pollbooks than the nine which (thanks to Potts and Rusher) exist.

vi. The results are taken from Williams W.R.J. (1899) *Parliamentary History of the County of Oxford*; the size of the electorate is given in the pollbooks.

Basic learning activities

i. Locate and map the places connected with political activity in Victorian Banbury: viz. Town Hall, Police Station, Railway Station, breweries, factories, inns and beerhouses, public meeting places, printers' offices, churches and chapels, other institutions (Mechanics, Tory and Liberal Corn Exchanges, Tory and Liberal Building Societies, Clubs etc.).

ii. Examine election literature (bills, pamphlets, press reports of speeches) and list (with frequency) key words viz. all -isms and -ologies, references to the Queen, to religion, and to individuals by name. Cross-refer by examining similar election material for Banbury in the 1974 election.

iii. Use a simulation exercise (similar to the Coketown example). A less hypothetical exercise could be to let pupils constitute a Banbury committee to secure (a) the unseating of Henry Tancred in the 1852 election, (b) to elect a working-man's candidate in the 1868 election. A somewhat high-level activity.

iv. Reconstruct a drama within the political process, e.g. an election meeting in 1859, or the White Hart non-electors meeting in 1859, and debate the issues and the effort at persuasion.

v. Set the problem of how one would set about (a) exerting pressure over a particular issue, (b) securing the defeat of an MP whose policies one dislikes, in the context of 1976 Banbury.

vi. Register the interlocking of political and other social and economic features by a range of quantifying exercises:

a. Use a pollbook (which gives the occupations of voters) to distribute votes by occupation: Tory butchers v Radical cobblers, or whatever relationships are shown (in fact, a striking link between skilled artisans (carpenters etc.) and emergent Liberal voting is shown in 1859). Use a Directory to see how many in each occupation appear to be without voting rights (for non-commercial and lower occupations, the census enumeration books would be required).

b. Use a pollbook to identify the 51 Chartists in 1841: find out as much information as possible from this, the Enumerators' returns and Directories. (They will find that a group of inn-keepers were all tenants of Austin's brewery, if they are persistent). Do these people seem the same as the Chartists described in general histories? If not, is Banbury different, or are the books wrong?

c. Use a list of members of a Banbury society (such as the Mechanics) and see how they vote. Suggest an explanation of their behaviour.

d. In the pollbooks of the 1860s, list the voters who live in North, West, East Street and South Place, Grimsbury. Go and examine the area today. The first inhabitants were enabled to buy the houses by an organisation interested in getting them on the voters' lists (see background handout). Could this have been their chief reason for wanting to live there?

e. Find out if people were 'loyal' in voting habits by taking a named family and following its votes through the pollbooks.

f. Construct an electoral 'genealogical tree' showing how voters behave when there is a confusing issue to sort out e.g. in 1859. (The handout shows how Bath voters coped).

g. Voters could be influenced by personality, money or some threat to their interest or livelihood, or they could vote on policies. Look at the election literature, to see which of the following policy matters are often mentioned, and add any which you spot:
Free trade
Temperance
Education
Resistance to State interference in industry
Public health and environmental improvement
Social welfare (including the Poor Law)
Royal family
Crime
Religion
British influence in the world
National leaders
Racial prejudice
What are the important issues in today's elections? Do people vote on these, or out of loyalty, personal respect, family background or 'like

their mates'.
N.B. The variety of approaches is countless, and by use of the census
enumeration, ages, birthplace, family relationships and much else
(especially servant-keeping) can be brought into focus.

3. Re-inforcement of concepts

a. Government

Power will emerge in the identification of elements of the Banbury
community with abnormal influence, be they property owners (North of
Wroxten), bankers (Tawney, the 1847 candidate), brewers (Barnes Austin,
the backer of the Chartist in 1841), industrialists (Samuelson, whose
nine employees secured his election by one vote in 1859) or dissenting
ministers of printers (like Rusher and Potts) or newspaper proprietors,
or carpet-baggers. This influence will be seen both as an individual
and a collective (by occupation, creed or class) factor.
Force will emerge, rather less clearly, in terms and in the a-political
lawlessness of Banbury (the suppression of racing, the destruction of
seedy lodging-houses to make room for the railway). Only in the Swing
rioting of 1830 will there be any local example of overt force in
Neithrop. Its absence may well be a source of discussion.
Authority will emerge, both in its dignified and efficient aspects. The
context of the force-less political disputes will illustrate both its
extent and impact; the place of monarchy in affection through the period
may illustrate the first.
Order will emerge as a circumstance, sometimes a thin veil, of all political life: again, only strongly challenged in the 1831 Reform agita-
tion.

b. Relationships

Law will emerge clearly as a process, involving the consent of some of
the governed; the correlation of national laws with the (often ana-
chronistic) notions of voters will be seen, and the role of an individual
MP shown by sloth (Tancred) and important committee work (Samuelson and
technical education).
Justice will be seen in publishers' nervousness over laws of libel, and
in the framing of petitions for greater voting rights and other demands.
Representation will be seen clearly in the electoral process and the continuing relationship of an MP to his constituents.
Pressure will be shown by the relative skill at bringing an 'issue' to
life, and obliging, within the system, authority to take notice.

c. People

Natural rights will emerge in the election literature, and a sharp focus
will be provided by the Chartist campaign and that of the ideologically-
committed Liberal in 1859. The demands of the non-electors will also
illustrate this.
Individuality will shine through the register of almost all the comments
encountered; the personal intervention of political figures on the
national scene (there are not too many) and the local adulation of
leaders will illustrate.
Freedom will be shown by the presence, or absence, of pressure on those
enjoying the formal voting rights; in a larger context it will be seen
by comparing the lot of electors with that of non-voters.

Welfare may well be shown by its absence as a concept: even the issue of public health (and the Chadwickian report for Banbury) will emerge as well-meaning intervention by an elite and not a response to popular pressure. This again should be an important source for discussion.

4. Balance sheet and legacy
The immediate and localised approach may need supplementing with other more far-reaching exercises, but the possibility of understanding of some of the concepts may be heightened by the active approach and the closeness of the evidence, in a way which Flora Thompson suggested:

'As they grew, the two elder children would ask questions of anybody and everybody willing or unwilling to answer them. Who planted the buttercups? Why did God let the wheat get blighted? Who lived in this house before we did, and what were the children's names? What's the sea like? Is it bigger than Cottisloe Pond? Why can't we go to Heaven in the donkey-cart? Is it farther than Banbury?'

5. Resources
Primary sources:
Banbury pollbooks (those for 1859 and 1865 published by OUP, 1973: others in Banbury Public Library)
Banbury Census Enumerators' Returns, 1841, 1851, 1861, 1871
Banbury Electoral Registers, 1836-50, 1864-6 (in Banbury P. Lib.)
Banbury Directories throughout the period (in Banbury P. Lib.)
Election handbills and posters (in Banbury P. Lib.)
Correspondence of H.W. Tancred with his constituents (Banbury Historical Society Records Series)

Secondary sources:
Step Back (Radio Oxford series): Using Census Materials (tape)
Tames R., *Disraeli* (*Jackdaw* No. 127: Cape 1975)
Tames R., *Queen Victoria* (*Jackdaw* No.131: Cape 1975)
Langdon-Davies J., *The Vote 1832-1918* (*Jackdaw* No.16: Cape 1965)
Addy J,, *Parliamentary Elections and Reform* (Longmans)
Rooke P.J., *People of Victorian Britain* (Wayland, 1973)
          The Age of Dickens (Wayland, 1970)
Lane P., *The Victoria Age* (Batsford 1972)
Healy S., *Town Life* (Batsford, 1963)

Teacher-oriented:
Best G.F.A., *Mid-Victorian Britain* (Weidenfeld & Nicolson 1971)
Dyos & Wolff, *The Victorian City* 2 vols. (1974)
Harrison J.F.C., *The Early Victorians* (Weidenfeld & Nicolson 1971)
Perkin H.J., *The Origins of Modern English Society* (RKP 1969)
Stacey M., *Tradition and Change* (OUP 1960)
          Power, Persistence and Change (Routledge 1975)
Vincent J., *The Making of the Liberal Party* (1965)
          Victorian Pollbooks, How Victorians Voted (1967)

(Geoffrey Stevenson)

3.2.7 <u>Specimen syllabus: The Radical Movement in Britain, 1815-1832</u>

1. Introduction
Since this topic is designed to form a component of established history
courses (most of which are geared to CSE. or GCE. 'O' Level examination
work), it is not envisaged that it will take up more than a period of
four weeks.
  'Peterloo' provides a useful starting point. It is a colourful event
which the teacher can use to create a vivid impact and to stimulate interest. It is suggested that the teacher initially outlines the events
of Peterloo with the aid of suitable visual material, (such as the print
which depicts soldiers cutting their way through the crowd that is published in Titley, *Machines, Money and Men*, pp. 202/3, or that of a similar scene which is published in Cootes, *Britain Since 1700*, p. 125), together with eyewitness accounts, (such as those of Samuel Bamford, the
Rev. Edward Stanley and the reporter of *The Times* who was on the hust-
ings. Extracts from Bamford's writings and Stanley's account can be
found in Kesteven, *Peterloo, 1819*, pp. 88/89 and 65/68 respectively. *The
Times* reporter's account is contained in the *Jackdaw* folder on Peterloo).
  Once the events of Peterloo have been outlined, the teacher can set the
scene for the topic by referring to factors such as: the background of
repressive Government; the important personalities of the movement (particularly Cobbett, Hunt, Place and Lovett); the main events leading up
to the gathering in St. Peter's Field; the radical objective of Parliamentary Representation; and the response in society to the violence at
Peterloo. In this undertaking, any basic textbook would need to be
supplemented by a more specialised book, such as Kesteven's *Peterloo*.

<u>Suggestions for pupils' work</u>

i.   A short description of the events of Peterloo.
ii. Finding the answers to specific questions, such as:-
     Why did people gather in St. Peter's Field on August 16th, 1819?
     What were they hoping to achieve? What kinds of people were they?
     Did they go there with violent intentions? What previous demon-
     strations had been held? Who was the principal speaker at this
     meeting? Who were the other radical leaders at this time?
     What do we mean by 'radical'? Why did radicals place so much hope
     in Parliamentary Representation? How did people in general respond
     to the news of the violence at Peterloo?

<u>Discussion point</u>

Was participation in a peaceful demonstration the best way for the ordinary working man to fight for better political, economic and social conditions? Were there other ways in which the working man could have striven
for reforms?

2. Main events
These are fairly straightforward, but will need to be taught, for the
most part, in chronological sequence, (since an understanding of the development of events is central in this topic), and through the use of
both visual and biographical material, (so that interest is sustained).
The main areas that need to be taught are as follows: the general situation after Waterloo, including conditions of high unemployment, declining
trade and low real wages; the response and attitude of the Government
and the 'comfortable' classes to 'Jacobinism' during and after the Napo-

leonic Wars; the electoral system prior to 1832, (the different types of constituency, the kinds of people who had the vote, etc.); the growth of radicalism and the belief among radicals that Parliamentary Representation would prove the remedy to all abuses, (such as poverty, unemployment and exploitation); the Luddites and the chance their actions gave to the Government to act against all reformers; the leaders of reform, particularly Cobbett, Hunt, Place and Lovett; the dissemination of radical ideas – Paine's *Rights of Man,* Cobbett's *Political Register.* etc.; the March of the Blanketeers; Pentridge; Peterloo; the Cato Street Conspiracy; the Six Acts; the general situation during the 1820s including the background of improving trade; the growth of working-class activity in other fields, particularly Co-operation and Trade Unionism; the events leading up to, and the passage of, the 1832 Reform Bill.

Suggestions for pupils' work

i. A written account of what conditions were like for working folk in general immediately after the Napoleonic Wars. (To include reasons why there was high unemployment, a decline in trade and low real wages, and a general fear of radicals on the part of the Government and the comfortable classes).

ii. A study of Parliamentary elections at the beginning of the 19th century. (To include a comparison with elections today).

iii. A visit to the local library to research into possible evidence of radical activity, such as radical meetings and popular unrest, in the locality in the years leading up to the Reform Bill.

iv. A written account explaining why it is true to say that in the years before 1832 only a very small proportion of working people were represented in Parliament.

v. A description of Luddite activities. (To include an assessment of the chance the actions of the Luddites gave to the Government to act against all reformers).

vi. A short biography of William Cobbett.

vii. Research into the life and work of one of the other prominent radical leaders, such as Hunt, Place or Lovett.

viii. A brief written description of (a) the March of the Blanketeers, (b) the Pentridge Rising, and (c) the Cato Street Conspiracy. (To include an explanation of the part played by the Government in each of these).

ix. A description of the events leading up to, and the passage of, the 1832 Reform Bill. (To include a statement of what the provisions were under the new Act, and an assessment of why radical leaders and many working people were very disappointed with it).

x. Preparation for, and the staging of, a radical meeting to advance Parliamentary Reform. Class members to represent: Henry Hunt, a spokesman for the middle classes (e.g. a factory owner without the vote and desirous of having it); a spokesman for the unemployed; other radical speakers; and members of the crowd.

Discussion points

i. Why did radicals place so much hope in the reform of Parliament?

ii. What does the passage of the Six Acts tell us about the Government of the day?

3. Recapitulation with concepts
Various basic points of political understanding, which can be given

specific reference to material already taught, can be discussed here. (It is suggested that such discussions, to some extent, take place concurrently with the later stages of the previous section). These points of political understanding should, between them, be handled in such a way as to involve most of the Basic Concepts identified in document 2.3. (As well as additional concepts like 'radical', 'revolution' and 'working classes').

It should be remembered that an important aspect of this discussion stage is that it should be used in such a way as to help pupils to develop their own opinions.

For the sake of simplicity the following structure has been adopted: (a) Point of political understanding to be examined. (b) Suggested basis for discussion.

i. (a) Change can be effected either within the existing institutional framework or by the destruction of the system (as in France and Russia). Early 19th century radicals who supported the objective of Parliamentary Representation were aiming to effect change within the existing framework.

(b) Discussion could be focussed on the following questions: What were the early 19th century radicals trying to achieve? What does this tell us about their attitude to existing institutions, particularly Parliament? Were there members of the radical movement who felt differently? To what extent were radicals already represented in Parliament? Why did radicals believe that by securing a 'fair' representation in Parliament they could achieve their goal of economic and social progress? What other methods might they have used? (Refer to the French Revolution.) What are the advantages and disadvantages of trying to bring about change by first destroying the established system?

ii. (a) In any society there are conflicts of interest. Thus, in post-war years the comfortable classes had good reasons for wishing to retain the status quo, while working people had good reasons for wishing for reforms.

(b) The class could be divided into three, with one third of the pupils being cast as factory workers, one as mill-owners and the other as comfortable landowners. Pupils in each group could be asked to write an account of how they would feel, in their roles, about Britain after the end of the Napoleonic Wars. The drawing together of the different accounts could provide the starting point for discussion.

iii. (a) At times, groups which have differing general interests can share a common objective. Thus radicals combined with many of the middle classes in the 1820s in the struggle to secure Parliamentary Representation.

(b) This could be linked with ii. above. Discussion should focus on what the radicals and the politically aware members of the middle classes were each trying to achieve, (their differences as well as similarities), and on why and how they were able to combine.

iv. (a) Groups of people, such as the early 19th century radicals, can agree about aims whilst having a diversity of opinion about methods.

(b) This could be discussed after reference has been made to various radical leaders and groups, (such as Cobbett, Hunt, Place, Cartwright and Thistlewood). It might be considered whether differences of opinion about methods actually weaken the general cause. (e.g. What was the effect of the abortive Cato Street Conspiracy?)

v. (a) Governments which are opposed to change, as the situation in England during and after the Napoleonic Wars suggests, are, on the one hand, likely to resort to repression, and, on the other, unlikely to be able to resist change indefinitely.

(b) Discussion might be centred on the following questions: What economic and social changes were taking place in the country? Why did the Government oppose the idea of change? When and why did the Government resort to repressive measures? and, Were these methods necessary (i.e. inevitable)? Was there any way or any situation in which the Government could have resisted the radical challenge indefinitely?

vi. (a) Individuals can normally best advance their welfare, rights and interests by association with others of a similar socio-economic standing.

(b) Discussion could revolve around the following: What do we mean by an individual's welfare, rights and interests? Why are people of a similar social and economic background likely to find themselves in the same sort of situation with regard to their welfare, rights and interests? In what ways did members of the working classes combine in the period under observation? (i.e. Co-operative groups, trade unions, friendly societies, radical organisations). What were each of these various types of combination trying to achieve? What were the advantages of combining with people in similar situations?

Concepts identified in document 2.3 that should be involved

(a) Government

Power The limitations in the power of the Government to wipe out, (through political intrigue and legal restrictions), 'Jacobin' tendencies.
Force Particularly, the Government's apparent use of force at Peterloo.
Authority The authority of the Government in dealing with the general situation after the Napoleonic Wars, and the way that it was challenged by the radicals and their supporters.
Order The aim of the majority of radicals to effect change in an orderly manner, (i.e. within the existing institutional framework), rather than through a breakdown in law and order, (as in the case of a rebellion or revolution).

(b) Relationships

Law Changes in the general body of rules made and endorsed by the Government in order to deal with the challenge precipitated by radical activity, (e.g. the Six Acts).
Justice The extent to which a feeling of justice was lacking on the part of radicals and their supporters amongst the working classes, particularly before 1820. (Including the sense in which the whole relationship between the radicals, on the one hand, and the upper classes and the Government, on the other, can be seen in terms of social justice).
Representation The claims of the radicals to represent the great mass of the working people of this country. The desire and failure of the radicals, in this period, to secure the representation of working people in Parliament through a reform of the electoral system.
Pressure Pressure exerted by the Government on the radicals and their supporters, particularly through repressive actions and legislation. The means by which the radicals and their supporters brought pressure to bear on the Government (pamphleteering, demonstrations, etc.).

(c) People

Freedom The radical desire to change society so as to maximise the free-

dom of the working man to live and work as he chose, and to be free to
join unions and other co-operative activities.
<u>Welfare</u> The belief amongst radicals that the welfare of the country's
citizens was the concern of the Government, and that this welfare could
be advanced through Parliamentary Representation.

An exercise in political literacy

The following written exercise, which is aimed at developing political
literacy, might usefully be undertaken at this stage. The pupils would
be asked, after some preparatory discussion, to imagine that they were
members of the working classes living in one of the new industrial towns
in the period under observation, and to investigate the various political
opportunities and frustrations by working through the following questions.
(The numbers and letters at the end of each question relate to the boxes
and questions in Diagram B of document 2.2).

    i. What were the main political points of view held in Britain in the
years after 1815? (1a)

    ii. How could you have become properly informed about the issues in-
volved? (1b)

    iii. Looking back on the period now, can you see different ways of
looking at the situation than were available then? (1c)

    iv. What political institutions existed at the time? (2a)

    v. In what ways were political disputes settled? (2b)

    vi. Were these ways in which the issues involving working people were
settled unfairly? (2c)

    vii. How could you have exerted any influence in that situation? (3a,
b)

    viii. How did these opportunities compare with those in Britain today?
(3c)

    ix. How would you have been affected by radical activity and the
Government's response to it? (4a,b)

    x. If you had become a member of a radical group, how would you have
justified your membership? (4c)

    xi. (a) Do you think that the Government's response to radical acti-
vity would have affected other groups in different ways from the ways
that it would have affected you? (5a, b)

        (b) How would the ideas that the radicals were proposing have
affected other groups in the community? (5a, b)

    xii. How easy would it have been to understand the points of view of
other groups at that time? (5c)

4. Balance sheet
  This stage, and the next (Legacy), can both be used to exemplify
further various political concepts, and ideally, like the previous stage,
should hold discussion to be central. Indeed, where written work is
given here, it must be directed towards preparing the pupil to discuss
the questions in hand and to arrive at some kind of reasonable opinion
about them.

  The importance and impact of the early 19th century radical movement
might be assessed by a consideration of the following:
(a) Was the movement really necessary? or Were radicals and the politically active members of the working classes at this time making a fuss
about nothing? These questions might, amongst other things, be used to
lead the pupils into a general discussion on the extent to which ordinary
citizens have a duty to work for, and defend, social justice.
(b) Did the movement make a significant contribution to the eventual

realisation of Parliamentary Representation for all adult males?
Thus: (i) Did it have a greater effect in bringing about the first stage
of reform (the 1832 Act) than Lord Grey and the Whigs or the rising industrial middle classes? and (ii) Did the movement contribute anything
towards bringing forward the date at which universal manhood suffrage
was attained (1918), or the dates at which progress was made in the
direction of this end (1867 and 1884)? (This would involve examining
briefly the circumstances in which the Reform Acts of 1867 and 1884, and
the Representation of the People Act of 1918, were passed).
(c) Did the movement bring forward the date at which the conditions in
society which lay behind the desire for Parliamentary Representation,
such as high unemployment, poverty and poor working conditions, were sub-
stantially alleviated; (This would involve plotting the progress of improved living and working conditions in general throughout the 19th
century, and in surveying the circumstances in which significant factory
and social legislation, such as the Factory Act of 1833 and the despised
Poor Law Amendment Act of 1834, was passed).
(d) Did the response in society to the violence at Peterloo benefit the
radical cause? If so, in what way?

5. *Legacy*
The significance of the early 19th century radical movement for the present day might be assessed by a consideration of:
(a) How much of the present Parliamentary structure do we owe to the early
radicals? Clearly the kind of representation which they envisaged is now
in operation, apart from the additional aspect of female representation,
but did the early radicals really make any contribution to the existing
structure? This question is very closely linked to, and might usefully
be discussed followed on from, (b) in the Balance Sheet section.
(b) Has the radical objective of Parliamentary Representation proved to
be the source of remedies for poverty, unemployment, exploitation, etc.?
The pupils might be asked here to prepare a list of all the important
measures of social justice, such as relate to housing, education, health,
etc., which have been passed since the Representation of the People Act,
1918. Following on from this, an assessment might be made of how important the various Governments which passed these and earlier measures of
social reform, (such as the Old Age Pensions Act, 1908), felt the electorate to be. (What would happen, and has happened, to a Government that
failed to live up to the expectations of the electorate in carrying through
measures of social justice?)
(c) Do the lessons of Peterlooo, and the experiences generally of the
early radicals, suggest that the radicals' methods, (protest meetings,
processions, petitions and so on), are likely to be successful today in
efforts for reform?

6. *Resources*
  i. One, or perhaps two, good general textbooks. The following can be
recommended: D.P. Titley, *Machines, Money and Men: An Economic and
Social History of Great Britain from 1700 to the 1970s*, (Blond) (C.S.E.).
F.J. Cootes, *Britain Since 1700*, (Longman) (C.S.E.). C.P. Hill, *British
Economic and Social History 1700-1939*, (Arnold). ('O' Level).
Pupils on examination courses will clearly already have at least one
general textbook.
  ii. Reference books (such as G.R. Kesteven, *Peterloo, 1819*, (Chatto
and Windus) which cover the following: (a) Peterloo and the radical demonstrations which preceded it. (b) Background information about economic, social and political conditions after the Napoleonic Wars. (c) The

growth of the radical movement in the early 19th century, including information about the dissemination of radical ideas. (d) Luddism. (e)
The various measures employed by the Government to control radicalism in
this period. (f) Biographical material on William Cobbett, Francis
Place, William Lovett and Henry Hunt. (g) The evolution of trade
unionism, friendly societies and co-operative activity in this period.
(h) The events leading up to, and the passage of the 1832 Reform Bill.
   Kesteven, which is quoted above, is a useful book and covers (a), (b),
(c), (d) and (e).
iii. *Jackdaw* folders on *Peterloo*.
 iv. Duplicated extracts from eye-witness accounts of Peterloo, e.g.
those of Samuel Bamford, the Rev. Edward Stanley and *The Times* reporter.
(These can be extracted from Kesteven and the *Jackdaw* folder).
   v. A series of wallcharts OR a filmstrip which depict:
(a) relevant scenes (such as Peterloo), (b) leading personalities (such
as Cobbett or Hunt), and (c) general background material (such as poor
living and working conditions).
   There appears to be as yet no suitable wallchart or filmstrip available
on the market.

(David Lambourne)

3.2.8 Specimen syllabus: Empires

1. Introduction
   i. The Romans - either visit to Hadrian's Wall or some other Roman
ruins in Britain.
  ii. Spanish Exploration - film strip "Cortes and Aztecs".
 iii. Scramble for Africa - Kimberley Diamonds 1867.
  iv. Russia - Hungarian uprising 1956 - newsreel film.

2. Main Events

a. Romans

Monarchy - Romulus legend, urbanisation, expulsion of Etruscans.
Republic - (a) constitutional set-up - patricians, plebeians etc.
   (b) local expansion - Latium plain, Gaul.
   (c) defeat of Greeks - enhanced Roman prestige and first class power
       status.
   (d) Punic Wars - Rome wealthier, aristocratic dominance.
   (e) internal dissension - Spartacus, Antony and Cleopatra.
Early Empire - (a) weakness of Republic e.g. mismanaged provinces, un-
       disciplined armies, thus need for Emperor.
   (b) Augustus' achievements - civil service, trading controls, citizen-
       ship extension.
   (c) relapse - Caligula, Nero - violence, debauchery, persecution.
   (d) restoration and expansion by Trajan - role of governors, local
       self-government, the curators, increased prosperity, responsibility
       to Emperor.
   (e) consolidation by Hadrian - standardisation of law, reduced taxes,
       strong army all led to unity.
       Self-government encouraged - latin right, municipalities, colonia.

Late Empire - (a) decline - power of armies, fiscal problems, adminis-
    trative problems, devalued 'citizenship' status.
  (b) external threats - Persians, Franks, Berbers.
  (c) division of Empire - Diocletian - grouping of provinces, tetrarchy
    of Emperors and Caesars, economic difficulties, his abdication.
  (d) Christian takeover - Constantine, autocracy, economic deteriora-
    tion.
  (c) fall of Rome - Goths, Vandals, last Emperor. (476).

b. Spanish Exploration - 'The Silver Empire'

Discovery - (To c. 1520)
  (a) motives - need for precious metals and spices, crusading spirit,
    converting the heathen, honour and fame, Government envy. Cultural
    link with Renaissance.
  (b) means - charts and astronomical innovations, technical improvements
    in ships, use of guns.
  (c) S. America before invasion - settlement patterns, tribes, advanced
    civilisations, organisation of society.
  (d) professional explorers - Prince Henry in Africa, Columbus, Vinland
    theory.
Consolidation - (1520-50)
  (a) the Conquistadors - Cortes, Pizzaro.
  (b) success - discipline, organisation, allies, faith,
    unscrupulousness.
Settlement - (after 1550)
  (a) role of Government - distrust of Conquistadors, feudal aristocracy,
    obligation to Pope.
  (b) ideas - political and civil rights of Indians, application of
    various laws.
  (c) administration - Spanish law, tributes, forced labour.
  (d) representative institutions - Town Councils, Governor, Church
    chiefs, military commanders, professional judiciary. System of
    checks and balances.
Eviction

3. *Scramble for Africa*
Background - native tribes and organisation, slavery coastal provinces,
    contrasts within the continent.
Acquisitions - (a) situation in 1840.
  (b) British, French, Portuguese before 1882 - e.g. British world in-
    clude - expulsion of Dutch from Cape, Great Trek, Kimberley.
    Diamonds, Suez Canal purchase, Transvaal annexation, Zulus, first
    Boer War. (c) Congress of Berlin 1884.
  (d) further conquests - other European powers involved.
  (e) conflict - British in Egypt, Sudan, S. Africa
                 - Fashoda 1898
                 - Germans v French, over Tangiers 1905, Morocco 1908
                 - Agadir 1911
Imperialism - (a) common features since 1870 - intense rivalry,
    aggression, improved means of colonisation.
  (b) motives - great explorers, profit, civilisation, political
    competition.
Control - (a) ideas - enlightenment e.g. Cromer in Egypt
                     - repression e.g. Portuguese in Mozambique
                     - assimilation e.g. French in Algeria
                     - exploitation

(b) effect on European politics e.g. 1911 Conference, World War, League of Nations, 1926 Imp. Conference, 1931 St. of Westminster.
Independence - just an examination of three issues:
  (a) 'wind of change' and Black Africa - Rhodesia.
  (b) Egypt and Suez Canal - Arab/Israeli conflicts.
  (c) Algeria and France - De Gaulle

4. Russia in Eastern Europe since 1939
Stalin's Russia - 1936 Constitution, Collectivisation, The Purges, 5 year plans establishing of control, economic power.
Weakness of Central and Eastern European States - rise and fall of Hitler in this area, Poland 1939-45, Russia's wartime efforts, The conference at Yalta, Potsdam, Teheran.
Russian expansion - (a) motives - buffer State, defence, ideology.
  (b) factors - FDR's death, Truman, doctrine, United Nations.
  (c) Cold War - Greece, Czechoslovakia, Germany.
  (d) Communist takeovers in Bulgaria, Hungary, Roumania, Poland, Albania.
  (e) Yugoslavia's position.
The established Iron Curtain - (a) military - Red Army, Warsaw Pact.
  (b) political - plebiscites, elections, constitutions.
  (c) economic - Comecon, currency, trade.
  (d) administrative - secret police, the wall, Gosplan.
Problems and resistance
  (a) East Germany 1953 - political parties.
  (b) Poland 1955 - economic liberty.
  (c) Hungary 1956 - nationalism - Nagy.
  (d) Czechoslovakia 1968 - 'Liberalisation' - Dubcek.
  (e) Within Russia - deStalinisation, personality-cult, leadership, literary dissenters.
  (f) Sino-Soviet relations - border clashes, aid rivalry.

5. Concepts

a. Government

Power The claims to legitimacy such as the establishment of the Roman Republic, East European plebiscites in late 1940s, the establishment (Cromer in Egypt?). Also the division of power - Diocletian's division of Roman Empire - and the external constraints on power in a state i.e. Papal intervention over Silver Empire between Spain and Portugal: USSR in Czechoslovakia 1967-8.
Force One of the practical means of establishing power and of overthrowing it too. Cortes compared with 18th and 19th century civil wars in South America.
Authority Roman acceptance of 'Imperium' but later weakening of it by Emperor's behaviour. The Conquistadors were perceived in such a role by Spanish Governments for a while (1520-50 mainly).
Order The need for an Emperor in early Rome because of the Empire's weakness could be contrasted with the establishment of Spanish type of administrative co-ordination by the professional judiciary in South America after 1550 and the totalitarian aspects of Soviet satellite regimes.

b. Relationships

Law The standardisation of Roman law throughout the Empire by Hadrian fulfilled this need, as did the harmonisation of Indian and Spanish law in the Silver Empire, and they contributed to the successful conquest and consolidation of the Empires.

Justice   The injustice of being conquered, and later persecuted, led to rebellions and other forms of dissent. Feelings intensified as development and educational advancements take place in the acquired Empire e.g. Czechoslovakia 1968.

Representation   The development of representative bodies was often encouraged by governments as a safety valve to avoid serious opposition to conquerors - Roman granting of self-government, colonia, Trajan's governors. However, there were established representative institutions in Rome - the Senate, the Assemblies, the Tribunes and perhaps even masters (for slaves). In the Silver Empire, representative elements included town councils, governors, Church leaders and military commanders.

Pressure   The application of pressure on the government to get change was economic (withholding tax revenues by provincial Roman Governors), military (regional armies after Hadrian's time), and religious (Christianity) in Roman period. In contrast government use of pressure in Modern Russian Empire was almost total, including economic (Comecon), military (secret police, Warsaw Pact 'manoeuvres'), social, administrative and literary even.

c. People

Natural Rights - a concept very difficult to perceive but often embodied in tribal customs in Africa (but only at the periphery of study) and Indian 'civil' rights in the Silver Empire. However, it is linked with Roman law, implicit in the Republic's Constitution and the Christian takeover, although of little significance, and largely abused, in Russian Empire since 1945.

Individuality   Perhaps it could be related to the explorers in Africa and paterfamilias in the Roman family, but otherwise suppressed (and thus significant?) or represented away.

Freedom   Clearly one motive behind revolutions against Imperial conquerors and other forms of opposition and dissent. There is a very interesting contrast between the freedom of Roman plebeians and the Russian peasants; but slavery in Rome too.

Welfare   The Communist model in the Russian Empire typifies the idea of government procurement of maximum community happiness and vividly compares with 'freedom'. Welfare was partly implicit in the establishment of Conquistadors but it was not really an issue in Africa where governments followed rather than led.

In the Roman Empire the welfare concept was not as total (as Crick's definition) despite the deification and illustrated by the patron-client relationship and paterfamilias.

6. Balance sheet

a. Romans

(a) Ordered society - law and loyalty to gods, state and family.
(b) Happy period - despite war conquest, Romans did not impose their culture, although they imposed peace, and they allowed and extended participation.
(c) Intelligent rule of conquered people.
(d) Importance of pageantry, ceremonial and tradition.
(e) Internal feuds and dissension.

(f) Debauchery, depravity, violence, persecution and belief in own invincibility.
(g) Administrative and economic problems of controlling such a vast empire.

b.   Spanish exploration

(a) Distinct change in life pattern of native society.
(b) Rapid improvements in navigation.
(c) Extension of slavery.
(d) Enhanced Spanish status in European eyes.
(e) New products, thoughts, wealth.
(f) Demolition of prevailing geographical theories.
(g) Quick, immediate and direct government intervention.
(h) Stimulated European colonial rivalry.

c.   Scramble for Africa

(a) Destruction of native cultures and disturbed tribes.
(b) Some beneficial developments e.g. trade, communications.
(c) Eased European tensions.
(d) Contributions of colonised to World War I.
(e) Governments followed rather than led.
(f) Created great interest and wealth.
(g) Limited international co-operation.
(h) Exploitation.

d.   Russians since 1939

(a) Suppression of dictators, principally Hitler.
(b) Increased USSR power.
(c) Instability in Greece and isolated Yugoslavia.
(d) Establishment of Iron Curtain.
(e) Precipitated USA active intervention in European affairs.
(f) Establishment of NATO and Warsaw Pact.
(g) Cold War.
(h) Rivalry over leadership of Communist world.
(i) Centrifugal tendencies within the Empire.
(j) Provoked closer West European relations, if not unity.

7. *Legacy*

a.   Romans

(a) Greatest Empire (in geographical extent) ever.
(b) Mixture of Roman with Hellenic and Oriental cultures.
(c) Spread of Christianity eastwards.
(d) West European unity through Catholic Church based on Rome.
(e) Impact of Roman ideas on cultures - literature, art, political theories, architecture.
(f) Language - 'imperium'.

b.   Spanish Exploration

(a) Systematic organisation of maritime reconnaissance.
(b) Maritime counterparts of mercenary armies.
(c) New products, thoughts and wealth.

(d) Unprecedented increase in knowledge about planet.
(e) Eventual self criticism of western governments as toleration and respect increase.
(f) Change in geographical emphasis of world trade.
(g) Temporarily shifted great power battleground.

c. Scramble for Africa

(a) Ending of imperialism was contributory cause of 1st World War.
(b) Racial bitterness.
(c) Undignified grab in Africa and European rivalry.
(d) African distrust of Europeans strengthened.
(e) Accentuated European patriotism.
(f) Violence and revolution.
(g) Neo-colonialism.

d. Russians Since 1939

(a) Europe deeply divided.
(b) New ideas of democracy.
(c) Totalitarian State and institutionalised violence.
(d) Indirect conflict by great powers through minor nations.
(e) Nuclear weapons.
(f) Space Race.
(g) Enhanced role for ideology in world affairs.
(h) Convergence theory.
(i) Emergence of new trading and political organisations and patterns.

8. *Political literacy through historical example*

Two examples:

a. Pre-Dubcek urban worker in Czechoslovakia 1968

Knowledge
(a) underlying ideas - government view, Dubcek's 'liberalisation' policies, politics of Western Europe.
(b) opportunities for reception - not equal - radio, TV, press, State controlled; party meetings, work place leaflets, conversation.
(c) historical perspective might include - attitude in other satellite nations of Empire, objective assessment of likelihood of use of force.
Institutions
(a) existing, e.g. party, parliament.
(b) settlement of disputes - internal and external aspects; use of force, value of discussion, argument and compromise, face-saving.
(c) was it fair? - consideration of Russian case.
Tactics
(a) individual influence - representative elements in Constitution.
(b) comparison with elsewhere e.g. Poland 1955.
Self Interest - If you had been there, in this position, what would you have done? - remain passive, protest in silence, criticise, fight on streets, accept the result, work to change the situation.

b. Plebeian in Ancient Rome

Knowledge
(a) many accepted ideas, but differences over methods.
(b) schooling, travel, libraries, social clubs, the Gods.
(c) changed status, information etc. over time as Empire expanded.
Institutions
(a) existing, such as the Assembly etc.
(b) dispute settlement - initially wise Senators, later forceful
    Emperors.
(c) Was it fair? - consider role of Patricians, slaves principally.
Tactics
(a) individual influence - representative elements.
(b) comparison with elsewhere, e.g. Greece.
Self Interest - what defects can you see in this sort of political system? - demagogues, static/dynamic.

9. *Resources*
Books   *Then and There* series - *Cortes & Aztecs*;   *The Romans*
        Roman Britain - Sellman;
        From Ur to Rome - K.M. Gadd
        Explaining the Americas - L.F. Hobley;
        Tropical Africa in World History - Book 3 'Africa after 18'
        Jackdaws: Columbus and the Discovery of America
                      Hadrian's Wall
                      Conquest of Mexico
                      Boer War
Film Strips *The Growth of Rome* (Gaumont Films), plus many on Roman
         Britain
         Three strips on Columbus (Hutton)
         The Sea and America series - Pt. 10:   Story of Africa
Games/Simulations   Longman's series - one on African Imperialism
                                      - one on Romans
Map Ordnance survey map of Roman Britain

(Keith West)

Appendix to 3.2.8

More detailed suggestions for teaching the Roman Empire*

(a) Monarchy - Romulus legend compared with the reality of Rome's Indo-
European origin; then Etruscan influence and the gradual urbanisation
of Rome. The removal of Tarquin the Proud, 509 BC.
Teaching ideas: Time line + significance of BC and AD map of Italy
Concepts: Definition of Monarchy + modern examples. Concentration of
power. Basic need for order. Use of pressure to secure end of the
Kings.

**This one illustration serves to show the depth of treatment that would
be required in each of the examples of empires, briefly set out above, if
comparisons are to be made. (Editors).*

(b) <u>Establishment of a Republic</u> - the constitutional set-up, embodying consuls, senate and tribunes. Initial neutrality of Roman army but later involvement e.g. Sulla 88 BC.
<u>Teaching ideas</u>: Describe a typical assembly meeting; write the dialogue for a debate on department cancellation; Pyramid diagram of hierarchy of consuls (2), proconsuls, praetors (8), aediles, tribunes (10), quaestors (40), '<u>The Plebeian in Rome</u>' - my earlier submitted example indicating his political literacy in terms of knowledge, institutions, tactics and self-interest:
<u>Knowledge</u>
(a) many accepted ideas
(b) schooling, travel, libraries, social clubs, the Gods;
(c) changed status/information etc. over time as Empire extended.
<u>Institutions</u>
(a) existing - Assemblies
(b) dispute settlement - initially wise senators but later forceful Emperors;
(c) was it fair? - role of Patricians, position of slaves;
<u>Tactics</u>
(a) individual influence - representative elements
(b) comparison of elsewhere, e.g. Greeks
<u>Self Interest</u>
What <u>defects</u> can you see in this sort of political system? e.g. Demagogues, means of change, problems of size.
<u>Concepts</u> Definition of Republic and modern examples. 'Citizen Power', via <u>representative</u> bodies such as Senate, Tribunes, Assemblies; legitimising of <u>law</u> through these elected bodies; the <u>authority</u> of these institutions accepted and hierarchy of power developed; symbolic <u>authority</u> of 12 lictors and fasces which Consuls had, plus imperium (military power); <u>pressure</u> by groups, but not really <u>parties</u> such as the Optimates and Populares (who sought land reform).
(c) <u>Expansion of the Republic</u> - local expansion in Italy (275 BC - control of Southern Italy); but later wider spheres of influence with the defeat of the Greeks (340 BC Pyrrhus), Punic Wars against Carthage (264, 218, 202, 146) and defeat of Syrians (190 BC).
<u>Teaching ideas</u>: Euro-Asian map - to show territorial expansion; draw/sketch etc. Roman soldier/weapons; film strip either *Roman Army* EAV or *The Roman Republic*, EAV.
<u>Concepts</u>: Expansion by <u>force</u> - use of army but respectful treatment of 'friends and allies' (unlike Greeks, etc.) thus extending peoples' <u>welfare</u> e.g. no attempt to change local customs; allowing <u>freedom</u> and extending <u>rights</u> to Roman citizenship; protection of provinces against wild tribes to preserve their <u>freedom</u>; fair treatment leading to <u>justice</u>, respect and acceptance of <u>authority</u> and <u>order</u>.
(d) <u>Results of the Republic's development</u> - increased wealth of patricians and wider distribution of wealth within Rome, leading to aristocratic dominance. Increased population and its structure e.g. exclusion of women, children, slaves, aliens from census figures. Enhanced prestige and first class power status. BUT internal problems such as social war (91-89 BC) between cities of Italian alliance which ended with Rome giving them all Roman citizenship. Spartacus and slave revolt (73-71 BC); conflict of Pompey and Caesar resulting in establishment of Caesar's dictatorship.
<u>Teaching ideas</u>: - imaginative writing - life of slave and/or wealthy patrician.

Film strip - *Slaves in Ancient Rome* EAV.
Literary - *Up Pompeii* TV, *Julius Caesar*.
Work based on population figures:

Census	Roman Citizens	Region's population in AD 14
130 BC	318,823	Italy 13m; Spain 6m; Gaul 4.9m;
114	394,336	Sicily, Sardinia, Corsica 1.1m;
85	463,000	Danube 2; Greece 3; Asia Minor
69	910,000	13; Syria, Palestine, Cyprus
28	4,063,000	6.5; Egypt 5.5; rest of Africa
8	4,233,000	6m.
14 AD	4,937,000	Total 61m.
47 AD	5,984,072	

Concepts: aristocratic dominance of government because unpaid offices;
slavery and its link with natural rights - general treatment, slave revolt, marriages not legally recognised, circumspect use of slave evidence, not allowed property.
Parameters of power - world wide rather than just Italy.
Importance of force - emergence of Caesar, dictator leading to diminution
of freedom.
(e) The Early Empire (44 BC - 180 AD) - significance of dates - 180 being
height. Augustus succeeds Caesar (27 BC - AD 14) and inherits mismanaged
provinces and undisciplined armies. Introduces important changes such
as salaried civil service, extension of citizenship, new Constitution 23
BC and provincial governors but with heavy reliance on senators.
   Claudius (41-54) responds to the growth of provincial cities by allowing important provincials to become Roman citizens. In 48 he admits
Gallic chieftains to stand for magistracies.
   Relapse under Caligula, Nero and AD 68-9 with violence, debauchery and
persecution but restoration and expansion by Trajan (98-117) - developed
local self-government supervised by his curators, increased prosperity
and encouraged Imperial help for the poor - free grain, free theatre
attendance.
   Consolidation by Hadrian (117-138) - standardisation of law and legal
procedures, reduced taxes and his strong army all led to unity. Hadrian
gave up his foothold in Armenia, Mesopotamia and also encouraged self-
government - Empire becoming more of a Commonwealth, with more towns
becoming municipia and colonia. Hadrian's wall and the Romans in
Britain.
Teaching ideas: Work on Roman Britain as a province - colonia at York,
Lincoln, Gloucester - VISIT.
Hadrian's Wall; Roman towns - plans; Roman roads - map; Roman camps;
Roman remains - historical evidence and work of archaeologists.
Concepts: Pressure by provincial cities for Roman citizenship - granting
shows Emperor to be fair/just; popular assemblies much weaker as
representative bodies and fall mainly under the Emperor's nomination.
Augustus's respect for law - new Constitution to justify extended powers.
Individuality encouraged e.g. use of talented freedmen in Imperial house-
hold (like PM's private office to some extent). Claudius increases
participation via Gallic chieftains. Nero's excesses lead to discontent
in Armenia 65 AD, revolt in Gaul 68 AD and eventually the 4 Emperors of
68-9 AD - Unjust Governments which limit freedom, lose authority and encourage the use of force against themselves. Power based on arbitrary
force PLUS respect for good/fair government, e.g. Trajan, Hadrian.
Usually religious freedom, once obligations to Romans paid but occasional

persecution, e.g. Nero. Citizenship further extended to discharged soldiers, later in 212 AD to all free men leading to continued pressure and respect for Empire's authority. Extension of roads/transport network as prerequisite for establishing order and welfare of citizens against wild opponents on fringe of Empire (Hadrian's wall).

Welfare - increase in philanthropy in Trajan's time + his giving of grain and free theatre to poor.

Standardisation of law but lacking justice i.e. discrimination against women, aliens, slaves.

Taxes (in general perhaps) illustrating power but possibly limiting individuality, freedom and furthering welfare.

(f) The Late Empire 180-475 AD - The Empire progressively declines after 180 AD with the increased power of the armies, fiscal problems, administrative difficulties - many weak, tyrannical, army-backed Emperors (211-284) and thus office-holding throughout Empire no longer seen as an honour. External threats from Persians, Franks, Berbers, Alemanni. In 284 Diocletian emerged as a temporary strongman and reformer - he divided the Empire into smaller, more manageable units and increased the bureaucracy, often now containing professional soldiers; fixed prices and introduced a regular census; introduced the tetrarchy of Emperors and Caesars which divided the Empire into East and West. In 305 he abdicated - the first Emperor to do so.

However, soldier influence returned and Constantine emerged in 324, the last of the Great Emperors. He reversed Diocletian's persecution of Christians, made the Empire christian but autocratic, building a new capital in the East, illustrating Rome's decline. Economic difficulties prevailed but his system of fathers succeeding sons in similar occupations failed; but impressive legal codes started 438 (completed Justinian 529, 534) which were a digest of centuries of laws, edicts and regulations.

The Empire based on Rome fell in 476, after a century of invasion by Visigoths, Vandals, etc. and several sackings, notably 410, 455; although the Empire in the East continued.

Why did the Empire fall? Suggested reasons e.g. persistence of barbarians, Roman citizenship allowed undesirable generals to emerge/work against the Empire, moral lapses, Christianity, general apathy.

Teaching ideas: map to show external threats to Empire, shrinkage of Empire and invasions. Increased bureaucracy:

| East Emperor | West Emperor |
| Caesar | Caesar |

each responsible for a quarter of Empire, on average 25 provinces each. Work based on an extract from Diocletian's *Edict on Prices* - food, clothing wages from p. 122-123, *The Ancient Romans* by O.A.W. Dilke. Essay - Why did Roman Empire decline? Was it inevitable?

Concepts: perspective of time - the late Empire not seen as a decline at the time; loss of authority of Emperor and the Senate. Tyrannical government - injustice and the negation of the law, reduction of freedom and elevation of force - military anarchy, extension of military influence into bureaucracy. Diocletian - restoration of order but ignores Constitution, bribes army - successful pressure. Confiscation of property of political enemies leading to diminution of freedom. Diocletian's attempt to control inflation shows regard for welfare but the means chosen (price fixing, later tradesmen/children fixed in occupation) limit freedom and individuality. Tetrarchy and division of Empire illustrate diffusion of power.

Constantine ended the religious persecution thus restoring some <u>freedom</u> - later Christian takeover showing his <u>power</u>.
Impressive legal codification.

(Keith West)

.

3.3 ENGLISH AND POLITICAL LITERACY
      Maureen Whitebrook

The English group experienced certain difficulties in drawing together
and sustaining a group of English teachers which could or would meet the
initial requirement that it '... should not issue anything like definite
curriculum but rather a series of examples of how particular literary
examples might be handled in political terms.' Out of three meetings,
correspondence with some thirty people, two or three of whom provided
material and/or comments, and the sustained commitment of Vicki Jones
(now Vicki Morley, formerly a mature student at Trent Polytechnic and
then English teacher in a comprehensive school), some material has been
gathered together. So this report contains: an earlier essay by the
convener that tried to identify the general relationships there are and
should be between English and politics (3.3.2); introductory curricula
material prepared by Vicki Jones and myself (3.3.3-3.3.5); a 'model'
lesson on Rights - all of which were widely circulated in the hope of
provoking responses and more exemplary material; some examples of classroom responses from pupils (3.3.7); together with a solitary but
interesting actual syllabus submitted by a school (3.3.8), and lastly
some comments from teachers (3.3.9).

3.3.1

However, the quantity and nature of this material does not sufficiently
indicate the lessons to be gathered from the experience of this group.
The subject groups were to be, to some extent, locally based: this
proved to be unfortunate in that teachers who might have become involved
in the Nottingham area had already been 'recruited' by the Social education project; in addition, as Convener, I was a newcomer to the area and
therefore lacked a base of contacts and potentially sympathetic colleagues. This might not have been so significant had I been in a more
senior position in my own institution. Not only would this have been ad-
vantageous in terms of resources I could have devoted to the work - from
access to a telephone to control of my own timetable! - but the status of
what I was trying to do might have been (more) guaranteed by my own
status.
  Other factors might also explain the relative failure of this group:
the pressures normally to be expected when both convener and members of
the group are all in full-time employment; the coincidence of the initial promotion of our ideas and the publication of the Bullock report
which then engaged the interest and planning of English teachers; the
concentration on literature to the - apparent - exclusion of other forms
of English.
  But it must also be said that despite much publicity for the work of
the group both locally and nationally, teachers of English were not able
to engage themselves with it. This appears to me to be for one of two
reasons:
  i. teachers felt that they lacked the knowledge of politics that would
enable them to make the kind of connections that we were suggesting (thus
there would seem to be a need for the provision of material that makes
the connection and provides a speedy introduction to political material
that could be used, and for the provision of short courses in 'Politics
for non-politics teachers')
  ii. 'Radical' English teachers claim that they are already making the
connections, that indeed their English teaching 'is political' (many
would seem to claim that their teaching is more, or more properly,

political than what they call our 'Hansard politics' approach). But these latter have not been able either to provide examples of their work or, except in a few cases, to state the principles of their approach. What remains then is, in the main, the advocacy of a particular approach (which predates the Programme), suggestions in outline of what might be done, by two of us who sympathise with that approach, and the comments of some of those who wholly or partially disagree with that approach and/or the notion of politics which underlies it.

3.3.2 The political element in English literature: some implications for teaching

(This essay of mine was originally published in *English in Education*, Vol. 9 No. 1, Spring 1975, pp 5-10, the journal of the National Association of Teachers of English. And for a fuller argument, see my "Literature and the Teaching of Politics", an article in two parts in *Teaching Politics*, Vol. 3 Nos. 2 and 3, May and September 1974).

The idea that a work of literature should be read for its own sake, that to 'use' it is to devalue it, is a common and valid one. But the connections to be made between English literature and politics are, I think, valuable both to the generalist teacher and to the specialist: the former may well derive a large part of his political knowledge (and, therefore, his political attitudes imparted to pupils) from literature; the latter may welcome the critical approach available through the study of literature - the teacher of English as an extension of the approaches to his subject, the teacher of politics as a means of providing breadth of experience and argument.

Modern literary criticism, notably that of the Leavis school, has focused on the relevance of literary works to their context in society within the general framework of 'culture', but there is little or no specific reference to the political in such criticism. I would like to argue, though, that certain works of literature have a political content, recognizably so and dealing with areas ordinarily thought to be political. While it is not possible to formulate a standard definition of politics and the political against which works may be measured for their political content, if such works are to be selected on anything but a completely personal, subjective basis (the selection of books which prima facie seem likely to influence political attitudes), it is necessary to indicate what I mean by these terms in this context.

The maximalist view of the political deriving (somewhat inaccurately) from Aristotle would equate it with society; but then 'literature is about life ... all life is political ...' - this is too loose to be useful. Limiting definitions can be roughly divided between the power and conflict type and the consensus type. The former, basically Hobbesian, is concerned with power - implying reciprocity and consent - coercion and legitimation. In contrast, there are the definitions which emphasize conciliation, with politics seen as concerned with decision-making and the meeting of interests. A common concept is that of community, the scene and subject of power struggles and the beneficiary of the conciliation of interests.

No single definition would cover 'the areas ordinarily thought to be political'; a work of literature with a 'recognizable political content' will probably draw from and contribute to both types of definition: it will be concerned with some aspects of the life of a community which is presently undergoing some form of struggle for power and/or conciliation of interests.

The 'social' novel or play will deal with what may be political problems in the widest sense, that is with individual problems of choice and action; but the political work will be concerned more directly with power or conflict, the conciliation of interests, the individual <u>against</u> society rather than the individual <u>in</u> society. Politics is concerned with the attempt to reconcile private freedom and public interests: the political work will treat of some aspect of the process of reconciliation.

Because works of literature are primarily orientated towards the individual, the political will be seen through the individual, and political works of literature will be those which deal with public, not only private, matters. This will not necessarily be their main theme, but will be a significant sub-plot which forms an integral, necessary part of the whole work, dealing with political problems to a degree which cannot be ignored in the total structure of the novel or play. *Lord of the Flies,* for instance, not only contains a large number of political analogies, but is generally concerned with problems of power and authority. To read and study the book and wilfully ignore the political is therefore to accord it a partial, if not superficial, treatment. The student who can connect will see that literature must be <u>about</u> something, to state the case at its most simplistic, and that something may well be a political matter.

It is to be expected that literature will, in general, deal with all aspects of life. It is therefore dishonest to deny the <u>political</u> aspect of literature. And it is as valid to extract the political strand as it is to extract the social, moral, Christian, or whatever. But it is preferable, at least from the point of view of the study of literature, not to extract at all but to take the political into consideration when subjecting the work as a whole to critical analysis. This will be not merely valid but positively justifiable if it can be shown that politics has any new insight to give literary criticism and the teaching of English.

Hoggart provides grounds for such an argument: English teaching may be suspicious of the social sciences because of their 'abstracting character', 'But this, I reason, is why the social sciences can be good for us. When put to the test by the generalizing, "objective" disciplines of the social sciences our truths ought to be confirmed or they are shakily held.'[1] From a different direct, Fred Inglis warns that we bring political values to our reading of literature that should be recognized and '... reading fiction is a cultural and social transaction which must take account of the total context within which our act of valuing must also take place'.[2] This point is taken up and expanded by Douglas Holly: political awareness allows literary criticism to be recognized and evaluated as part of the (for him) perpetuation of elite values.[3] And for literature that is overtly political in content, 'If political scientists are as informed about politics as they ought to be, they have a critical role to play in correcting misinformation and distorted emphasis in fiction, whether these proceed from reasons of politics or reasons of literary expediency.'[4]

There are, then, a variety of arguments (from within the area of literary criticism and concern for English teaching) for what politics can contribute to literature. The most telling, for my case, I take to be the Hoggart-Inglis concern for the quality of teacher training and the necessity of teachers being aware of connections. Thus Inglis suggests that teachers in training must realize that their work will be essentially political and, 'Some may find discomposing the necessary political nature of such work ... but most would agree that some version of

historical movement is necessary to understand (say) the change from
verse-drama to novels.'[5] So I would argue that teachers of English need
to be aware of, and be prepared to explicate, the political content of
works they are using and studying in school as well as being prepared to
place works of literature in their general political context.

Possibly literature is being used in schools in this way, but in the
absence of relevant research findings it can be assumed that the connections which I am advocating are not widely acknowledge. Teaching
notes, criticism for school use and school editions of novels and plays
give little or no indication of an awareness of the political content
of these texts.

I have said that the political should be taken into account not so much
by the picking-out of political analogy, but by considering the political
element in the book as a whole. This approach may best be illustrated by
reference to some of the texts commonly used in secondary schools. *Lord
of the Flies* has already been referred to: criticism usually emphasizes
the moral aspect of the fable, '... examining what human nature is really
like if we could examine it apart from the mass of social detail which
gives a recognizable feature to our daily lives'.[6] Though this approach
is both obvious and rewarding, the book as a total work is also political.

The emergence of evil and savagery is the principal underlying theme
but this is expressed through the study of the boys and their island
society. There is a crude characterization of types of society ranging
from the adult, 'ordered' society left behind to a tribal savage society
with a changing pattern of leadership. Golding tends towards a Hobbesian
argument: without an imposed and accepted law and order, life is reduced
to barbarism. The novel assumes the political in that it conveys the
idea that where the institutions of ordered society are lacking, something must take their place. It may be accounted political, too, because
it is concerned with power, authority and leadership - issues central to
a consideration of politics.

Another commonly-used text more obviously political is *Animal Farm*.
Here the political element may indeed seem inescapable. But the use of
the book at second and third year secondary level encourages the belief
that it can be regarded as just a fairy tale, a modern bestiary. Again,
a moral, if not distinctly Christian, slant can be attached to any book,
and this has been done for *Animal Farm*, thus avoiding the specifically
political. Orwell's human belief in right reason, i.e. reason fused with
compassion, is seen as a presupposition underlying the tale - when reason
is divorced from compassion it degenerates into mere animal cunning.

But it is very difficult to ignore the political analogies (attention
is drawn to them in all teaching guides to the book) and they are essential to understanding. Thus it is argued that the meaning of Chapter 7,
the slaughter of the animals, cannot be appreciated without a knowledge
of the Moscow trials, especially in that Orwell's disillusion is an integral part of the writing. But such an emphasis on political *facts*, modern history is, I think, misplaced. The political importance of *Animal
Farm* is not in its usefulness as an analogous history of Stalinist
Russia. The political content of the book lies primarily not in its
detailed analogies and parallels but in its central theme and the
questions it poses: the revolution failed - why? There are clearly two
possible answers: either the aim of an absolutely egalitarian society
was impossible of achievement, or the animals were less than true to
their purpose. The former is what Orwell himself may well have believed,
and the book may be read as a satire on egalitarianism. But this theme
is only implicit (if present at all) in the book, whereas Orwell makes
it clear that the pigs were corrupt, and '... his hatred for the pigs

is not simply because they exploited their fellow animals and were corrupted by power, but specifically because they betrayed the great egalitarian and libertarian ideals of the revolution: "All animals are equal".[7]

Close attention to political analogy would lead to the argument that only a sixth form would be able to understand these analogies. Rather I would argue that below the sixth form there might be a knowledge of political facts but hardly the political sophistication necessary to distinguish the separate strands of Orwell's thought and to see the importance of the questions raised – but not answered – about egalitarianism, class, and the possibility of revolution. This is a fable – a generalized statement of the corrupting nature of power, the possibility of failure of ideals matched by corruption; unusually and outstandingly there is the presentation of an extreme alternative in politics – to lie and distort to achieve preconceived ends or to appeal to common sense and sympathy to achieve what ends are then possible.

Not all literature that appears to have a political theme is necessarily helpful to the development of insight and political empathy which I am suggesting is the reason for emphasizing, or at least taking into account, the political. Thus *Cry the Beloved Country*, still popular as a school text, presents not only a dated, slightly Uncle Tom-ish view of racial problems but gives a caricature of 'the politician' (cunning John Kumalo) as against 'the Christian liberal' (upright Arthur Jervis). And there is an ambiguous attitude towards law: conservative, reactionary calls for increased protection from the authorities are parodied, but Paton, if his remarks are to be taken seriously and not as sarcasm, admits that the law is white law but then goes on to count it as an achievement of the society to be upheld, and 'If the law is the law of the society that must be changed.'[8] – which in the context of the book is ironic or pathetic – or both. There is nothing here of the debate on the morality of the individual justly disobeying some laws within society

It is just this connection between morality and politics which works of literature might be expected to bring out. An outstanding example of this, and of the need to take the political into consideration for a full understanding of the work is Arthur Miller's *The Crucible*. While the play has obvious parallels with McCarthyism, Miller himself says: 'It was not only the rise of McCarthyism that moved me, but something which seemed much more weird and mysterious. It was the fact that a political, objective, knowledgeable campaign from the far Right was capable of creating not only a terror but a new subjective reality, a veritable mystique which was gradually assuming even a holy resonance.[9] The connection between the existence of evil and political action which Miller postulates is important for an understanding of the whole play.

The action of the play depends on an assumption of evil: 'A wide opinion's running in the parish that the Devil may be among us.' This belief was used for political purposes, to unite a society which was changing and liable to question authority. Miller discusses the 'political use of the devil' and suggests that this is still relevant: political resistance is united to malignant forces and consequently, 'A political policy is equated with moral right, and opposition to it with diabolical malevolence.'[10] These issues brought out in *The Crucible* relate to the arguments of such political texts as Lipset and Raab: *The Politics of unreason* and Hannah Arendt: *The Origins of Totalitarianism*.[11]

The Crucible deals with the close relationship between private and public, especially in matters of conscience: thus it is concerned with questions about the freedom of the individual and the power of the state. Both Proctor and Hale stand against authority (again there is an interlocking of public and private, authority based on religion and 'political policy is equated with moral right'). The essential question is that of authority and the justification of the limits to private action; whether survival is more important than the preservation of identity. Thus Proctor's question and decision: 'It is no part of salvation that you should use me ... How should I live without my name?'[12]

In England, and at an increasing distance from the 1950s, there tends to be an emotional response to this play, a concentration on the witchcraft and the psychological. It is the more necessary then to explicate the political elements of the play if it is to be seen as anything more than a vehicle for a hero-figure. The hero-figure is to be shown as acting politically. The political issues in *The Crucible* are those concerned with the inter-relationships of authority, individualism, and moral right. What are the justifications for limiting individualism? What are the criteria for the individual's obedience of authority? Essentially, the play examines the area where public and private overlap and a balance must be found between order and freedom. These questions which are central to the play are also central to any consideration of the political.

I have argued that novels and plays, including several of the texts commonly used in secondary school English teaching, may include a significant political element which should not be ignored in the critical consideration of these books. They may be a source of political knowledge: this may well be an important but unstructured way of acquiring such knowledge, or the political element may be acknowledged and used – both within the area labelled English on school timetables and as a means of bridging the gap between the disciplines of English and the social sciences – and politics in particular.

References
1. Richard Hoggart, *Contemporary Cultural Studies: an approach to the study of literature and society,* University of Birmingham Centre for Contemporary Cultural Studies, Occasional Paper No. 6, 1969, p.5.
2. Fred Inglis, 'Reading children's novels: notes on the politics of literature', in *Children's Literature in Education* No. 5, 1971.
3. See, for instance, his letter to *The Times Educational Supplement,* 26th January 1973.
4. J. F. Davidson, 'Political science and political fiction' in *American Political Science Review,* Vol. 55, 1961, p.857.
5. Fred Inglis, 'English: an academic discipline in the training of teachers' in *English in Education,* 1970.
6. Ian Gregor and Mark Kinkead-Weekes, introduction to William Golding, *Lord of the Flies,* Faber, London (School edition), p.iii.
7. B. R. Crick, 'An introduction to the introduction that Orwell suppressed' for the Italian edition of *Animal Farm* (private communication).
8. Alan Paton, *Cry the Beloved Country,* Longman, London, 1966, p.175.
9. Arthur Miller, *Collected plays,* Cresset, London, 1958, p.39.
10. Arthur Miller, 'The Crucible' in *Collected Plays,* op. cit.
11. Hannah Arendt, *The Origins of Totalitarianism,* Allen and Unwin, London, 1967. S.M. Lipset and M. Raab, *The Politics of Unreason,* Heinemann, London, 1972.
12. Miller, 'The Crucible', op. cit.

3.3.3 Introduction to the Work of a Politics and English Working Group

In discussion it has become clear that there are diverse strands of English teaching in schools[1] and correspondingly different groups of teachers involved with English studies; it has, therefore, proved difficult to produce an example of what English teachers might use to link English and politics. We think that there are five types of teacher for whom we want to produce useable material: four are representative of points on a spectrum of ways of teaching English, the fifth is the teacher of politics as such.

  i. The (young?) 'committed' teacher who claims that he is already aware of the political dimension of his work - basically he has some sympathy with the Programme. But we might call his 'political', 'social'; and his political interests might be more gut-reaction than political literacy as the Programme defines it. We think that this teacher could use a clarification of his probably diffuse and incomplete knowledge, a 'crash course' in Politics into which he could slot his interests in English teaching. This would be accompanied by a matching of the fashionable (i.e. recurring in the course books and anthologies, at least) topics in English with the recurring political concepts and problems.

  ii. The specialist teacher associated with English studies - in particular, perhaps, the drama specialist - who, again, deals with the 'fashionable' topics, recognises their political content, but is not able to develop this recognition into useful teaching material or strategy in either English or Politics. Again, there is a need for systematisation to fit these topics into a framework of political analysis; there is also a need to extend the English/Politics analysis into the whole field of English studies.

  iii. The 'ordinary' English teacher who does not recognise the political content of his work, but would be willing to consider it, and not necessarily averse to using it, if it was pointed out to him. Initially, this teacher might simply require an analysis of the field of English studies in political terms: then, if his interest is aroused, he might move on to the material suggested for type i.

  iv. The conservative (older?) English teacher who would reject the notion of a political element in English teaching, and would not want to be associated with the work we are doing. If we feel any missionary zeal towards this teacher, it will have to be expressed in an exercise which combines gaining their confidence with reinforcing our message. Perhaps this might be done by beginning, again, with the topics likely to arise in English and considering how the political connection may act as a link and as background and stimulus for the 'English' which focuses on them. This might be done by reference to the systematising framework already suggested.

  v. The teacher of politics who is, or may be, or ought to be, concerned both with improving and extending the teaching of his own subject and the breaking down of subject barriers. In the latter area, he might be 'institutionalised' into an integrated studies or humanities type team-teaching situation or he might simply be concerned to relate politics to other areas of the child's experience. It would be useful to reverse the English/Politics analysis for this teacher, to show how English topics relate to political material and how literature might contribute to the teaching of politics.

[1] See John Dixon, *Growth through English*, 2nd ed., NATE, OUP 1975

150

It has been possible – and seemed to us to be potentially useful – to identify some areas where connections might be made, and to provide some suggestions of how this might be done. We are, though, aware of the dangers inherent in such formalisation, and expect them to be criticised: indeed, such criticism is necessary, especially if it can be accompanied by examples of alternative approaches and current practice. The material which follows is within the framework, then, of an attempt to

a) simply tie up the recurring topics (and literary texts) in English to <u>political</u> concepts (to indicate where the political might be explicated in English teaching);

b) to link political concepts to English material, with some suggestions for 'further study for teachers' to provide <u>political</u> background.

What we would see as a helpful order of work would be to look at this material, criticise it, as suggested above, and <u>then</u> to meet and discuss the implications for English teachers of document 2.2, the 'literacy tree', and the succeeding papers on concepts, values, and issues. This order is suggested by the <u>initial</u> response of many English teachers to the diagrams in document 2.2, namely that these (only) express aims and objectives of their English teaching – it is felt that the diagrams could be looked at again in the light of some actual examples.

3.3.4 <u>Political Concepts : English Themes</u>

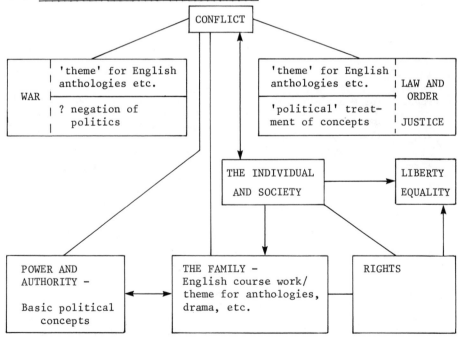

Group and individual proposals

3.3.5 English themes: developments from 'political' concepts

1 CONFLICT: THEM AND US: *power* and *authority, trades unions, school systems, gangs*

    LAW AND ORDER: *justice, capital punishment, corporal punishment, vandalism, shoplifting, squatting*

    INDIVIDUAL AND SOCIETY   *rights, liberty, equality*

    FREEDOM AND RESTRAINT: *pollution, advertising, consumer protection, pressure groups*

    FAMILY: *women's lib, children's lib, pocket money rules, sibling jealousy, responsibilities*

2 LINKS WITH ENGLISH MATERIAL:

(a) LAW AND ORDER/JUSTICE

Short Stories

Ray Bradbury, *The Pedestrian*
Sillitoe, *Saturday Afternoon*   ) individual falling foul of unsympath-
       Uncle Ernest   ) etic law
       Ragman's Daughter   'pleasure' of stealing
       Long Distance Runner   'honesty' us v them

Plays

Antigone
Caucasian Chalk Circle
Measure for Measure   the nature of the judge's authority and strict observance *(Angelo)* v humane handling of law *(Duke)*

Arden's Prefaces
Land of the Mighty   clowns and constable Roman reason v
Workshop Donkey   Celtic imagination straight lines v curves; develops representative order: creative anarchy. All his plays involve this idea, i.e. *Live Like Pigs* (a reasonably balanced view).

(b) ORDER V CHAOS/ANARCHY

Dionysus and *The Bacchae*
J. Bowen, *Disorderly Women* (Metheun)
The Just (Camus)   wordy, dialectical discuss of politic-al justification of assassination, with strong dramatic moments
Priestly, *An Inspector Calls*   morality
Hopkins, *This story of Yours*

Novels on similar themes

Conrad, *The Secret Agent*	sixth form only; brings out clearly the similarity between 'in laws' and 'outlaws' in methods – v jaundiced view of police and Home Office
Koestler, *Darkness at Noon*	(police state)
Burgess, *A Clockwork Orange*	

3.   RIGHTS

Possibly arising out of work on: *the family, conflict, individual and society.*

Topics   for drama/discussion/projects/writing:

                     should children have the vote?; school government/democracy in school; racial prejudice; and family troubles – responsibility, rules

Kit materials   Humanities Project; General Studies Project

Supporting literature *Antigone, Animal Farm, A Man for All Seasons, Cry the Beloved Country, Billy Budd, Kestrel for a Knave*

                     Each of these books may lead on to consideration of: *equality, liberty* and *justice.*

3.3.6 'Model' lesson on RIGHTS

At least a double lesson (eighty minutes?), second year?, mixed ability group. Preceding work – on the family: nuclear and extended families family conflicts – generation gap roles in the family – parents, responsibilities.

Aim of lesson: to open up discussion of rights

(a)   as against responsibilities (assuming that previous discussion has contained some element of 'parents can do as they like ...');
(b)   to explore idea of different roles within a given situation (in this case the family) leading to different – and conflicting? – RIGHTS;
(c)   to extend consideration of child's role from family (defined role) to wider world (less clearly defined role).

Procedure:

i. Blunt beginning – for reference purposes for rest of lesson – ask for list of what <u>people</u> (children and adults) consider to be their rights. (Response expected: freedom of speech; making own decisions; ?right to work; welfare benefits; fair trial; etc.) (see iii below).

ii.   Ask for examples of common expressions, including 'right' or 'rights' e.g. 'You've got no right to ...' 'I know my rights ..' Ask class to explain what the speaker might mean ... Divide class into small groups, ask them to prepare, in five minutes, a short sketch incorporating one of the phrases provided in ii., act it to class.

iii. Now return to list on board, with reference to sketches, distinguish RIGHTS, needs, demands, preferences etc. (Depending on ability of class, introduce idea at this stage of 'Are there any natural rights?').

iv.   Discuss and add to the list of RIGHTS as eliminated in iii. Discuss which of these might apply to children.
      (a)   ideally
      (b)   in their real world
      (refer to *Lord of the Flies* – matters could be different in a children's republic?).

v.   Read to class two extracts –
      from *Kestrel for a Knave,* any one of the passages where Billy, Jud and their mother are involved – possibly the passage where Billy discovers his kestrel has been killed
      or *Timothy Winters*
      and from *To Kill a Mocking-Bird*, any passage where Atticus' attempts to treat Scout reasonably are countered by her perception of how things ought to be.

vi.   Prepare work for finishing at home – or in subsequent lesson – to write a Bill of Rights for class's own age group up to ten points; and to prepare a newspaper report of the court proceedings when the first person is accused of violating the Bill.

Teacher could usefully read:
Margaret Macdonald, 'Natural Rights' in Laslett & Runciman eds.
Philosophy, Politics & Society 1st series
Joel Feinberg, *Social Philosophy* Chapters 4 and 6
R. S. Peters, *Ethics and Education,* Chapter VII
Benn and Peters, *Social Principles and the Democratic State,* Chapter 4.

possible extensions:

In political terms	In English Terms
justice and fairness	drama – extend, with larger groups, the
equality	best of the situations in ii.;
	write 'The Man who insisted on his
	rights ...' (...imagine a man who never
	gave way...);
	debate – Women's rights
	should school children have the vote?

Examine newspapers for examples of people claiming rights or appearing to be denied them.
Read *To Kill a Mocking-Bird*, bringing out the ideas of right and rights...
To lead into consideration of how to achieve one's rights – skills, political and communication
knowledge – of what rights are, how to find out
attitudes – when to give in and when not...

3.3.7 Some Examples of Responses from Pupils

POWER AND AUTHORITY

Double period (eighty minutes) lesson with third year mixed ability class in comprehensive school, outskirts of city, with teacher in her first year at the school.

Outline of lesson

POWER AND AUTHORITY

Aim - to develop the understanding of the concept of authority by discussing power.
Method
1. "Suppose a person asked you what power was, what would you reply?" Discussion of answer.

2. Different grounds for people having power.
    Weber's classification - traditional, legal-rational, charismatic. Charismatic was put across in terms of personality. Examples used included Prime Minister, the Queen, a judge, a teacher, Che Guevara and Jesus Christ. Children discussed the different grounds for each example.
3. Read 'Dangerous experiment' by John Davy, a *Sunday Times* review (26.5.74) of Stanley Milgram's book, *Obedience to Authority*.
    Several children had seen the television programme about this experiment. Discussion.
4. Write down (a) What is power?
                (b) Who has power?
                (c) Why do they have power?
                (d) Do you have any power?
Discuss written answers in small groups.
5. Read extract from *Lord of the Flies* p.21-25.
    Write down (e) Why was Ralph chosen as leader?
                (f) What sort of power did he have?
                (g) Why was Jack expecting to be leader?
                (h) What sort of power did Jack have although he wasn't elected as leader?
                (i) Write a story about the day when you have all the power you want. Would you run things differently? Would you take over the Prime Minister's duties?

Examples of class written work

POWER AND AUTHORITY   Kay

(a) What is power?
     "Power is one of two sorts, it may be either physical or otherwise. The Prime Minister and the Queen both have power over others. Physical power is when someone is bullied into doing something against their will. The other sort of power is when someone is respected and wanted as a leader because they are clever or sensible."

(b) Who has power?
"The Queen; the Prime Minister; Politicians; Headmasters: Teachers; Parents and Older Children."

(c) Why do they have power?
"Because they are respected and people think something drastic would happen to them if they did not obey."

(d) Do you have any power?
"Yes, I think I have, in our groups anyway. I'm not sure if it is because I'm bigger than them or if it is because they respect me. I think it may be the first because I used to have a rather bad reputation of smacking people up in 2nd year."

(e) Why was Ralph chosen as leader?
"Because he had suggested the idea and people respected him because the things he made them do were for them and not for himself."

(f) What sort of power did he have?
"He had a strong personality which made people want to do things for him."

(g) Why did Jack expect to be leader?
"Because he was a big-head and thought he was the best. He always got his own way through bullying."

(h) What sort of power did Jack have although he wasn't elected as leader?
"Jack was in charge of the choir as hunters."

(i) Write a story of the day when you have all the power you want. Would you run things differently? Would you take over the Prime Minister's duties?
"On the day I have all the power I want I would get rid of nasty people like the IRA bombers and other such organisations. I would make sure that everyone was given an equal chance in life, such as job availability, scholarships etc. I would put food prices down and make everything cheap."

Richard

(a) "Power comes in different forms, things such as electrical power or human power. People that have power have the ability to make people do what they want, either by their personality or by physically forcing them."

(b) "People in places like the House of Commons have to have power over the public to get them to vote them. The Prime Minister has power over his fellow men because they have to elect him."

(c) "The people I have mentioned have power because of their personality, they are able to make people do things, even against their will. They may be good at something also."

(d) "I have power over smaller children because my size normally means authority."

(e) "Ralph was chosen as leader because although he was not very talkative he possessed the conch and was not bossy but could have his way if he wanted."

(f) "Ralph had power because he seemed sensible and not as overpowering as Jack. I have already described his power in question (e)."

(g) "Jack expected to be leader because he had been leader of the choir. He was too bossy for everyone. He had previously been able to have his way with everyone."

(h) "Jack had physical power over people as well as being very dominating."

Peter

(a) "I think power consists of many different sorts. The power of a leader or the power of electricity or a force. The Prime Minister has power, power over people, factories and many different other things."

(b) "People like the Queen and the Prime Minister have power. Cleverer people have power, and older people also have power."

(d) "I also have power over younger people, on some weekends because I act as a Cox on a four-man speed rowing boat."

(i) "I had all the power for one day. I would first have all the drinks and visit other countries. I travel luxuriously. And I order the day to go slowly."

Elaine

(a) "Makeing poelpe Doe What you Want them to Doe."

(b) "God has power beuses poelpe say he is the best."

(c) "Beuses poelpe say he is the best."

(d) "I have power oveth my Brother."

(e) "Beuses he was Umain And he had power."

Joanne

(a) "Power is being able to make something or someone do something."

(b) "Most people have some power, though some people have a lot more power than others. Even small children have power over small animals and pets."

(c) "They have power either because they are big and can bash people in who don't do what they want or because they have an outgoing or dominating personality."

(d) "I have power over my pet rabbit because it couldn't live if I didn't feed it and look after it. I have power over my sister because she is younger than me."

(e) "Ralph was chosen to be the leader because he was sensible and not too bossy also he had the conch shell."

(f) "He was quite friendly so the others didn't mind doing what he told them. Also he had sensible ideas."

(g) "Because he had always been the leader of the choir and was used to frightening people into doing what he wanted and he thought that he could frighten the other boys into obeying him."

(h) "Jack was bossy with a dominating personality so he could still boss some of the choir around."

Darren

(d) "I have power over some relay teams in the swimming club because I am the team captain and also the oldest. But more people have power over me than I do over them."

Ian

(a) "Power gets things going and makes things move."

(b) "the Queen has power and lots of other people."

(c) "Because it is tradition that they are elected."

(d) "Yes I have power over small people."

(e) "Because he was sensible and he knew they had to get off the island and they liked him."

(f) "Ralph had power over all the other people on the island."

(g) "Jack had no power because he wanted to be chosen because he could have bossed people about."

(h) "Jack had power because he had power over the choir because he made them hunters."

(i) "As I was walking along the road when I was suddenly I was changed into that I had all the power I was stronger than anyone else and I saw one of my worst enemies and I have the power. So I did them in without any trouble. I was glad because they never touched me again."

Example II GOVERNMENT

With the same class as in Example I. Discussion of laws and rules, based on reading of *Lord of the Flies*.

Writing: 3. How are rules decided upon or changed?: i. in Great Britain
ii. in ... Comprehensive School.
4. How did our system of government develop?
5. Are there any other ways of running a country?

Examples of written work

Debra

3.(a) How are rules decided upon and changed?
i. "Because of the behaviour of the people the government decide which rules there are and the local governments decide which school you go to."
ii. "The head mistress decides on which rules we have and the local education committee decide which rules to change."

4. How did our system of government develop?
"The people started to get tired of being told what to do by the King and no government, and in the Victorian times they decided they wanted to speak for so they elected MPs to speak for them."

5. Are there any other ways of running a country?
"You could just have the King ruling or just one rich person ruling the country."

Helen

3.(a) How are rules decided upon or changed?
i. In Great Britain.
"The governments National and Local."
ii. In our Comprehensive School
"Headmistress, the behaviour of the children change the rules."

S

3. i. "The rules changed by the Government because of the behaviour of people."

ii. "The Local Government tell us which schools to go to."

4. "Poor people didn't want to stay at the bottom and they wanted to get an education, so they elected some people to talk for them so they would get some rights, so their children can go to school."

Paul

3. i. "The rules in Great Britain are decided on by Government and are changed by the need for a different rule."
ii. "The rules are made in our Comprehensive by a headmistress and changed by heads of year and the headmistress usually for the good of the school."

4. "The people voted for certain people to be put in Government because the people thought they would be fair."

5. "There are other ways of running the country but they are not all very nice. For instance, there is communism, or a King or Queen who must be obeyed."

Kay

3. i. "The Government decide rules and they hold elections to change them.
ii. "The headmistress and the behaviour of the pupils form rules and good or bad behaviour changes them.

4. "The subjects of the King revolted against him and they wanted their say in the matter so they elected people to speak for them. These people were MPs and the people voted for the different ones for their constituencies."

5. "You could have just one ruler but that would not be very good because only he would get what he wanted."

Stuart

5. "Are there other ways of running a country?
Yes, you could grade people to their Jobs."

Peter

3. i. "People in Great Britain can elect and choose their own Government, and put their own views against something."
ii. "The headmistress can decide which rules to have and not to have."

4. "People at the bottom of an imaginary list were getting a bit fed up. So they wanted to elect their own Government."

5. "There are, but ways like Communism."

Darren

3. i. "The government thinks what will be a good idea and they have debates and bills passed to try and make it general. They are changed in the same way."
ii. "In this school when problems arise in the present rules then they are tried out and announced on the daily notices."

4. "When problems come up in the old system of king over country such as the men inbetween thinking why should they be below the king someone was elected who was thought suitable for being in charge."

5. "Yes, by Communism, Socialism and Dictatorship."

159

3.3.8 Syllabus from the English Department of
      a Boys' Independent Day School

LITERATURE 'POLITICS'

First Forms: (a) Penguin English Project, *Family and School* (kinds of ed.).

Second Forms: (a) Sci. Fi. *War of the Worlds, Time Machine* etc. (different societies)

Third Forms: (a) *The Chrysalids, The Day of the Triffids, Fahrenheit 451* (different societies)

           (b) *Kestrel for a Knave, The Leaping Lad, Joby* (social backgrounds)

           (c) *The Spy who Came in From the Cold, Roque Male* etc. (systems)

           (d) Others: *Animal Farm, Glencoe,* Penguin Connexions Series:- *Lawbreakers, Fit to Live in, All in the game*

           (a) War *All Quiet on the Western Front, The Long and the Short and the Tall, Men who March Away, The Cruel Sea, Goodbye to all that, O What a Lovely War, Wilfred Owen's Poems, The Reason Why, Arms and the Man*

           (b) America: *The Grapes of Wrath, 8 American Poets, Shane, The Grass Harp, Miama and the Siege of Chicago, Guys and Dolls*

           (c) Prejudice: *To Kill a Mocking-Bird, Language of Prejudice, The Experience of Colour, Mr. Johnson, Cry the Beloved Country.*

           (d) Satire: *Gulliver's Travels, Candide, Scoop, Rasselas.*

           (e) Adolescence: *Conflicting Generations, That Once was Me, The Receiving End* (PEP)

           (f) Others: Connexions Series: *Disaster, Living Tomorrow, Break for Commercials, Z Cars, St. Joan, The Royal Hunt of the Sun, Luther.*

At fifth and sixth form level we have used:
essays by Orwell and Lawrence; *Secret Agent;* various novels by Dickens;
and by Hardy, Huxley, Kafka, Lawrence, Lee, Orwell, Pasternak, Forster,
Golding, Heller, Hemingway, Salinger, Snow, Waugh etc.; and plays by
Arden, Beckett, Barnes, Behan, Bond, Brecht, Miller, etc.

O Level English Literature Courses 1974-5

A <u>Power Games</u>

Ambition, jealousy, cruelty, greed, revenge: some of the more primitive
drives and emotions which continue to work beneath the 'civilised'
surface of modern life are explored in:
   The Visit (play) by Friedrich Durrenmatt. An ageing millionairess
   with a wooden leg, nine husbands and a score to settle plans to 'buy
   up' the town of her birth. The power of money allows her to mount a
   terrifying vendetta against the community that rejected her in youth.

   This Sporting Life (novel) by David Storey. 'Getting to the top' in
   a tough, hostile northern town isn't easy, but one outlet for ambition

is to become a rugby league star. The rules of the game, however turn
out not to be confined to the field alone, and the basic problem is to
discover precisely who makes them.
The Birthday Party (play) by Harold Pinter. Why, sensitive Stanley,
cosily holed up in his seaside lodgings, has some unexpected birthday
visitors. Through a series of sinister party 'games' they take him
completely into their power and destroy him. Why?
Selected Tales of D. H. Lawrence. Some short stories, set in or around
Nottingham, which show how personal relationships are often dictated by
dominance and aggression.
Little Malcolm and his Struggle against the Eunuchs (play) by David
Halliwell. Art student Malcolm Scrawdyke, self-appointed Che Guevara
of Huddersfield, leads a spectacular revolution designed to overthrow
the College authorities and establish a power-base for his Party of
Dynamic Erection. Some revolutions, though, are not quite as pure as
they seem when tested by the pressures of reality.

B Systems

The systems referred to in the title are political and ideological.
The gooks deal with unheroic figures whose stubborn individualism leads
them to fall foul of the prevailing beliefs and practices of their
world. They do not succeed against the odds:

In Koestler's *Darkness at Noon*, Tubashov, the Communist intellectual
imprisoned in a Stalinist purge, and awaiting interrogation, reviews
his past life and beliefs.
In Orwell's *1984* , Winston Smith in a chillingly perceived future is
found guilty of 'thought-crime', perpetrated in an act of rebellion
against a society in which his every movement is monitored and controlled. Can he ever love Big Brother, the mythical ruler of his
world?
In Brecht's *Galileo*, Galileo's revolutionary discoveries in physics
bring him into conflict with the Church and Inquisition, whose account
of the world requires a different explanation of physical phenomena.
In Golding's *Lord of the Flies*, religion is again the concern; this
time with the primitivism and communal terror that underlies supposed-
ly civilised life. A group of boys find themselves marooned on an
island. All goes well until the Beast appears:

C The Individual in Society

A study of how people (both authors and their characters) cope when
external events impose serious pressures on their individuality.

A Man for All Seasons by Robert Bold. Sir Thomas More is a Catholic.
He is also a politician. At what point and why does the Catholic
conviction refuse to yield to political realities?
A Day in the Life of Ivan Denisovitch by A. Solzhenistsyn. One day
of one man's experience in a Russian labour camp. How does he try to
protect himself, and what individuality does he have left to protect?
Short Stories by Graham Greene. Four or five stories tracing different types of individual anguish, varying from that of a schizoid
paranoic, who is chasing himself, to that of a 14 year-old boy whose
position as gang leader is threatened at the crucial moment.

Poems: a selection of up to ten, from sixteenth to twentieth centuries, looking at aspects of threatened individuality in contexts such as love, war, ambition, and the apparent transience of human life.

D Literature as Social Comment

The course demonstrates the ways in which the writers reflect the nature of the twentieth Century in their work. These authors have all had some influence upon later literature:

The Caucasian Chalk Circle (play) by B. Brecht. A look at tyranny and justice in the story of a servant girl who disappears with the heir to the throne and meets, among others, Azdak, the unusal judge.
The Plague (novel) by A. Camus. The effects of the disease of individuals and their community.
The Machine Stops (short story) by E.M. Forster.
The poems of Edward Thomas.

E Journeys

A consideration of the ways in which writers use the idea of a journey to consider the significant experience and development of their central characters facing problems posed by their worlds:

The Captain of Koppenick (play) by C. Zuckmayer. A Prussian ex-convict buys an army uniform and takes over a town hall in his 'journey' of rebellion against his society.
Watership Down (novel) by Richard Adams. A fable about a group of rabbits and their quest to set up a new community against overwhelming odds.
The Ancient Mariner. Coleridge's poem tells of an unusual sea voyage.
Narrow Road to the Deep North (play) by E. Bond. Basho seeks enlightenment by travelling to the north, 'gets it', but then has to relate it to his role as adviser to the two conflicting rulers of his town.

3.3.9 Comments from teachers of English about the Programme:

1. From a Head of an English Department in a mixed comprehensive school

"I do see English work as being in a wide sense 'political', especially if one takes the current trend in either the 'linguistics' English or 'the English of communications' as closely involving thinking about language and therefore developing one of the prerequisites or sensible political involvement and understanding.

We do not take the 'thematic' line in English, so much as basing what we do on skills - development, and in this context, therefore, we do not have a programme of political content - it may well come in, of course, in the sociological work that may be the framework for a half-term or so. What I am trying to explore, largely through oral work in the CSE, is the 'aural' effect that an approach based on 'Language across the Curriculum' may have. The 'Language across the Curriculum' approach, I feel, enables me to limit my attention to the skills that, I hope, may be of value in political awareness. A 'theme' approach not based on such skills doesn't either suit well the efforts towards an individualised curriculum that we strive for.

For this latter reason, too, namely the striving for an individualised curriculum, we tend not to look systematically at a group of books that may be of value in this context of political ability, although, no doubt, some of the books may be of value individually. In short, it may be said that I hope that political education may be implicit in what we do.

Care should be taken over looking for a 'political' link in, say English texts - there is at present a reaction against 'thematic' teaching of English, in and out of IDE. Some flexible notions needed of a half-way house' between theme-based learning and the 'pure literature' school. Both approaches tend to a rigid approach to language, and therefore both could forget what English is generally reckoned to be about these days.

BUT the oral side, provided its aims and objectives are clear, could well provide the half-way house; such aims and objectives could be, in this context -

(a) equipment for understanding of the 'persuasive' element in language;
(b) equipment for listening carefully;
(c) equipment for a use of language that is flexible enough to enhance sympathy.

Similar aims and objectives could be drawn up, of course, for writing or reading, but it seems likeliest that the oral element provides greatest scope for reaching the language-level of the individual, whether one uses talk as a way of teaching politics or politics as a subject for talk. There might be a good chance of improving the quality of attitudes and values - an important part of socialisation is facilitating language.

... isn't is a problem of politics (cf. the current debate over the referendum) that we emphasise the complexities and therefore create apathy? Shouldn't 'political education' better spend its time reforming and simplifying rather than identifying or creating awareness (a useful parallel is the misuse perhaps built into the 'Language in Use' kind of approach, which tends to harp on the interest in the varieties of language rather than using or seeing through it.)

(Some of the material, especially that trying to match English themes to political concepts, would create awareness for the teacher, but too abstract for the pupil).

I very much like the Simulation/Drama approach of 'Who's to blame' - Why?

(a) controlled drama creates a situation where you have to keep stopping to take stock - this seems a vital political skill;
(b) such a simulation brings people into contact;
(c) the people involved are usually aware (in a way that seems rare in discussion/reading/writing) of objectives that are relevant and meaningful - perhaps this is (a) written differently;
(d) the combination of (b) and (c) creates dialogue that is concerned with unravelling and simplifying - see the very valuable process of the whole group and the sub-groups including the controller/ teacher that would be involved in the work in 'Introducing the incident' on p.2.
(e) such a simulation involves skills of rapid reading/concentration/ assimilation that are vital for participation in our sort of democracy (as opposed to the entirely school-sited skills that seem involved in a place like Countesthorpe ..."

Group and individual proposals

2. From a teacher of English, mixed comprehensive school

"Having read through the material which you sent me there are a few comments which I would like to make about it.

The choice of literature as noted in the syllabus seems to me an interesting one although, particularly in the early years, I would have thought that a slightly greater variety could be introduced. (I may, of course, be misjudging the situation as the information on the first years is only scanty). There seem to be so many books available to teachers which carry a political content at a variety of levels and I think there might be a great argument for teachers producing, for their own purposes, anthologies and collections of examples along the lines of the Penguin *Connexions* series.

A couple of examples of areas which we studied are as follows (materials being prepared by individuals and groups of teachers):-

1. The Family - roles and relationships within the family, its relation to the outside world, conflict within and without the family.
2. Law and Order - the desirability of an ordered society, factual history of the growth of the police force, problem solving exercises e.g. what would you do in a certain situation?

If we examine the two areas above there are obviously many ways in which they can be approached. When I was looking at these areas in an integrated studies context we approached both areas from a point of view which covered many and varied situations both in terms of time and geographical location.

One can think that through such a study, one is teaching, amongst other things, some basic political concepts e.g. an individual's responsibility, an individual's rights within both small and large communities, but I often wonder, and this applies to many areas of secondary education, how much of what is actually taught transfers into the experience of life of the children concerned. Therefore, it seems to me most important that practical, meaningful and real opportunities for some kind of political involvement must be provided for children and students in order that such theoretical studies may take on a significant place in their education.

If one looked at the whole of the school curriculum in such terms, then obviously much of it would be found wanting and such a look might indicate necessary areas for change."

3. From a Director of Sixth Form Studies

"My main interest is not in how 'literature can be useful in politics teaching', but in how the teacher of English can be made more aware of the political content/assumptions/ideological background of the books he teaches/reads with his students/reads on his own.

... while I know that an argument like 'literature is about life ... all life is political' is, in your words, 'too loose to be useful', yet I am continually appalled at the naivete, not so much of my students (some of them are very aware indeed) as of my colleagues teaching English - who are likely to say things as asinine as "I'm not really interested in politics" or "English is concerned with individuals, not society".

164

Take for example the books I have taught for 'A' level this year:

> *Mister Johnson*
> G.M. Hopkins, *Selected Poems*
> W.B. Yeats, *Selected Poems*
> *Tess of the D'Urbervilles*
> Tennyson, *Selected Poems*
> *A Passage to India*
> Owen, *Collected Poems*
> *Our Mutual Friend*

(I teach half-sets, so inevitably tend to choose the set-books which are more 'political, since I am 'political'!). There's not one of these which isn't of political interest (even Hopkins, whose Victorianism – attitudes to urbanisation, the unemployed, Ireland and England, the soldiery etc. – has to be taught as carefully as his aesthetics; even Tennyson – how else to teach *Locksley Hall* and *Locksley Hall Sixty Years After*, or *Ode on the Death of the Duke of Wellington*, or the *Idylls*, and so on?). A politically aware English teacher can't help but dwell on the political implications of these texts; when I teach *Lord of the Flies*, I automatically deal with the power-struggle between common-sensical and decent Ralph, scientific Piggy, saintly Simon, barbaric and power-hungry Jack, sadistic Roger; the fragility of democratic authority (the conch); the way the situation on the island mirrors the outside world (the "message" of the dead parachutist; the "rescue" by an officer who rests his hand on his gun, who looks to the "trim cruiser" in the bay, who jokes about "having a war or something", who believes in *Coral Island* as a paradigm of boys' behaviour on an island while fighting a presumably nuclear war), and so on. I also base my critique of the novel on its overwhelming view of Original Sin, its narrow view of potential salvation, its essentially 'liberal' i.e. non-socialist view of the boys' society. All the students I teach know that I'm a socialist; I make no bones about it, and believe that being open removes the possibility of charges of indoctrination! I am sure that part of the reason for the appeal of *Lord of the Flies* in schools (i.e. to teachers) is that it confirms a lot of their views both of Original Sin and of the nature of society!

My feelings is that the curricular limitations on the development of Politics as a separate school subject (at the most, it would be an option at sixth form level) make it essential for our efforts to go towards developing the political side of, say, English and History (or Social Studies) teaching – that is, to make the political content (which is already there for those with the eyes to see) more obvious to everyone. That way we are likely to reach more people anyway; I suspect that old-fashioned liberalism is so strong in schools that attempts to introduce political education as a major and separate (or even minor and separate) part of the curriculum ("Won't it be indoctrination?" is the cry I've already heard. And "What will it replace?" – if Politics, why not Psychology, why not Sociology, why not Anthropology?) will be in effect counter-productive.

For fun I drew up two 'A' level syllabuses which someone politically committed (but presumably rather stupid) could brand as 'right-wing' and 'left-wing'.

```
Right wing syllabus:
Henry IV, I and II (hierarchic views of society etc.)
Coriolanus (fascist)
Yeats, Selected Poems (Irish nationalist and fascist)
Pound, The Pisan Cantos (effects of solitary confinement on a fascist)
Eliot, Four Quartets (Anglo-Catholic royalist ...)
Wordsworth, The Prelude (1850 edition) (ex-radical turned Tory)
Disraeli, Sybil (Tory-radical feudalist)
Orwell, Animal Farm (anti-revolutionary)
Koestler, Darkness at Noon (reactionary)
Dickens, A Tale of Two Cities (anti-revolutionary)
```

(You haven't forgotten that I am joking, please!)

```
Left wing syllabus:
Richard II (the people's king)
Lear (Kott's version of the tragedy of history)
Wordsworth, The Lyrical Ballads radical approach of common people ...)
Shelley, Selected Poems (idealist radical)
Mrs. Gaskell, Mary Barton (the failure of reformism ...)
Dickens, Dombey and Son (the capitalist ethic)
Conrad, Nostromo (the evils of imperialism and the corruption of
silver)
Achebe, Things Fall Apart (colonialism)
Hemingway, For Whom the Bell Tolls (the struggle)
Camus, The Plague (Nazi occupation)
```

Seriously, when one thinks critically about what one teaches, there is hardly a book which isn't going to be illuminated by political awareness. I can't honestly see much point in circulating lists of books which might be taught in politics, or treated as political texts; what we need to do is to show just how political the kind of texts already set are.

How to make English teachers more politically aware? I'm a devotee of Raymond Williams (especially of *The Long Revolution* and so tend to put it and *Culture and Society* in the way of my colleagues. I have also started recommending Fred Inglis's new book, *Imagination and Ideology*, (CUP, 1975). Jan Kott can be very useful on Shakespeare ... But the difficulty here is that one is talking about the whole approach to literary study, at a time when some other approaches (e.g. the struct-uralist) seems to be making considerable inroads into critical methodo-logy. While I think it essential that English teachers (all teachers for that matter) have a smattering of at least some of the modern work in linguistics, I tend to share the kind of suspicion of the structura-list and purely linguistic methods which F.W. Bateson outlined in the latest *New Review*. I am sure that the Raymond Williams school offers a much more healthy way forward in the study of literature.

You will presumably gather from this that I am almost by definition unhappy about overly conceptualist versions of the teaching of politics (and about similar versions of the teaching of ethics, sociology, psy-chology etc); I am intersted in enactment. While I'd like students to have more terminology available to them, I would like to see literature used to complicate those terms (and so enrich the concepts by enacting them). As you say in your paper, the enormous virtue of imaginative literature is that it complicates, presents 'complex images of a dynamic reality', rather than illustrates concepts. It follows that I am al-together in favour of attempts to make teachers and students of politics

166

(and politicians for that matter) more literate and imaginative (in the broadest sense of the words). My primary text is a quotation from Iris Murdoch from her essay "Against Dryness":

> We need to return from the self-centred concept of sincerity to the other-directed concept of truth. We are not isolated free-choosers, monarchs of all we survey, but benighted creatures sunk in a fatality whose nature we are constantly and overwhelmingly tempted to deform by fantasy. Our current picture of freedom encourages a dream-like facility; whereas what we require is a renewed sense of the difficulty of the moral life and opacity of persons.

How to make teachers of politics more imaginative? Well, for a start they have got to read especially fiction, and be taught to read properly ... They've got to be taught to <u>particularise</u>, <u>complicate</u>, <u>enact</u> their categories and concepts. One might start by putting D.H. Lawrence, "Why the Novel Matters", at the head of the list, and then getting them to read *The Rainbow* and *Women in Love*.

Is this any use to you? Or too tangential to relate to the work you've done? I suppose what I am really expressing is my terror that the kind of version of 'politics' which seems to emerge from some of the material you sent is dangerously narrow. David McLellan's essay on 'Political Theory' in *Literature and Environment* (ed. Inglis, naturally) says what I feel pretty exactly:

> 'Not to be politically minded is not to have an interest in one's society and, ultimately, not have an interest in oneself. For politics is not solely about the way institutions work, the means of acquiring and preserving power, the impersonal techniques of government. Fact can never be entirely separated from value, and the ambition of many writers on politics to make it into a purely descriptive science with the consequent prestige associated with neutrality and objectivity, has proved a chimera. Behind every description there lies a point of view. More important, however, such an attempt to narrow the definition of politics is extremely dangerous. It carries with it the conclusion that the most intimate values and beliefs of individuals belong to a 'private' world separate from the 'public' world of politics in which, it is implied, they have no place. Politics thus becomes a specialised profession in which only the opinions of 'experts' have any weight. Hence a growing gap ... between what most people experience as important to themselves and the increasingly irrelevant and mystifying manoeuvres of the public world.
>
> In fact this divorce between the two worlds is itself a specifically political ideology designed to exclude from the political process all those who do not possess an expert opinion; and, by the same token, to remove political discussion from the sphere of values - where all men start equal - to that of techniques - where professionalism can reign supreme. And since techniques are easier to deal with than values, those wielding them can afford the added luxury of not having too much.'

It might be worth passing that quotation and the Iris Murdoch piece around to the others involved ..."

4. From a Teacher in a Comprehensive School

"Not surprising, the major difficulty in this whole discussion seems to be one of definition. In attempting to define 'political literature it is obviously quite appropriate to reject the 'literature is about life ... all life is political' idea as being too loose to be useful. The distinction drawn between political content and social content as being that of the individual against society as opposed to the individual merely in society seems to be helpful, but then by accepting J.C. Davies's definitive themes of political fiction - "power-survival and liberty; criticism of the *status quo*; status distinctions; equality and the dignity of the human being", an equally loose and, by implication, useless framework seems to have been adopted.

For in a typical comprehensive school's list of literature, how many texts would actually fall outside Davies's categories? Those read in the first year or even in the primary school could well be interpreted as containing these elements. *The Family from One End Street, One Hundred and One Dalmations*, the *Narnia* books, *The Weirdstone of Brisingamen, The Hobbit, Gumble's Yards*, and *The Silver Sword* are novels taken from one such school's list, and all could, without too much thought, be interpreted in the light of Davies's categories.

And the categorising of books/plays/poems under various headings e.g. 'governing' concepts seems to be no more than thematic lists of texts and extracts, a feature of 'English' publications familiar to all English teachers. Indeed, many anthologies and sections within anthologies reflect a similar interest in 'political' matters: *Reflections* - 'Family, Community and Work', 'The Mass Media', 'Questions of our Time'; *Living Expression* Bk. 4 - 'Crowds', 'It's Forbidden', 'The Older Generation', 'Prejudice, rights and Responsibilities', 'Violence', 'Love and Hate'; *Conflict 2* - 'Self versus Society', 'Self versus the System'. And even in poetry anthologies, sections on war, work, town and country, conflict etc. etc.

Does the work of the Politics and English Working Group do anything more than these anthologies, in drawing together complete texts in perhaps a more politically systematic way?

The debate as to how far English literature should be subject to this process of thematic anthologising is well known; but within the context of political education, it may be worth restating the view that literature is essentially about the total complexity of human experience, and to claim *Lord of the Flies* for a political education programme is to ignore similar claims from programmes of psychological, theological, anthropological, moral, sociological ... education, all of which highlights the difficulties of treating a piece of literature as an example of any one, or number of themes or issues.

If it is the purpose of the Politics and English Group to provide systematic anthologies, then, this has been done to a certain extent in many schools, especially those who teach an integrated social studies/English CSE. scheme. Many of these schemes have as a declared aim the teaching of social/political awareness through literature.

Perhaps the main difference is in approach: the Politics and English approach is to look at the set texts and to decide how these can be grouped 'politicially'- whereas the integrated CSE. type approach is to decide which social/political issues should be taught and then find texts and extracts to add the extra 'literary' dimension to the issues. (This would seem an acceptable use of literature as long as some texts were studied in their own right and not as part of the theme).

The teaching of political concepts through literature seems to me to be process demanding a level of conceptualisation beyond that of the average 13-16 year old pupil - one target area of the project. Mention is made of games and simulations, but even nearer to reality is the pupil's own experience of politics via the workings of the school. This 'hidden curriculum' of the power structure, the rules and regulations, punishments and rewards, the staff-pupil relationships, streaming and mixed-ability - the whole ethos of the school - will teach the pupil far more about the reality of politics than any discussion of the issues via the vicarious experience of literature. It is not difficult to parody a situation in which the pupils are studying *1984* in English, the growth of parliamentary democracy in history, the iniquities of Apartheid in social studies and St. Lukes Gospel in RE; and all this in a school situation which is overtly elitist, denying any individual participation in its running. A caricature, of course, but more realistic examples easily come to mind where the 'hidden curriculum' of the school teaches the pupils the realities of political issues far more effectively than any carefully structured syllabus.

The Schools Council Social Education Project (Working Paper No.51) clearly had some things in common with the Programme for Political Education. In this Project a clear definition emerged - not in any sense to judge other notions of social education - but rather to set the limits on the work of the Project. Social education was defined as "an enabling process through which children may acquire skills which will allow them both to achieve a greater understanding of society and to effect change within it". Simple social skills are enumerated, such as the willingness to approach others to ask relevant questions, to initiate group activity, to work in groups, etc; and these skills are practised through socio-drama and the realities of building up various profiles on, the class, the family, the school, and the local area. Great emphasis is laid on pupil initiative and in the final profile of the local area, pupils are encouraged to take action in the community. This may result in nothing more than having faulty street lighting corrected, getting a farmer to make good a ploughed over right-of-way, or persuading the council to build a bus shelter; but this type of action brings pupils face-to-face with the frustrations of bureacracy and the realities of politics.

Within the political education literature, political literacy is seen as 'knowledge, skills and attitudes', but there are no real opportunities given pupils actually to practise these skills. The Social Education Project, whilst placing no great emphasis on the acquisition of knowledge about society, does see the practising of defined skills as an absolute essential.

From the point of view of the use of English literature, there are other similarities in the two projects. I have always been committed to the opinion that literature should be used to add this dimension of vicarious experience to any profile of social groups, but there is a body of opinion within the exponents of social education that all the resource material used should come from the information the pupils themselves collect. A rather esoteric debate, but one in which I would see a real contribution from an English-social education element, parallel to work of the English-Politics Working Group. But perhaps again the emphasis is slightly different; from the social education point of view, I see the English contribution as offering extracts and poetry to highlight issues already raised, but in no way providing a systematic framework for the teaching of social education.

Group and individual proposals

So the work of the English-Politics Group seems to have suffered from a lack of a clear definition of 'political-education' and of 'political' literature. This has led to what seems to be little more than a systematic grouping of texts under political themes, a service provided by many anthologies and paralleled in many schools' English/social studies syllabuses. And finally, in contrast to the Social Education Project, the concepts and skills seem largely academic ·and in no way exploit the realities of the school's political structure, or give opportunity for the skills to be practised."

(Adrian Knight)

3.4   FURTHER EDUCATION AND POLITICAL LITERACY
       LINDA ANKRAH-DOVE AND GEOFFREY STANTON

3.4.1 Aims of the group

The objective of our working group was to produce an introductory module
of approximately 4 x 1½ hour lessons intended for trial use with students
in further education in their general studies time on second and third
year technical, and fourth year craft courses or their equivalent.[1] We
decided to aim at a small module simply to increase the chance of its
adoption.

   The package produced and set out below (which went out with a full
explanatory letter to all teachers involved) includes:

   Overall objectives (3.4.2 - 3.4.5).
   A rationale, explanation and suggestions to the lecturer in general
   terms.
   Three lesson plan outlines *(not reproduced here as included in 3.4.2 -
   3.4.5 Editors),* with suggestions for timing, teaching and learning
   activities, content and the relevant political literacy skills which
   might be developed (3.4.6 - 3.4.8).
   Teaching materials, e.g. newspaper extracts, exercises (included in
   above). A detailed follow-up schedule to provide feedback on the
   success or failure of the suggested format, objectives, content and
   strategies *(not reproduced here. Editors).*

   Let us briefly summarise some of the lessons learned from the trial.

3.4.2 Concept of politics

At the time the module was designed, only documents 2.1 and 2.2 of the
Programme were available. From the discussion there of political
literacy and the procedural values, a concept of politics has to be
inferred; it is nowhere explicit. In a teaching situation where most
students are being introduced to politics for the first time, we felt
that a conceptual framework must be supplied.

   Although we would have some reservations about the consensual
overtones of the documents 2.1 and 2.2, we felt that the notion that
politics is fundamentally about methods of allocation of scarce
resources is not incompatible with the approach of the Programme.

   The first lesson plan focuses therefore on the ideas that:

a.   there are <u>alternative</u> methods of allocation. (The list of methods
     suggested are examples and are not exhaustive as some teachers
     thought.)
b.   some of these methods will be political, i.e. using discussion,
     persuasion, consent, etc. within agreed institutional frameworks.
     Others will be non-political, e.g. market forces or military.
c.   the important point is that whatever method is chosen the making
     of the choice of method is also political.

[1] *So important is this field that the Hansard Society began early in 1977
a further project of curriculum development specifically aimed at craft
apprentices, called 'Political Literacy in Further Education', under the
direction of Dr. Robert Stradling, funded by the Anglo-German Foundation
for Industrial Society, and it hopes to report next year. Editors.*

Group and individual proposals

Our impression is that the strategies we suggested for introducing this notion went some way towards providing a conceptual framework within which political literacy could be developed. We would emphasise, however, that feedback to us from teachers in the field was less than we hoped. Future programmes need to pay detailed attention to the problems involved in communication and liaison between "ideas-producers" and "experimenters".

3.4.3 Political literacy

The items on the political literacy tree in document 2.2 are not strictly teaching/learning objectives since they are at a level of generality which prevents their being used in behavioural evaluation. Rather, we think, they form a useful checklist of knowledge, skills and attitudel which, learned singly, help the development of political literacy and which, as a collectivity, delineate the characteristics of a politically literate person. One checks one's teaching activity against them, rather than derives the lesson material from them.

As many as possible of the political literacy items were incorporated into the module as guidelines for the teacher but the success or failure of the module can only be assessed by reference to the list of objectives designed specifically for the module. Lessons 2 to 4 of the module attempt to start the student off on skills which are prerequisite to political literacy (e.g. extracting information from a document and communicating it orally). Later modules in the series would obviously build on this.

Feedback on these lessons has revealed the complex range of skills needed for political literacy. Even assuming a student had all the skills, we feel that a learning experience such as this may be useful in revealing how he/she needed to assemble the skills in order to act (i.e. understand, evaluate, do) politically. The design of this module seemed well suited to demonstrating to the teacher what additional remedial packages are needed which would concentrate on specific skills found lacking.

3.4.4 Political situations

Our route into political literacy is through situations (not problems or issues, since situations only become problems or issues for the student when he sees them as such). The situations are ones which the student meets in everyday life (e.g. seating allocation on a bus). Prior to the trial we felt that this approach would lend itself to adaptation to all ages and 'level' of student but that the nature of the concrete situations introduced as case studies (here, aspects of housing) need to cater to the interests of the specific students involved.

Even then there is no guarantee that the students will be motivated, interested or enthusiastic. Feedback from lecturers suggests that students may use their freedom to opt out (a procedural value) in the following ways:

i. They may fail to see the situation presented as a problem relevant to a political context, e.g. some students thought that the price of a house was a fact of life, and failed to see it as a human mechanism for allocation. In this case, the understanding of the concept of what makes up a political context was dependent upon a prior understanding of the concept of market forces.

ii. They may think quite reasonably that the 'issue' or 'problem' though real, may be left to others to deal with. A student is action rationally if in a learning situation he has listened to the 'problem' and decided to allocate this own scarce resources of time and energy to other things. He has his own priorities.

iii. They may decide that the 'problem' is not relevant to their own interests or needs. It is always tempting for teachers to try to motivate students by appealing to their self-interest. Yet there is an ethical problem here. Do we want to put over the idea that political activity should be used exclusively for oneself and never 'purely' for the common good?

3.4.5 Learning context

As with all evaluation in curriculum development, it is not easy to disentangle factors arising from variables in the teaching/learning context from those to do with the objectives and content of the module. There were obviously disadvantages in the somewhat prescriptive approach we adopted here. But we have found that personal contact with the teachers and their understanding of and sympathy with the purpose of the exercise prevented the prescriptiveness being seen as irksome, constricting or disrespectful.

The approach has given us greater control over the number of intervening variables than we could otherwise have hoped to have and feedback has therefore been more precise. Although detailed changes are required in the material, the consensus of opinion seemed to be that the approach as a whole was a fruitful one.

L. A-D.   G.S. (October 1976)

3.4.6 Lesson one: Allocation Exercise 1

The idea behind the start of this lesson is to generate a situation in which a group of people (in this case a class) have a problem to which there is no answer satisfactory to everyone.

Student learning activity	Teaching strategy	Content development	Lit. Tree
	Remove some of the chairs from the room, or ask the class to imagine that you have done so.		
Answering questions	Ask how they would decide who got a seat	Methods of Alloca-tion	Gen.
Giving opinions (15 mins)	Elicit answers ——→ display on board	'first come, first served'	1a,b
		'need'	2a,b
		'status'	3a,b
			4a,b.c
		'market forces'	5a,b.c
		'lottery'	6a,b
		'avoid the problem'	
Giving examples (10 mins)	Ask for real-life examples of each method of allocation display on board		specif- ically
	Introduce the concept of ——→	'A decision making procedure'	2a,b 3a,b
Answering questions	Ask for each of the above examples ——→	Who decides which procedures to use, etc.? What is the decision-making machinery they use? This is a political matter.	
Writing (a) listening (b) describing (15 mins)	The students list some of the formal and informal groups to which they belong, and briefly describe how decisions are reached within them, and about what.	Identification of groups. Identification of decision-making procedures.	4a,b 5a,b
(10 mins)	Let them report back, discuss answers		and
Selection of alternative answers. (10 mins) Written opinion and justification.	Give out handout (Collect in when comp-leted - check them before next lesson)	Check on learning/ re-inforcement. Expression of student's personal personal views.	4c,5c

A correct solution cannot be calculated; instead some decision-making procedure has to be agreed upon. This introduces the concept of 'politics' at two levels. Firstly, some would say that politics is essentially concerned with such decision-making, and therefore we cannot replace the 'dirty game of politics' with 'common sense' as some would have us do (including some of our students perhaps). Secondly, the choice as to which decision-making procedure to adopt may well be, in itself, a political decision.

It is very likely that 'first come first served' will be the first suggestion made by the students. If other suggestions do not arise spontaneously, the teacher will have to introduce other factors (supposing one of the available chairs was behind the teacher's desk, and he was last in the queue; supposing one student was disabled, supposing the situation went on week after week, supposing one of the students was six feet and a bully, etc.). This approach, as lightly handled as possible, should enable the teacher to elicit the required list.

To ensure some degree of transference, he/she then goes down the list asking for real life examples of each method at work (allocation of new potatoes, seats on a bus, supplementary benefits, private housing, or whatever). In some cases, of course, it will be found that a mixture of methods is used. It is interesting to get on to such fairly recent problems as the sugar shortage, and to raise the issue of what happens when one procedure is thought to be in operation, whereas another is being used in fact, i.e. when the 'rules' are changed.

The next phase of the lesson is intended to hammer home the point that we are all members of many groups (the class, the football team, the town, the family, etc.) and that each of these groups probably has a 'procedure' for deciding such issues as the above, though this procedure may have been determined 'formally' or 'informally', and may be (by the same token) open or tacit. The students are therefore asked to list the groups to which they themselves belong, and to describe briefly how one 'formal' and one 'informal' grouping reaches decisions.

The final phase is a very simple multiple choice, which should take only a minute or two to complete, but will allow the teacher to check on the reticent students and for any blatant misunderstandings (a student has been known to answer a. to question A6, on the grounds that there is a queue when it's crowded). This is followed by an opportunity for written opinion and reasons (some students prefer this mode). These should be looked at before the next lesson in the series, and used to 'tune them in', and to lead them on to a consideration of the implications of their decisions.

(For the purpose of the exercise, this lesson has been 'timed' for a one hour slot. This is not, of course, prescriptive. Priority should be given to the first phase of the lesson, which is the most important one. Within reason, it should be allowed whatever time it seems to need in practice. Extra time could be 'won' by moving consideration of Section A of the handout to the start of the next lesson, and by curtailing - or even omitting - the last but one phase (on their own group membership).)

Students will be able to
   i. identify the groups to which they belong, and describe the methods by which they reach decisions.
  ii. Use the concept of 'decision-making procedure' in a political context.

iii. Be able to define the terms 'agenda' and 'minutes' and be able to list the conventional order of items on an agenda.

iv. Select a method of influencing public events, and justify its appropriateness in a given situation.

v. Predict who is going to be affected by given policies.

vi. Differentiate between matters of fact, matters of expert opinion, and matters for public debate, given a list of issues.

vii. Given the problem of allocating scarce resources, students will be able to describe four different methods of allocation:

be able to recognise examples of the methods in use;
be able to justify their own choice of method given a specific example;
be able to analyse the consequences of their choice; and
be able to describe how particular methods have been selected in practice.

viii. The students will have been given the opportunity to put over a point of view orally, (three minutes) in a simulation of a committee meeting, and will have received an evaluation of their performance from the tutor, and comments from their fellow students.

(These objectives are not intended to be stated precisely in behavioural terms. They vary in how complex they will be to achieve, both in terms of time required and amount of prerequisite skills, knowledge etc. needed. Some may be achieved within a few minutes, others may require further practice and development in subsequent modules. Nevertheless, they may give an indication as to priorities in the teachers organising of the students' activities and the planning of his/her own.)

3.4.7 Lesson Two : Housing

This lesson should begin with the handing back of the brief written work that the students did at the end of the first lesson. We suggest that you do not give 'marks out of ten' for the short answer section, but tick those answers that are obviously correct, and query those that are not. Discuss any discrepancies briefly with the class at this point. You will have read the paragraphs they wrote in answer to the second question. Ask for a cross section of replies to be read out, take an interest in as many of their opinions as possible, and then move on to a consideration of the implications of some of their decisions. Do this by question and answer and by asking for other students' comments. You will know who to ask from their written work, but think (before the lesson) about the factors they may have overlooked, the hard cases, and what questions to ask.

If you ran out of time at the end of the last lesson, give the short answer test quickly at this point. Check the answers orally, and use it as re-inforcement, feedback to you, and an introduction to the main part of the lesson.

You start this by asking some of them to tell you what sort of housing they live in themselves. You are looking for such answers as privately owned by their family, privately rented, council rented, student residence, etc. Then ask them how it was decided that they should have this particular accommodation. They will probably not understand this question at first, but remind them that we are considering methods of allocation of scarce resources, and elicit from them what elements come into it: being first, being able to pay the going price, having greater need, knowing someone who mattered, etc.

Having 'tuned them in', so to speak, move on to the more specific issue of allocation of public housing and ask them who will have opinions about how this should be done, and make a list of their replies, prompting them if there are any obvious gaps. Do not spend too long on this exercise: the aim is simply to get them to use their imagination in this connection, and perhaps to realise that there will be some conflict of opinion. You might also draw their attention to the fact that some groups involved are likely to be better organised and more influential than others, though this point will be picked up more fully next lesson.

Then split them into small groups of three or four. Hand out the newspaper extracts, together with the questions, if you have been able to get these duplicated. (Otherwise write them up.) Give each group one extract only, and encourage them to discuss it amongst themselves and to come to a joint conclusion. Move among them to check on any difficulties, but do not be too obtrusive as one of the intentions is to provide an opportunity to debate in a less formal 'register' should they need to. Then ask a spokesman for each group to describe the case (to the rest of the class) and their analysis of it. Open this out into a more general discussion about what their opinion of the issues is.

Student learning activity	Teaching strategy	Content development	*
Listen, discuss (5-10 mins) Reasoning	Hand back last week's work. Elicit consequences of their decisions	Feed back/reinforcement. Analysis of consequences of their choice of policy.	
Replying factually (5-10 mins)	Ask where they live, what sort of housing, how allocated.		
Imagine/guess (10 mins)	Collect list on Board. Prompt if necessary (Political parties ⟨local ⟨national Housing officers, Shelter and other pressure groups existing owners/residents, neighbours, ratepayers, etc.)	Who has opinions about allocation of housing, in the public sector in particular?	1a
Read, discuss, report back to rest of class. (20 mins)	Give out newspaper reports. They consider them, and some specific questions, in small groups.	What are these opinions?	1a
Discuss (10 mins)	Ask for their views, and elicit the criteria they are using (make them explicit - on board if suitable.	What are their opinions?	4b

* In document 2.2, 'Political literacy'

Group and individual proposals

Apart from the obvious practice in communication of various kinds involved here, the intention is to give them knowledge of what opinions do exist, practice at recognising examples of methods of allocation, and insight into the criteria on which they are basing their own judgments. (Make a mental note of individual differences here, for use in the last lesson.)

Questions on newspaper extracts

1. How does the council mentioned in the report allocate housing?
2. What reasons are given in support of this policy? If they do not say this outright, what reasons would you suppose they have?
3. Do you agree with this policy? If so, can you think of any problems that would be produced? If not, what would you recommend them to do?

HANDOUT

ALLOCATION OF SCARCE RESOURCES.

a. 'First come first served'
b. 'Market forces'
c. 'According to need'
d. 'According to status or position'

A. Which of the above methods is used in the following cases:

Allocating

1. Seats on a bus.
2. Private housing.
3. New potatoes.
4. Invalid cars.
5. A new issue of postage stamps.
6. Social security payments.
7. An old, rare, postage stamp.
8. Company cars.
9. Secretarial help at work.
10. Hospital beds.

B. Which method, or combination of methods, would you like to see used to allocate either:

1. Telephones, or
2. Parking places at the college or your place of work.

Give your reasons.

PETER HILDREW on the plight of families with nowhere to go   18. AUG. 1975

Locked doors for the homeless

MARY ROBERTS came to Solihull from Wiltshire to look for a home and a job. Eight months later, she had a steady job with the Post Office, but she and her son were still living with the friends who had temporarily agreed to put them up. The domestic strain was showing, and they told her she would have to go.

At the Solihull housing department, where she presented herself as homeless, she was turned away. A housing official went to see her friends, to remonstrate that they must take her back. After four more unhappy days and a fruitless intervention by Shelter, she threw up her job and returned to her brother's doorstep in Wiltshire, her effort to launch out on her own as a one-parent family in ruins.

The tragedy of Mary Roberts is doubly serious because there is nothing in the Government's current policy proposals for the homeless which would make any difference to her plight. Solihull council maintains that it acted properly; she had "somewhere else to go," if not the friends' house, then the relatives in Wiltshire that she had "come from." Shelter maintains the council acted improperly — by putting unreasonable pressure on the friends to take her back, and by effectively operating a residence qualification of at least eight months before accepting anyone as homeless.

This, says Shelter, is contrary to the Government's famous circular 18/74 on homelessness, which reads: "It is the authority of the area where the need exists on whom the responsibility falls for helping to meet it." But circulars are only advisory, and the Government is now coming under very heavy pressure from voluntary organisations to define exactly what it expects councils to do in terms of legal obligations.

It shows every sign of refusing. The Department of the Government's homelessness working party took 11 months to produce a desultory consultation paper, described by Lord Soper in the Upper House debate as a "wheezy, evasive document," which explained that this was not the "appropriate time" for a "legalistic approach."

Shelter has submitted a detailed list of authorities not complying with the circular, pointing out the disputes which have arisen in non-metropolitan areas where housing and social services are at different tiers of government. Not all housing authorities have accepted responsibility for the homeless even in principle, and where they have arguments have arisen over the priority categories listed in the circular.

Some councils, such as Salford, refuse to house the homeless unless they have lived in the area for nine months; they offer "repatriation" travel warrants, but in practice shunt the burden on to their neighbours. Some councils still refuse to accommodate husbands; a woman expecting a baby may be defined as a "priority family" at four, six or eight months pregnant, depending on the area.

The trouble is that homelessness is increasing everywhere, not just in London and the other cities. "I find every authority in this region thinks it has become a stopping off point for the itinerant homeless," said one Shelter organiser. But most housing managers know that the increase in homelessness is taking place mainly in their own district, and the reasons are increasingly clear.

They include the steady shrinking of the privately rented sector and the slump in housebuilding in 1973-4, but the most important trend is the increase in marital breakdown.

The non-metropolitan districts have been telling the Government that they cannot handle the homeless without more resources. Salaries for the extra staff required, and money for bed and breakfast bills should, they say, attract full subsidy, because they are not allowed by the Treasury to increase their own expenditure. But the most important resource of all is housing itself — and new building is the one area which has so far been spared from the public expenditure axe.

The crucial question in any case is not whether there are enough houses, but whether the homeless will be given first priority on those becoming available. The voluntary organisations argue that there can be no greater need than homelessness, and if allocations systems put somebody else first, then they need revising. Residence qualifications are especially harmful, acting as a barrier to mobility, and in Shelter's view reinforcing a narrow view of a housing authority's role.

But the controversy centres on the legal obligation: the voluntary organisations, and the county councils, would like a statutory duty to be imposed on housing authorities to house the homeless, similar to the duty formerly placed on social services departments under the National Assistance Act. The district councils are resisting this, but their argument that they already have a duty — under the 1957 Housing Act — to meet housing need, seems flimsy; the more substantial reason is that "priorities can only be determined by the local authority at the local level in the light of local resources" — in other words they want to retain their own freedom to decide who comes first, and to drag their heels on the homeless.

A legal obligation, like the duty on councils to look after the handicapped in their areas under the Chronically Sick and Disabled Persons Act, would shift the burden of proof. It would not stop councils putting off the homeless, but it would lead to a clear definition of who they are, and it would strengthen the moral position of the campaigning organisations.

Housey-housey out of a hat

By PETER COLE   ?1 JAN. 1975

Last night, in a London borough, saw the merging of two expressions as old as homelessness itself. "A home of your own" and "the luck of the draw" blended, happily for some, to the anger of others, as the mayor of Tower Hamlets made the draw.

In the wake of Ernie, the Maltese Government, and the secretary of the Football Association strode the mayor, Councillor George Chaney. Not a large sum of money (and a letter from every charity in the land), not a home tie with Manchester United, but a house, a place to call your own.

Perhaps the final comment on the state of housing in Britain was made in Tower Hamlets last night, with the council's frank admission that these days it's no more than a game of bingo.

To get a council house, especially if you're young and newly married, you put your name down on a waiting list currently running at 7,000, or you let your name go into the hat, pray hard, and hope that the hand of the mayor will find its way to the piece of paper carrying your name.

There are entry qualifications for the Tower Hamlets housing bingo. You must be under 30 and have lived in the borough for two years. Last night the entrants sat in hope and waited to hear if the squat was over.

As a special bonus at this first housing lottery there were 50 winners. For the rest of the year there will be 10 winners a month.

The new scheme of dealing with homelessness not by planning, not by careful sifting of applications but by throwing the problem over to the great God chance, met with some opposition. There were about 20 demonstrators from a Tower Hamlets group calling itself Faceless Homeless in the hall where the draw was taking place, and as soon as the first new householder had been drawn from the hat there were cries for the lottery to be stopped.

One of the demonstrators, Mrs Ann Mills, said that a home should be given to those most in need, not those with luck on their side. Mrs Mills squats, with her husband and five children. But old chance had one up his sleeve. Later in the draw a squatter from the same squat as Mrs Mills won himself a council house.

There were 700 under-30s at the draw, hoping to be among the drawn 50. And those who won were predictably thrilled at the news. "This is better than winning the pools," said a ventilation contractor who will now be able to think about ventilating his own house.

In fact the process was remarkably similar.

179

Flats discount for the few

housing council

By ADAM RAPHAEL

10. DEC. 1973

The Royal Borough of Kensington and Chelsea, which has one of the most acute housing problems in London, is selling off 484 prestige flats to wealthy council tenants at discounts of up to £10,000 on market value.

The borough has more than 5,000 families on its housing waiting list. Negotiations for the sale of 80 of the " higher income " flats are now in progress with the tenants who include BBC compere Jack de Manio, the actress Joyce Grenfell, a former Mayor of Chelsea, a director of a city public relations company, and several business and advertising executives. As well as discounts of up to 30 per cent, the council is offering mortgages of 10 per cent, 1 per cent under the market rate, for up to 60 years.

Mr de Manio is planning to buy his penthouse flat, which

has a terrace overlooking the Thames, for £18,900—30 per cent less than the council's valuation. He said he appreciated that he was very lucky but added that most of his neighbours appeared equally " well-heeled."

Mr Peter Senn, a Daily Mirror reporter, explained that he was hoping to buy his four-room flat for 20 per cent less than the council's valuation of £18,000. " Any suggestion that we are some sort of élite class is nonsense," he said. " We are just a lot of ordinary working people. This deal is in the interest of the council, the tenants, and the ratepayers.

" I have been on the housing list since 1957 and I badly needed rehousing. Before this I was in a basement flat infested with slugs and mice."

The chairman of the borough's

housing committee, Councillor Douglas Eaton, explained that the purpose behind the policy of maintaining separate housing lists for those earning above and below £2,500 a year was to maintain the neighbourhood's character.

" The idea behind selling these houses is that we believe that home ownership should be extended as far as possible. The Jack de Manios of this world thought that most of our ' upper income ' tenants are not all that well off."

The borough's lower income housing list is not as exclusive. The waiting list has been as high as 7,000 but many families have given up hope after years of waiting and have moved to other boroughs or out of London altogether.

" As far as we are concerned, the housing list is a farce," said

a voluntary social worker who vainly attempts to help a continual flow of families under threat of eviction.

" We have practically given up hope of getting families rehoused by the council. They just push them into bed and breakfast accommodation, which means in effect that they have to be out on the street all day."

Councillor John Keyes, the senior Labour representative on the housing committee, said the borough's policies were so disgraceful that the Labour Party would call for a district auditor's investigation.

The Labour MP for North Kensington, Mr Bruce Douglas-Mann, said that many members of the council were reactionary and stupid. " They are a damned sight better about dealing with the problems of the middle class than those of ordinary families with children," he said.

Picture, page 6 ; Crosscheck, page 11

...the year, and both are Olympic medallists

Squatters accuse council of double dealing

Housing homeless

19. OCT. 1973

BY OUR OWN REPORTER

Squatters yesterday accused their local council of hypocrisy in its dealings with the homeless. The squatters, say the Hackney council—through some of its social workers—tells the homeless to squat, and then proceeds with evictions through its legal department.

Squatters who are supporting a woman with three children who is squatting in a council property in Cecilia Road, Hackney, and who is threatened

with eviction by the council, said yesterday that they were being made the scapegoat for the council's inability to deal with its housing problems.

A small group of squatters met yesterday in Cecilia Road, where Mrs Patricia Bobb and her three children have been squatting for three months in a first floor flat which the council says it needs for a homeless family already on its list. The squatters made various accusations against the council, including a charge that houses in neighbouring streets have been left empty for months.

The squatters denied the council's claim that the majority of them came from outside London. They also denied the council's official line that squatters were simply queue-jumping on the official housing list—which now numbers over 11,000 people.

Mr Ken Tyrell, a Hackney squatter, said : " The housing list hasn't moved in two years except for slum clearance, and the odd family with special needs. It's virtually static, so how can we be queue-jumping ? "

Mrs Ann James, who has been squatting for three months in a council flat, told a story which appeared to sum up many of the causes and effects of London's housing crisis. She was evicted from her home when the private landlord decided to renovate the property in order to sell it. She was then homeless, and was given bed and breakfast accommodation by Hackney council. She was later moved out of that accommodation, and lived with a friend for a short time. But the friend was not allowed to sublet, and Mrs James was told that her foster child might be taken into care. So she squatted in the council flat.

The council said yesterday that it was concerned about illegal squatting, and had asked for possession orders on certain of its properties.

Alderman Lou Sherman, chairman of the social services committee, said that the council had people who had been legitimately and patiently waiting for a house for over 20 years. The council could not accept squatters from other areas, who had moved into the area in the past few months.

3.4.8 Lesson Three : Location of Housing

The 'issue' for this lesson is a slightly different one - that of
location rather than allocation of housing. Tell the class this, and
point out that another of the political problems involved with housing
is where to put it. This political debate can again come down to the
problem of the allocation of a scarce resource, in this case land, but
it can also be concerned with disagreements over priorities, and
aesthetics, and personal freedom, etc, etc.

The idea is that the teacher describes in some detail the piece of
land in question, and what exists on the site at the moment (see lesson
plan). The plan of the houses and land should be drawn on the board.
The students are then asked to say what land and buildings lies just outside the site. Perhaps one of them could come up to the board and draw,
again in plan form, what his colleagues want to be there. Prompt them
if really necessary, but there may, for instance, be a local park, rows
of shops, a main road, factories, a school - or there may not, of course!
Ask them to specify what sort of housing borders the site. The hope is
that this procedure will involve the students in the situation - it will
become 'their' locality, so to speak.

Having set the lesson up in this way, the teacher asks the students
to say who is going to be affected by the proposals, making a list of
groups and individuals. The students are then asked to speculate about
what point of view each is likely to have, in view of their vested
interests or known attitudes. The newspaper reports examined last week
may have given information about some of the groups, and the rest could
be commented on from the students' own experience, or just common sense.

The teacher then splits the students up into small groups, and labels
each as being one of the interests listed. They are then given a list of
possible courses of action 'their' group might adopt, and asked to select
some, in order of priority. Get them to report back on their decisions,
and discuss which actions are generally thought to be effective, which
might be counterproductive, and the difference between groups in terms of
power to influence and access to influence. The discussion will probably
broaden out into what the students themselves would decide about this
particular site.

Supposing that they were the council committee responsible for deciding this matter, what information would they require to be laid before
them so that they might reach an informed decision? Lead the class on to
this consideration (and emphasise, incidentally, that this is a Local
Government matter, at least at the outset). Make a list on the board and
distinguish between those things which are factual, if anything is (such
as the area in square metres involved, the traffic on neighbouring roads,
etc.); those matters which are not as factual, but might be a matter on
which to consult an expert (e.g. the length of time it will take to build
new houses on the site, the cost of repairing the existing houses, the
legal position, etc.) and those things which really are matters of
opinion, and therefore open for public debate, as anyone is an 'expert'.
This would presumably include things such as the comparative value of a
regency facade and extra homes, the 'atmosphere' of the area, alternative
uses for the site, etc.

(If you find that the students have difficulty in analysing the issues
in this way, it would be worth spending some time on this matter alone
on another occasion. This could be said to be a political issue, because

Group and individual proposals

one method of removing an issue from public debate is to make a claim about 'expertise' being required, or to 'convert' it into a matter of fact rather than opinion. Many students are weak in this area – there is a tendency for instance to suggest that an issue to which we happen not to know the answer is, *ipso facto*, a matter of opinion, and conversly to think that an incorrect 'fact' is an opinion. A suggested exercise is given in Questions and answers.

Student learning activity	Teaching strategy	Content development	*
Listen, imagine, create 'surroundings' for houses. (10 mins)	Teacher presents example of five houses under a compulsory purchase order. (see note 1 below)		
Answering, imagining (5 mins)	Questioning	Who is going to to be affected? (See note 2)	5a
Answering. Some recall. (10 mins)	Questioning	What are they likely to want to say?	5b
Discussion in small groups. Students select courses of action for one 'interest group'. (10 mins)	Divide class into groups of two or three. Give out list of options. Students select.	How are they going to try to try to influence event?	3a 3b
Large group discussion. (10 to 15 mins)	Leading on from their above selections, and their justifications, to what they would decide about these houses.	Why are certain actions to be preferred? What would the students decide?	
Question and answer (10 to 15 mins)	Encouraging distinction between factual info., opinion/value judgments, and 'expert' judgment.	What information do they need first?	

*
Relates to the political literacy diagram in document 2.2.

Note 1. There are five regency houses in a row that have escaped local redevelopment in the past. They have large gardens, and the land they occupy could give space for 35 two-bedroomed flats if the houses were to be demolished. They look good, but are actually in need of much restoration. Three of the houses are owner occupied; two of these have 'professional' people living in them, couples with young children; the other one is lived in by an old lady who rents bed-sits to students. The remaining two houses have absentee landlords, and are split up into flats of not very good quality. In fact, one of these houses has a badly leaking roof, and the top floor is derelict.

Note 2. For example the majority and opposition parties on the local council, the Ministry of Housing and central government, Council officials, local shopkeepers, existing occupiers, the landlords, neighbours, environmentalists, architects and planners, local homeless, etc.

Consider these possible courses of action in the discussion

Letter to the local paper.
Letter to a national paper (say which).
Letter to your local councillor or, going to see him.
Letter to your local M.P. or, going to see him.
Set up a petition.
Form an association. How would you start to do so? What would you call it?
Approach an existing association.
Get in touch with the T.V. people. Which ones? How?
Get in touch with the radio people. Which ones? How?
Put up posters in the local shops.
Get some car stickers printed.
Have a sit-in. Where?
Put a motion forward at a council meeting.
See or write to, the housing manager, or city planner, or some other full-time council official. (Say which)
March in a demonstration.
Or what else would you do?

Questions and answers

A.   Write down the number of each of the following statements, and indicate whether you think they are matters of fact (f), matters for expert judgment (e), or matters of opinion (o). If your answer is (e), say which sort of expert you would consult. If you are undecided, write (u), and say why, if you can.

   1.   London is 95 miles from Bristol.
   2.   Bruce Forsyth is funny.
   3.   This man will be fit to return to work in 10 days.
   4.   The best material for making electrical cable from is copper.
   5.   Gold is a better conductor than copper.
   6.   This court case is not worth fighting.
   7.   Books are more educative than television.
   8.   Churchill was a great man.
   9.   Chelsea is a more stylish team than Fulham.

B.   Your local council is considering knocking down a funfair in one of its parks, and replacing it with a sports centre. Describe

   a.   one matter of fact,
   b.   one matter for expert judgment, and
   c.   one matter of opinion.

3.4.9 Lesson Four : The Committee Game

This lesson can be linked into what has gone before by saying that if a question can be identified as being one of fact, then we should investigate it scientifically to determine the right answer; if it is one on which we should get expert advice, then we should go to the right expert with the right question; and if it is one of opinion essentially, then we need some public debate before taking a decision on it. One such issue 'for public debate' is the method we should use as a community to allocate the scarce resource of public housing, and one way for deciding on that is a committee meeting of elected representatives. We are going to pretend to be such a committee for a short while.

183

If at all possible, get the room set up as for an official committee meeting. Certainly get the class sitting round in a square or circle facing each other, and perhaps prepare labels to place in front of each student giving his new name.* Announce that you are going to be chairman (unless you have a student whom you think will be able to handle this complex job at the first attempt). Issue the agenda, and before you get into the role, check with them that they know the terms used on it, and discuss the reasons for having an agenda at all, and why minutes exist, why a motion cannot be put forward if it is not on the agenda, etc.

Next, issue them with their 'briefs'. There are five different ones – if there are fifteen students then there will be three 'Browns' (each with a different first name of course), and so on. In this case, one of them should present the points missed by his colleague, and the third should listen carefully to the case from the other side, ask appropriate questions, and make the final speech at the end, taking any new points into account when he does so. If there are fewer students then the arrangements can easily be adapted, but if there are many more then, very unfortunately, two meetings will have to be held in different weeks. Those not directly involved at the time can be asked to be the 'public gallery', and asked to evaluate what went on.

Be very strict about the length of time any one person speaks. Make sure that the 'Martins' do state a position by the end. It may be necessary to create amendments to the main motion; if so do this yourself and legislate about how the vote is to be taken and when. (If the group is very familiar with committee procedure, then this issue of amendments and voting could be dealt with here (with some practice voting exercises perhaps), but in most cases this will have to be reserved for a later lesson.) The idea is that there should be a genuine vote at the end, in that the issue could go either way – there are people in a position to be persuaded.

You may be able to allocate roles, to students on the basis of the opinions they have expressed in previous lessons, but do not be squeamish about setting someone the challenge of representing a view that is not his/her own.

With a small class, and if the exercise goes smoothly, you may find time at the end to discuss how well various views were expressed, what opportunities were missed, etc. To some extent, the vote may be an expression of some of this. If you can, make notes of the features of different student contributions, and at a later stage find time to discuss each one individually, if briefly, with the person concerned. At least, make notes immediately afterwards. Having a colleague present to help with this task while you concentrate on chairing the meeting can be a great help, and can check your subjective reactions.

---

* Borrowing the college board-room has been known to be very effective at setting a good, constructive atmosphere. In some colleges it may be possible to video the meeting. The resulting tension is not unrealistic.

Student learning activity	Teaching strategy	Content Development	*
Listen, recall (5 min)	Link to previous lessons. Introduction of this week's activity.	need for machinery of decision-making.	
Listen, answer (5 min)	Describe, elicit.	How one such set of 'machinery works.	2a 2b
Read, ask questions (5 min)	Allocate roles. Deal (briefly) with any queries.		
Presenting a case listening responding deciding (10 min)	Chair a simulation of a committee meeting.	Applying inform- ation and ideas acquired in earlier lessons. Practising the communication skills required by this sit- uation.	6b 7b 4b
Discuss, evaluate (5 min **)	Discuss how well views were presented, responded to, etc.	Feedback on above.	

*
   Relates to the political literacy diagram document 2.2.

**
   Should also be continued later.

Group and individual proposals

<u>Inglewood Borough Council Housing Committee</u>

Meeting to be held on Tuesday 30th February, 1976 at 7.30 p.m.

<u>AGENDA</u>

1.   Apologies for absence.

2.   Minutes of the meeting of 30th January 1976
     (previously circulated)

3.   Matters arising

4.   Allocation of the newly completed housing on the Eastwood
     Estate Extension

         Proposal: "that the new accommodation be allocated to
         those inhabitants of the Borough who are at present in
         the worst housing in terms of overcrowding and condition".

                         Proposed by   A. B. Brown
                         Seconded by   L. M. Brown

5.   Any other business

(Additional information. The Eastwood Estate was started twenty years
ago, when 2,000 houses and flats were built. An extension to the
estate is now being built - this contains 300 houses and flats.)

<u>Councillor Brown</u> You want the houses and flats to be allocated to those in greatest need. You are in favour of a points system that gives points to those families who have the most young children, the worst health, the worst living conditions at present, etc. The families with the most points are housed first.

<u>Councillor Green</u> You think that the fairest system is a very simple one – first come first served. Anyone over the age of sixteen should be able to put his or her name down on a list, in any one borough. (They do not have to be married: single people are also eligible.) They are then re-housed in strict order – no-one being allowed to jump the queue for any reason.

<u>Councillor Jay</u> You think that the new houses should be put on the market at a realistic price (10% more than it cost the council to build them, for instance). The houses will therefore go to those people who are prepared to work hard, save efficiently, and make the most sacrifices. People will have to put down a deposit of 10% and pay the rest of the money off (plus interest) over the next twenty years. If too many people want to buy the houses and flats, then the price should be increased, and the extra money used to build more houses.

<u>Councillor Sparrow</u> You think that preference should be given to those people whose families already are on the estate. In your opinion, this is the only way that a community will be built up in the area. In any case, the council should take care of its own people first.

<u>Councillor Martin</u> You are undecided at the start of the meeting. Do not put forward any strong point of view at first. Ask questions if you like, particularly if you see any problems arising out of the suggestions put forward. If you develop a clear opinion towards the end of the meeting, then put it forward. In any case, you must vote one way or the other at the end.

Acknowledgements
We thank the following for assisting in the work of the group:
Peter Fox; Inder Gera; Jack Guest; Kate Hoey; Peter Jackson;
Jean Jeffcoate; David Logan; David Morgan; Peter Morrison;
B. O'Connell; Bill Page; Margaret Rogers; Diana St John; Edward
Sallis; G. Stanton; T. Stygal; E. Sudale; Christopher Townsend.
(Linda Ankrah-Dove was a senior lecturer at Middlesex Polytechnic and
is now a lecturer at the Institute of Education, London; Geoffrey
Stanton was a lecturer at Garnett, now seconded to the DES)   Editors

3.5   POLITICAL EDUCATION AND TEACHER TRAINING
       Tom Brennan

This is a very difficult time to assess values and tendencies in teacher
training. The year of 1976 has witnessed mergers and closures of colleges
on an unprecedented scale and we are likely to witness a continuation of
this process in the early months of 1977. The decade of expansion has
ended and for those colleges which survive new ways have to be found of
catering effectively with the greatly reduced quota of teachers in institutions which are no longer monotechnic in character. The change to
higher entry qualifications and the imminent phasing out of the teaching
certificate introduces a whole series of new considerations but tutors in
some colleges are at the moment understandably more preoccupied with
devising survival strategies than with rethinking educational assumptions.
But paradoxically the current era of rationalisation and retrenchment,
together with the temporary fluidity which it engenders may offer
opportunities for new developments which the imperatives and rigidities
of the older and now crumbling structure of teacher training denied. The
old structure made virtually no provision for the encouragement of political education and for the training of teachers in politics what then
should be the place of politics in the institutions which are now being
developed?
   Originally, the intention of the Programme for Political Education in
considering the role of politics in teacher training was to see if there
was a place for 'a small adaptable unit (of study) as part of any
teacher's programme';   it was later agreed to try to obtain a picture,
however sketchy, of developments in training institutions and to consider
what steps might sensibly be recommended in the light of the situation
revealed.   Accordingly, questionnaires were sent during 1975 to all
institutions concerned with teacher training and a statement indicating
the general nature of the responses was appended to this paper. *It is
now so dated that it has not been included in this published report, but
the Hansard Society retains copies of it for loan. Editor*
   Any picture sketched from such scanty and partial evidence can be indicative only and is inevitably coloured by the observer's prejudices and
predilections. Nevertheless, it is possible to make some provisional
assessment and it is hoped that what follows will assist in the ongoing
process of discussion and provide a framework upon which a more systematic
investigation can be based.   The fundamental questions being asked at this
stage are: By what means can training institutions best be encouraged to
provide a climate favourable to the development of political education in
schools, and what provision should be made to ensure the availability of
teachers professionally equipped to undertake the task of educating for
political literacy?

3.5.1 The education course

Since the James Report and the establishment of the Diploma in Higher
Education some colleges have moved away from 'concurrent' training to
'consecutive' training models, i.e. instead of being pursued throughout
the course, theoretical and practical studies in education are concentrated in the third or fourth year of training[1]. The idea of a
'general' course in education, as opposed to discrete approaches to the
history, psychology, sociology or philosophy of education, dies hard
and all students proceeding to a teaching qualification, whether Certificate or B. Ed., are required to pursue educational studies in one form
or another;   in the past this course has figured strongly as a form of

professional socialisation. It is suggested that the most effective way of encouraging attitudes favourable to the concept of political education in all or most intending teachers at the pre-service stage lies in stressing the political dimension of educational studies and including within the education course an overtly political perspective in theoretical studies together with a consideration of the aims of political education in curriculum studies[2]. If the policy-makers can be persuaded that political education is a necessary ingredient in the core curriculum the task of persuasion would, of course, be greatly facilitated.

To achieve this end would necessitate for many education tutors an enormous shift of attitude and assumption because a recognition of the political perspective runs counter to the whole tradition and ethos of the training institutions whose task initially was to assist in the process of gentling the masses and to ensure respect for the established social order[3]. It has to be said that, in this respect, the responses to the question asked in the survey 'to what extent does the education course deal with questions of a political nature?' do not generally provide a very encouraging basis.

3.5.2 <u>Tradition and consensus</u>

The comments reflecting the approach and content of education courses under the old dispensation were in the main apolitical, ersatz-political or anti-political. Some tutors perceived themselves to be focussing significantly on political issues when discussing the comprehensive or independent schools controversies (see references in statement to 'socialist policy programme' and 'background for political ideologies'), the historical arguments on control by Church or states of the administrative context of the schools system. The roots of the present lie deep in the past and the reason for the low premium placed on the properly political aspects of the educational process are probably to be found in the values traditionally adhered to by a large number of college tutors influenced by the relatively isolated environment of monotechnic institutions which gave rise to a distinctive professional sub-culture.

Danny McDowell argues that for a long time, teacher education rested in 'an inherited set of unexamined assumptions about the nature and purpose of education and the nature of teaching which are largely irrelevant to contemporary schools and the personal and professional needs of students'[4]. The predominant emphasis in the approach of Education tutors to both theoretical and practical studies has been 'child centred' rather than 'subject centred' and there is some evidence to suggest that this both reflected and encouraged, however unconsciously, what can only be described as an anti-intellectual ethos in which pride of place was given to the capacity for 'good relationships' rather than intellectual attainment[5]. There has been a preference in educational studies for what passed as 'integration' or synthesis rather than a consideration of educational phenomena via the disciplines of sociology, philosophy etc.

Although paying lip-service to the idea of encouraging a sympathetic and questioning attitude to issues of social concern, the questions asked and issues raised were normally confined within strict limits; many teacher educators, without perhaps being aware of it, have accepted their role as agents of social control and trusted upholders of the societal *status quo*. Professor William Taylor shows how the bulk of social criticism that the dominant value orientations of teacher educators embodied were 'directed not at the major structure and economic features of society ... but the less significant and peripheral working of these larger structures[6].' Danny McDowell observes: 'In such an ethos there is no place for fundamental disagreement ... There is an impatience with politics and political issues, a relentless search for consensus[7].'

3.5.3 <u>Modern trends</u>

There have, of course, been exceptions to the pattern outlined above and the predominant assumptions have been actively challenged by the influx of young lecturers in sociology and political science who entered the colleges in the expansionist phase. The tendency has been, however, for two value systems to co-exist uneasily and sometimes explosively; the underlying intellectual and ideological tensions have yet to be finally resolved.

More positively the survey revealed a number of courses in which the approach to education is by way of the relevant disciplines, incorporating elements of philosophy, psychology, history and sociology, several of which focus on the political themes. In the more direct philosophical approach, for example, the concepts of power, authority, justice, and equality are systematically examined. One hopes that in these situations the tutors concerned take cognisance of Professor Bernard Crick's caveats on the false dichotomy between ideas and institutions and encourage their students to engage in something more than interesting but abstract discussion and consider the political relevance and ramifications of these important ideas and underline the fact that 'all ideas seek institutional realisation and institutions embody purposes[8].' (Perhaps an article in one of the educational journals written by an appropriately oriented political philosopher and systematically exemplifying this viewpoint would be helpful?) Similarly, sociology has established a foothold alongside the more traditional psychology of education; in hands of experts this can only have a beneficial influence in the analysis of educational problems bringing into question the traditional orthodoxy. The main danger is that when undertaken by those less skilled in the discipline there will be an over-readiness to succumb to the temptation to settle for a purely functional treatment and not give due weight to other perspectives[9].

Under the new dispensation a number of interesting courses usually available as options in 'unit' or 'modular' curriculum structures are being developed: these include, in addition to systematic courses in sociology, history, or philosophy, education courses under such titles as 'Ideology and Education', 'Decision-making in Education' etc. All of these, in their own way, probably serve to minimise the impact of the tendency to 'manipulative socialisation' which was implicit in the more traditional courses in education, and are certainly much more likely to create a climate more favourable to the consideration of political questions. Part of the answer to criticisms that the approach to education through distinctive disciplines is likely to create confusion and disfunction in the minds of students is that the more disciplined study at least offers opportunities for more detailed systematic analysis and encourages the students to pose questions which are educationally, socially and politically pertinent. It is, arguably, more rewarding for both tutors and students to have asked important questions than to have learned 'correct' answers. Pertinent corrections are of vital importance but they are best made by the student himself rather than being presented, pre-digested on a platter.

3.5.4 Politicisation of educational studies

If an appreciation of the role of political education is to be encouraged
in the general run of those students preparing to be teachers, the most
fundamental and urgent need is to attempt a conscious 'politicisation'
of their educational experience and knowledge. The claim can plausibly
be advanced that if this were done it would not only create a generation
of teachers more sympathetic to the idea of political education but it
would also serve important purpose of making more coherent the impact of
the myriad strands which properly inform the subject matter of educational studies. The political dimension of human experience and
educational problems has for the most part been grievously neglected in
teacher-training. It is perhaps not unreasonable to suggest that in the
rethinking which is now taking place its just claims should be carefully
considered.

That this suggestion is not wildly unrealistic is indicated by the
observations received from a large college of high reputation. This institution which submitted a thoughtful and detailed statement, set out
its approach to the study of education in the following terms:

'Students are encouraged to see the provision of education in relation
to social and political pressures in the widest sense and not simply as
the projections of a platonic ideal. For example, we attempt to foster
a consciousness that educational provision, at the macro-level of the
system and at the micro-level of the classroom, is in a state of con-
tinous change, and development and perceptions of a variety of social,
political and economic forces'[10].

This college also takes the view that the achievement of political
understanding by students is affected by the inter-relationship of the
curriculum and institutional patterns. It asks "Is not the will and the
ability to co-operate with one's fellows, to display initiative in the
management of one's affairs, to participate in decision-making and imple-
mentations, to engage in community activities, to develop a sense of
identification with others, a more potent influence in the development of
political sophistication than perhaps all the units of work academic or
educational that can be devised by student's mentors?"

This is an aspect of political education which will, in due course,
have to be investigated.

3.5.5 Academic courses

Over thirty years ago, the McNair Report on Teacher Training, concerned
to 'lay the foundations of an interest in public affairs and of the
practice of being a good citizen', recognized the value to a college 'of
having on its staff some teachers who have made a special study of the
social services and of the machinery of government, central and local;'
it also recommended that 'in each training area there should be one or
more training institutions which include these matters in their curricula
as an optional subject under the name of social studies, public administration or some similar title.' It went on to forecast that 'In some
areas the existence of a university department of Social Science will
help to meet this need'[11].

For more than a quarter of a century this modest but sensible proposal,
in common with other suggestions in the report, lay in abeyance. Indeed when
Derek Heater made a survey of the colleges in the late sixties he could
not find more than two colleges which offered anything approaching a
systematic course in political studies. No college offered a main course
in politics and government in its own right; such studies that did
exist were to be found in the form of options within other main courses,

but mainly sociology, and owed their existence to the interest and enthusiasm of individual tutors who were prepared to battle against competing claims which, at the time, had more obvious 'legitimacy' and professional appeal[12].

The implementation of the James Report on teacher-training has brought forth a small but vigorous crop of new courses wholly or partly concerned with aspects of government and politics. These are usually in the form of 'units' or 'modules' available to be taken singly as a main interest, or, in combination with kindred units, as a more specialised programme at Certificate, Dip.H.E. or degree level. Academic studies in politics in teacher-training institutions may be conceived of in three main ways: firstly, as being approached through the medium of the distinctive disciplines of political science; secondly, as part of multi-disciplinary studies; and thirdly, as dimensions with other disciplines such as history or geography. What we are primarily concerned with here are those units of study which are recognisable as falling firmly within the category of studies in political science.

Although such courses remain the exception rather than the rule, they are much more in evidence than at the time of Derek Heater's survey. Thus one college has units in Politics and Government in Britain and the U.S.A., and in International Politics; another offers Political Sociology; others include Political Theory, Public Administration, Contemporary Politics, Soviet Studies and Post-War International Relations. This development appears to stem in part from the opportunities for new courses offered by the reorganisation of colleges and the response to demands for 'diversification' and in part from the merger of former colleges with polytechnics and other institutions which already had established politics departments whose facilities were now extended to a new clientele. There are also indications that courses in other subjects like history and geography, and multi-disciplinary or inter-disciplinary subjects such as environmental studies, European studies and American studies are also more likely to take cognisance of the political dimension in their respective spheres of interest than was formerly the case. It has to be recognised, however, that colleges which offer courses which, in terms of content, would enable teachers to offer politics as a specialist subject in secondary schools, are still very few in number; an advance has been made but, viewed against the total provision of alternative courses, it is exceedingly small. The worrying feature is that the present wave of rationalisation and retrenchment will have a depressing effect on the colleges involved and that they will be forced to cut back on these courses and concentrate their efforts in the more traditional subject areas. It would be ironic indeed if the effect of reorganisation was to excise those developments which the new pattern was in part designed to achieve.

3.5.6 <u>Pre-service training</u>

If the provision of courses in the academic study of politics is minimal, the situation in respect of professional training facilities in the teaching of politics is even more deficient. The main reservoir of teachers specialising in political studies in the schools has been the limited number of political science graduates who have taken up teaching, and established history and economics teachers who have taken in the teaching of politics as an alternative, or, more usually, as a supplement to the teaching of their main discipline. Derek Heater's survey revealed that in the late sixties not a single college or university department of education offered a post-graduate certificate course in the teaching of

politics and that 39 out of 114 graduates with politics as an important
component in their degree were pursuing their post-graduate Certificate
in Education at the only three university departments, Aberystwyth, Lei-
cester and London, which provide properly planned and developed courses
in social studies[13]. Although the climate of opinion in some departments
is much more sympathetic than at this earlier stage and attempts are
being made in a few institutions to cater more satisfactorily for the
needs of politics graduates, there is still no post-graduate certificate
course which provides a fully systematic methods course for those mainly
interested in the teaching of politics. It is, in fact, those colleges
concerned with the training of teachers in further education, including
Southlands, Huddersfield and Wolverhampton, which have progressed
furthest in this direction.

Apart from the post-graduate certificate courses, methods courses are
few and far between because under the arrangements for the teaching
certificate the colleges have been inhibited from undertaking such
developments by the Balance of Training agreement. Notable experiments
have, however, been undertaken at two or three colleges. The nature of
the problem will alter when the Certificate is phased out and consideration needs to be given to the ways in which courses in the teaching of
politics can be introduced into those colleges which are now concerned
with academic courses in politics[14].

The University of York Department of Education, which houses the
Political Education Research Unit, has initiated a first degree in education and politics but, by design, is not directly concerned with
teaching methods. The University of London Institute of Education has
recently made the first ever appointment of a Lecturer in Education with
special reference to the teaching of politics. These developments are
among the most significant of the last decade and indicate that two
important centres are prepared to pave the way in an educational sphere
to which they attach importance. Now that the lead has been given it is
hoped that other centres will find it possible to follow suit.

Derek Heater's survey ended with a passionate plea for training
institutions to respond to the need to provide courses to equip teachers
of politics professionally. He wrote:

'The Training Institutions are placed in a crucial position with opportunities to investigate the most appropriate methods and to train a
body of teachers in these principles so that they will assume responsibility when they enter the schools. If even a single UDE and half a
dozen colleges were to seize these opportunities, a sense of direction
could develop to dispel the present confusion, and the way be opened up
to the education of a politically literate citizenry. Duty, challenge
and opportunity are clear, only the response is awaited'[15].

The pattern has altered, but the need and challenge remain.

3.5.7 In-service courses

Developments in in-service work in the field of teaching politics and
political education have been largely restricted to short one-day or
weekend courses offered by University Institutes of Education (including notably London, Cambridge and Belfast), University Extra-Mural
Departments (especially Newcastle and Manchester), Politics Departments
(e.g. Liverpool), and Local Education Authorities (including Northants,
Avon, Kircklees and others), and the vast majority of these courses have
taken place within the last three or four years; before this time such
courses were virtually non-existent. Welcome though this development is,
it can manifestly only scratch the surface of the problem.

Group and individual proposals

A few LEAs are now co-operating actively in teachers' groups, which it is hoped will follow up, in a practical way, recommendations of the Programme for Political Education on curriculum development. This is a promising but small-scale development and the main problem would appear to be that of financing the groups and finding an effective method for the dissemination of their findings.

A few of the University Institutes and Schools of Education, apart from London and Cambridge, have taken an interest in the work of the project and have already developed work and courses which have a close relevance. The Liverpool University School of Education houses the Schools Council Project on History, Geography and Social Science for 8-13 year olds, which has been concerned, *inter alia*, with the political education of children in the middle-school years. The University of Bristol School of Education offers a course in 'Politics, Culture and Education' as part of its programme of Advanced Studies for serving teachers. The Keele Institute runs two advanced diplomas, one of which is concerned with the Teaching of World Studies and the other with General Studies for the 16-19 age range.

It is suggested that one of the most effective ways of advancing political education in the schools in the short run would be to offer substantial training courses lasting for an academic year which would include both academic and professional studies to experienced teachers who already have some interest in this work, but feel themselves to be ill-equipped because their initial training was undertaken in other fields. This group represents a valuable reservoir of talent and enthusiasm and could make a very important contribution to the development of political education. Is it beyond the bounds of possibility that one Institute or School of Education could be persuaded to establish an advanced certificate or diploma in Political Studies perhaps following the Keele model? If an interested institute or other institution was willing to undertake the organisation of a validation of a course of this kind, it would surely not be difficult to arrange for the cooperation of associated university departments and colleges to ensure a suitable mix of academic and professional studies at the appropriate level.

It seems likely also that a few of the colleges or former colleges would be well-placed to plan and offer one-term courses for serving teachers who wish to undertake responsibility for the development of political education in their schools. It appears that the growth of in-service work generally will grow much less quickly than was hoped when the James Report was first published, and that financial constraint in local education authorities will severely limit the number of teachers who can be seconded for a term or longer. Nevertheless it would be defeatist to accept this as a continuing situation and it would be unfortunate if tentative plans could not be made in anticipation of an easing in the present restrictions.

In the last few years significant things have begun to happen in connection with the development of political education in schools, colleges and universities but it is clear that, if the venture of enhancing political literacy is to succeed, a much more systematic provision for teacher training in this field will have to be evolved. In this task, universities, polytechnics, colleges, LEAs, and the schools themselves, all have a part to play. The way forward is now fairly clear: it remains to be seen if there is the will to provide the means.

References

1. The Department of Education & Science: *Teacher Education and*

Training, H.M.S.O. 1972.

2. The only college known to me which has seriously attempted to involve all students in civic or political education is the former City of Leeds College where, in the early 1950s, there was a compulsory course in Civics. This situation presumably derived from the personal interest and commitment of the then Principal, Dr. R.W. Rich, who wrote a book on *The Teacher in a Planned Society*. I hope shortly to obtain further details on this interesting development.

3. See D.V. Glass 'Education and Social change in modern England', in A.H. Halsey and J. Flood (eds.), *Education, Economy and Society*, Collier-Macmillan, 1961.

4. D. McDowell, 'The Values of Teacher Education' in T. Burgess (ed.), *Dear Lord James*, Penguin, 1971.

5. See W. Taylor, *Society and the Education of Teachers,* Faber, 1969; F. Musgrove and P.H. Taylor, *Society and the Teacher's Role*, Routledge & Kegan Paul, 1969.

6. W. Taylor, op. cit.

7. D. McDowell, Op. Cit.

8. B. Crick, *In Defence of Politics*, Penguin, 1964.

9. See: M.A. Coulson & D.S. Riddell: *Approaching Sociology: A Critical Introduction*, Routledge & Kegan Paul, 1970.

10. Statement received from Didsbury College.

11. Board of Education, *Teachers and Youth Leaders*, H.M.S.O. 1944.

12. See D.B. Heater 'Teacher Training' in D.B. Heater (ed.), *The Teaching of Politics*, Methuen, 1969. For a description of the relevant courses in one of the colleges, see T. Brennan, 'Studying politics in a college of Education', *Education and Social Science*, July, 1969.

13. D.B. Heater, ibid.

14. D. Robins and A. Kidd of Worcester College of Higher Education are currently preparing a paper provisionally entitled 'Politics, Teachers: Initial Training and Employment in 1975-6'. The core of this investigation involves (i) the collection of PGCE, B. Ed. and Cert. Ed. figures for teachers completing initial training in 1976 who were deemed to have the 'ability to teach politics', (ii) the collection of data on the employment of 1976 college leavers with special reference to the proportion who actually found posts involving the teaching of Politics.

15. D.B. Heater, Op. cit.

(December, 1976)

The following met on one occasion only, under the chairmanship of Tom Brennan:

Mr. G.N.D. Beavan, Crewe & Alsager College of Education
Mr. C.H. Brown, West Midland College of Education
Mr. D.P. Gabriel, Madeley College of Education
Mr. B.M. Jones, Sheffield College of Education
Mr. E. Fearn, Sheffield College of Education
Mr. P.G. Squibb, Bingley College

They agreed to the form of the enquiry to be undertaken, were informed of its results, and agreed to the content of the Chairman's report.
Editors

4

THE TEACHING PROGRAMMES IN COOPERATING SCHOOLS AND COLLEGES
Alex Porter

4.1 INTRODUCTION

Having set out the theory in the project documents and then arranged for working groups of teachers to suggest what this might mean in practice, individual teachers were then encouraged to try out the suggestions together with their own ideas in their schools.

This was done to study the feasibility of the theory of the project and the suggestions and ideas based on the theory: to provide a commentary on how they could be implemented in the classroom. It therefore involved identifying the difficulties of implementation and concentrating on those aspects which presented least difficulty and greatest opportunity and scope for development on the project's lines. The reactions of teachers and college and school students (hereafter 'students') to the details of implementation could also be observed; and all of this could be studied in as great a variety of contexts as resources allowed. The schools were selected to provide both a self-contained group of broadly representative contexts for the purposes of comparative study, as well as to provide a range of institutions which would complement those selected by the York Research Unit.

The conclusions which follow are really little more than a general summary of the separate commentaries on the teaching programmes given later. There were too many variables for reliable comparisons to be made between the different teaching circumstances and the sample was too small for generalisation to be anything other than tentative. Nevertheless some general conclusions appear to emerge. The evidence for these

conclusions is set out at some length so that the reader can make a reasonable judgement of how far the inferences are valid.

This section is mainly a commentary on each of the teaching programmes
in six schools. These commentaries and the accounts given of selected
lessons have been derived from a systematic analysis of field notes, interviews and lesson observation schedules. The particular pictures which
have been developed must depend ultimately on the criteria and the techniques which were used for defining and collecting relevant data, and for
subsequently analysing and presenting it. (So that the reader can make
up his/her own mind on the reliability and validity of the commentaries,
the Appendix on page 240 sets out detailed accounts of the research
design, its application and modification in practice and of the criteria
of evaluation employed in the analysis. This Appendix also explains our
useage of terms, such as 'successful', 'consistent', 'residual', 'specified practice', 'incident' etc., which are used frequently.)

4.1.1 The Teaching Programmes - Construction, context and content

The six schools observed can be grouped into two fairly discrete categories: those whose programmes were developed for the project to include
distinct elements of political education and those whose programmes
existed already, with different objectives, and to which project objectives were later adapted.

School A had devised its teaching programme, a general course for
fourth and fifth years, during the first year of the project and quite
independently from it. Nevertheless, the programme embodied nearly every
feature of the political literacy specifications and was perfectly suited
to the project without modifications. School F, after reading our specifications in the project documents, devised the politics modules for
its social education programme and tried to cover these specifications as
closely as possible. College E had a choice of examination courses to
allocate to the project. After one had been agreed, the teaching syllabus was extensively amended so as to give complete priority to the project specifications.

However, in School B the teaching syllabus continued to reflect closely
the history examination syllabus of which it formed only a small part.
To meet the project specifications certain emphases were made and some
parallels were drawn between the historical material of the syllabus and
contemporary institutions. Similarly in School D, the examination syllabus dominated the programme and although it was exclusively concerned
with political institutions, there were difficulties in adapting it to
the project specifications. And in School C, the history teaching syllabus had existed for some time prior to the project. As in School B,
emphasis was given to those parts which appeared to accord with the project specifications but the fundamental objectives of the history syllabus dominated throughout.

Other classifications are possible, but these turned out to be less
significant than those mentioned above. The programmes can be divided
into those which were taught through traditional curriculum subjects
(history in the case of these studies) and those which were predominantly
politics courses. However, this division is rather obscured by other
factors. Of the two history programmes one, in School B, was a small
part of a two-year non-examination programme. Two of the politics
courses were directed towards external examination, making three examination courses altogether. The programmes in Schools A and F were politics modules incorporated with general social education courses. Also the
proportion of courses devoted to the programme ranged from the full

197

Table I The programmes in their school settings

	A State Comprehensive	B State Secondary Modern	C Independent	D Independent	E F.E. College	F State Comp. & Community coll.
The School	Coed. 11-16	Coed. 11-16	Boys 13-19	Boys* 13-19	Coed. 16+	Coed. 11-18
	675 students	1200 students	500 students	600 students	850 full-time 3000 pt.-time	1250 students
	Small village	Small coastal town	Near small coastal town	Small country town	Inner-city suburbs	Small coastal town
	Recently a sec. mod. intake	Grammar school nearby	Mostly fee-paying boarders	Mostly fee-ing boarders	Split between 3 sites	Formed from amalgamation of grammar & two sec. mod.
The Programme Basic subject	Social education	History GCE	History	Government & Politics GCE	Government & Politics COS	Social education
Age group	14/15	14/15	13/14	16/17	17+	14-16
Approx. class size	50	30	25	14	5	30
Weekly t/t allocation to subject	1 x 40 mins	2 x 80 mins	3 x 45 mins	1 x 43 mins + 1 x 86 mins	1 x 120 mins	1 x 75 mins
Proportion of year's t/t given to project	Spring term	4 weeks	Full year	Full year	36 weeks	4th yr - 9 wks 5th yr - 7 wks
Objectives	Distinctly political educ.	Adapted for project	Adapted for project	Adapted to project	Distinctly political educ	Distinctly political educ.
Emphasis	All aspects	Concepts	Concepts	Concepts	Issues	Issues

*A few girls in sixth form

course, two years in the case of School F, down to about six weeks in the
case of School B.

A further classification that can be made concerns the basic way in
which the project specifications were adapted. The two history programmes were intended to concentrate almost exclusively on the political
concepts. This narrow but intense approach was largely determined by
the nature of the subject and some of the ensuing difficulties are described below. In School B's programme a little more mention was made
of the recommended knowledge and issues than in School C, but this was
within a much shorter programme. The teaching programme of School E
also featured certain political concepts.

The other three programmes paid particular attention to political
issues rather than concepts. These three also, therefore, included the
kinds of knowledge etc. prescribed by the project although not necessarily ordered on the lines of the political literacy diagram. School A's
programme was the only one which paid attention through gaming and
simulation to skills and consequently it dealt with political concepts
in quite a different way to the two history programmes. This programme
also featured some of the procedural values in the same direct way.

The teaching programmes which were most successful were those which
were devised after the project had made its initial recommendations
rather than those which were adapted to the project. Here the comparison
is being made between similar courses rather than among all courses.
This factor appeared to be more important than the nature of the course.
To be precise, those teachers who constructed a new coherent teaching
programme around the project recommendations were more successful in
implementing the recommendations than those who in good faith intended to
adapt their usual teaching programme on an *ad hoc* basis as the opportunity presented itself.

The general non-examination courses tended to be more successful than
the others which used history or British government. This was because,
for both the teacher and the students, the basic subject objectives
were always dominant. These objectives therefore present constraints on
the time and on the opportunity to make significant innovations. For the
history teacher, the subject objectives may be quite different from the
project objectives. In the case of British Government examination
courses, there is an awkward tension between the objectives: the teacher
naturally feels the need to stress the examination syllabus' objectives
in order to distinguish those from the project objectives. Drawbacks
inherent in the use of history or political science as a source of analogous material is referred to later.

It was not possible to evaluate success by the proportion of time given
to the project. Time promised to the project ranged from the full year
down to a few weeks. In practice the time actually devoted to the project recommendations was less than promised - in some cases a little less
and in others considerably less. It could be concluded tautologically
that the more time actually given to the project, the more successful the
programme was. But a more accurate observation is that the more successful the teacher was in the implementing project recommendations, the more
time was given consequently to these recommendations. Moreover, in the
most successful cases, detailed and enthusiastic planning was undertaken
for the allocation of more time to, and/or more opportunities to engage
in teaching, the project objectives.

The use of issues as a vehicle for political literacy is a fundamental
recommendation in the project Documents. (See, for example, document
2.1, paragraph 10 or document 2.2, paragraph 3.) This was interpreted in

199

various ways. The more successful programmes were planned to focus on one or two issues and to explore them in depth. Those programmes which touched on several issues per lesson or which were not planned but rather were opportunist, exploiting issues as they arose incidentally in the lesson, were markedly less successful. The more successful programmes dealt with issues to which the students could themselves relate. Issues of political science and, in particular, historical issues were far removed from their experience.

Within our small sample the use made of political concepts did not appear to relate to any observed factors. There were no apparent differences between the frequency of use of concepts in those programmes based on issues and those based on concepts, between those devised for the project and those adapted to it, or between the various subject bases etc. For the time being, therefore, we are unable to suggest the conditions which will be more conducive to the coverage of political concepts. It may seem trite but is probably true to say that the variations observed could depend a lot on the educational background and the confidence of individual teachers.

The use of 'procedural values' is considered in the section which follows.

4.2 GENERAL COMPARISON OF THE PROGRAMMES EXAMINED

We must consider the different settings, school atmospheres and patterns of classroom interaction of the places observed.

The differences between the secondary modern, comprehensive, further education and independent contexts were interesting because they did not all correspond to expectations. The teaching programme in the secondary modern school was at least as successful as those in the independent schools. The students at independent schools had a wider general knowledge, but on the other hand appeared to be much less interested in political issues and problems. These two characteristics tended to balance each other out. The students at the secondary modern and comprehensive schools participated in lessons with greater enthusiasm and less knowledge. Their growing knowledge served to fire their enthusiasm even further.

There were no important differences between the success of programmes taught to the part-time further education students and those taught to the full-time school students. Part-time students are more interested in the end-product of their course and a little impatient about embellishments which are not strictly confined to the syllabus; these facts presented a slightly greater challenge to the teacher.

In the coeducational schools the girls generally appeared less willing to answer, or to ask questions. Question and answer, being, after all, a basic and primary form of participation, this could prove significant.[1] As no single sex girls schools were involved in the study, no observations can be made as to whether a class of girls alone might present greater or lesser difficulties for the teacher.

The effect of the age of students is slightly obscured. The older (16-19) students were studying to examination syllabuses and claimed to

1 See Stradling, R., *The Political Awareness of the School Leaver* (Hansard Society, 1977). This survey of political ignorance among school leavers conducted in 1976/7 shows that boys had significantly more political knowledge than girls on all five indices used. This raises important questions. Is politics thought to be a boy's subject? If so, then by whom? By boys, or by girls?

be less satisfied with teaching which did not appear to be directing them towards effortless examination success. On the other hand the older students had a greater general knowledge, especially of current affairs, and they were more confident when participating in lessons. The younger (13-15) students, it seemed, had more open minds and were more ready to enquire and to learn. The older students had deeper prejudices and tended to be cynical rather than simply sceptical. Those teaching programmes with the younger age groups were generally more successful.

All the schools were similar in their characters – very friendly, relaxed and welcoming. Students were happy and cooperative. They were not the sort of places where, for example, one would expect truancy and discipline to be a problem. The FE college had a slightly different atmosphere. As most students were older and a large majority were part-time, they seemed to have a keener sense of their rights. Most staff were sensitive to this and there was a more relaxed and natural relationship between staff and students – a mutual respect. In the schools, although the teachers associated with the project were all exceptionally conscious of the personalities and rights of their students and were all very highly regarded by them, there was a much greater likelihood of the students encountering other staff who would treat them quite differently. In two of the schools in particular, the students had a poor view of teachers in general, referring to them as unjust, arbitrary and oppressive. Whereas in the three other schools there was a generally more relaxed and informal relationship between most teachers and students and considerable give and take in the expression of opinions, the choosing of what to discuss and so on. Inasmuch as the usual processes of decision-making tended to involve the students and in that the teachers tended to be less arbitrary or authoritarian, the atmostphere in these schools (and the college), as far as the project specification is concerned, could be regarded as not undemocratic – at least fewer things seemed to go on which negated democratic values. The project recommendations were implemented notably more successfully in these more 'democratic' schools.

Much of what has so far been remarked about degrees of success probably has rather less to do with the teaching programme or type of school etc., and rather more with the style of teaching. The most significant of the differences could be attributed to this; and variations existed not only between the participating teachers but even between lessons given by the same teacher. To dispose of a few variables, there were some characteristics which made apparently no significant difference. These were use of blackboard or overhead projector, use of books, use of written exercises, the general level of noise (up to a point) in the class and the amount of individual attention given to the students. The problem of low levels of general knowledge has been mentioned above, but this was adequately compensated for in some classes by the use of prepared handouts, films, tapes or other devices such as outside speakers.

Without doubt the most important feature was the extent to which, and the way in which, teachers enabled their students to participate in the teaching programme.

For example, it was possible for teachers to take an issue, to show with admirable objectivity and empathy the differing viewpoints and groups associated with it as per the political literacy scheme, but for the students to be wholly unaware of these references having participated in the lessons only to the extent that they were physically present in the room at the time.

There were a wide variety of ways in which students were enabled to become involved in lessons. The objectives of the course and/or of the

lessons were discussed with them. They were involved in the course planning and given some choice in the course or lesson topics; or they were
involved in determining the direction, pace and content of the teaching.
Their active participation in lessons was extended in various ways.
Their interest and therefore awareness was heightened by such things as
those mentioned above or by the skills of the teacher. Appropriate use
of questions improved participation although never as much as student-
dominated discussions did. A sure indication of student interest and
participation was a high frequency of student-initiated questions and
spontaneous comments (what some teachers might regard as interruptions
to their well-prepared lessons). Small group work and especially gaming
and simulation exercises resulted in a very high degree of involvement
for most students. A further (and possibly unusual) technique was to
conduct a post-mortem analysis of lessons.

This close correlation between student participation and the success
of the programme arises not simply because some of the project recommendations depend on such participation, but also because it seems likely
that the teaching and learning of concepts and procedural values in
particular is better undertaken in this way than by the formal stance
of lecturing. The teachers invariably encountered difficulties when
attempting 'straight' explanations of political ideas. The chances of
success increased with more versatile and adaptable teaching language
and style. Douglas Barnes' comments on a history lesson observed in
1969 could have been written for many of the lessons observed in these
studies.

"For all this teacher's vividness and flexible variation of intonation
and vocal quality, one cannot but feel that this would have been
better done with the aid of pictures, and by the pupils talking more
than the teacher.
    It is not difficult to point to several passages ... in which the
teacher's intentions could probably have been carried out more effectively if visual or other materials had been available. Yet this does
not seem to exhaust the implications of the domination of lessons by
language - and mainly the teacher's spoken language it should be
noted. <u>The domination seems to amount to an unintended restriction</u>
<u>on the kinds of learning which go on in the classroom.</u>"[2]

The use of visual materials has been remarked on above and it was noted
that only insofar as they compensated for lack of general knowledge did
they affect the success of lessons. The point being emphasised here is
the use of language. Several lessons depended on a question and answer
routine. Most were 'factual' or 'closed-reasoning' questions[3] which
were used to elicit quickly a single acceptable response or an acceptable response from an understood narrow range of options. If an acceptable response was not quickly forthcoming, the question was either re-
formulated or answered by the teacher. Thus the student is, by this
method, being used by the teacher to set up a 'cue' for the next predetermined piece of the lesson. Where this method is used the student is
actually hindered in reasoning about policies, procedures, attitudes,
alternatives, etc. and consequently the teaching was not consistent with
the project specifications.

2 Barnes, D., Britton, J., and Rosen, H. *Language, the Learner and the*
  School, (1969), p. 64 (emphasis added)
3 For a general taxonomy of teachers' questions see Barnes, Britton and
  Rosen p. 17

Analogies were quite commonly employed to add 'colour' to the lessons. The use of analogies is characterised by greater pupil response and interest. This in turn appears to reinforce the teacher's approval of this technique. However, interviews with students indicate certain problems. The direction of the analogy is important because, to be of any use whatsoever, the analogous example must be familiar. It is impossible to teach the unfamiliar by reference to the obscure. The British political system in the twentieth century cannot be explained by reference to events in the nineteenth century, or to eighteenth century France, if the latter are also unfamiliar. There are as many difficulties when these analogies are reversed, for students appear to receive analogies as low-status material which serves a limited purpose but which is not necessarily to be remembered. Thus the political illustrations are forgotten.

Simulations and the use of examples drawn from the students' own experience provided more appropriate analogies, more opportunities for student talk and involvement and less chance of teacher dominated lessons.

4.3 GENERAL CONCLUSIONS

Thus, from this limited evidence (detailed in the commentaries which follow), the circumstances most conducive for a successful teaching programme appear to ideally be as follows. The style of teaching and general atmosphere of the school should be versatile, open and reasonably 'democratic', that is, enabling considerable student participation in as many aspects of the programme as possible. If the students are not actually involved in the preparation of the programme and the selection of subject matter based on the objectives of the programme, then the objectives and the means to those objectives should be made explicit to them and they should have a chance of criticising them. The course should be taught by a group of staff and the procedure in lessons should depend as much as possible on student contributions and actuations. It should have been devised with predominantly moral, social and political education objectives rather than adapted from, or to, a course with other competing or overriding objectives. The political literacy objectives are best conveyed through a programme and lessons which consider a limited range of issues supported by 'packaged' presentations of background information. The successful programme is one which has been constructed in accordance with these factors and is considered by the staff to be a crucial part of the school's curriculum.

We found no evidence that an indirect approach, on which we had earlier pinned some hopes, would work. The problem may be simply too difficult and the motivations too low if politics is only considered through something else.

In short we believe that the accounts which follow provide ample evidence that political literacy teaching is only really successful where it is done through courses which have been constructed with exclusively political literacy objectives.

4.4   THE CASES

4.4.1 School A: Comprehensive

This was a coeducational five form entry 11-16 school located in a rural community. Although now classified as a Comprehensive School it was until recently a Secondary Modern. It is a school that is likely to continue to have generally lower than average ability students for the foreseeable future.

It was suggested as a possible school for project purposes by a member of the Working Party with some knowledge of the school curriculum. A point of particular interest arose from a change in the staff involved during the observation period. The original contact had been with the head of social studies who was responsible for devising the teaching programme and coordinating the rather complex teaching arrangements. During the Autumn term she accepted another appointment commencing from the beginning of the Spring term, coinciding with the start of the political education component of the social studies programme. The interest was therefore the question of to what extent the teaching programme could survive the departure of its author and organiser.

The Teaching Programme: The syllabus reproduced below is a slightly abridged version of a handout prepared, for members of the social studies department, before the school had been approached about participating in the project. The handout was itself a slightly amended version of a syllabus taught in the previous academic year. The 'focal points' are a summary, for students, of the political education objectives which include virtually all the political literacy specifications.

Objectives: Through the experiencing, analysis and understanding of issues that arise as a result of differing opinions (conflict), to trace the action, and the mechanisms of change.

CONFLICT - ACTION - CHANGE

Focal points to which reference should be made throughout:
(a) How individuals and groups come towards a point of action or reaction (the dynamics of change)
(b) What is positive and what is negative in action, drawing from current examples (industrial action, Ireland, Spain, etc.)
(c) What is socially acceptable and socially unacceptable
(d) The process of change and the part the individual takes in it (or does not take) - a realisation of the responsibility of the individual

Media: Video; film; visiting speakers from appropriate sources (councillors, M.P., local specialist groups) - debate; simulation; tape; written work; radio; TV; press.

January 9: Explanation of terminology. What we mean by the words 'conflict' 'action' 'change' 'authority'. Draw from local press examples to illustrate. Outline the course. Distribute pupils' hand-outs and explain the requirements of the exercise. Devise school-based situation. Give verbal instructions and supportive handouts. Situation must be easily identifiable. Divide into groups; role play; question and answer sheet.
January 16: Move from personal situation within the immediate environment into the community. Show BBC TV film *Last Bus* to illustrate local

and personal action theme. Identify conflict/action/change theme, and
questions posed by the film.

   Moral issues will naturally arise, but emphasis lies in the direction
of 'personal responsibility' of the individual towards his neighbour, the
group, as well as the rest of society.

January 30: Move forward into the immediate community. Where does
action really start? How does it start? - A study of the techniques of
local procedures. This is designed as an information session, outlining
what the local council is, how it is elected, the role of the ratepayer
and the councillors. Councillor P. and two other members of B...
Council will discuss a local problem - probably one on which there is not
complete agreement, but is one which is under discussion currently. The
three visitors will represent different political groups, and they will
also explain the procedure as they go along.

February 6: Simulation Game: *The Swimming Pool*. Invite speaker to represent 'anti' ratepayer, and headmaster to speak in favour. Game di-
vides pupils into groups representing different local areas of opinion,
with the specific task of carrying through their wishes. The game aims
to show how political and social groups and pressure groups play an important part in policy formation and decision-making, as well as opening
up the range of activities a group can engage in in order to win others
to support it.

February 13: Where does power really lie? For the purpose of this
exercise 2 major groups have been chosen: <u>the Trade Unions</u>: <u>the Govern-
ment</u> The Trade Unions - give some insight into the growth of the movement, its role and power. Show video-film from TV *Scene* programme.

February 27: Simulation Game: *Tea-break*. Simulation of industrial action, showing how groups differ in reaction, how the managers exert their
power on employees and vice versa. An exercise in resolving conflict.
Invite speaker to represent manager.

March 5: The Government - The rights and privileges of the voter. How
do you get to know about politics? Who do you vote for? What are M.P.s
supposed to do, and do they do it? What do we mean by democracy?

March 12: Visit to Houses of Parliament. Meet M.P. and invite him to
take the session there.

March 19: Follow up on Parliament visit - reinforce variety of roles
played. Ask for questions on the efficiency and effectiveness of the system. Pupils to complete questionnaire (an evaluation exercise).

March 26: Rights and privileges of young people.

   and   Divide into groups to prepare a 'Young People's Charter'.

April 2: A chance for the pupils to air their own views on what they
might like to see changed. Make into a display, school news-sheet or
wall newspaper.

   The context of this course is important for it stands as an integral
part of a much larger social education programme. The full programme
takes up one afternoon per week in the fourth and fifth years. The first
half of the afternoon is usually a classroom based session whereas in the
second half the students are subdivided into small optional group activities many of which are community service type activities based outside
the school. The political education course therefore occupies half an
afternoon (1.30 p.m. to 2.45 p.m. approx.) per week during a ten/eleven
week term.

   Six of the teaching staff of the school worked together in the programme and, in addition to these, speakers and other participants from
the local community (police, youth workers, clergy, university staff,
councillors, etc.) were also regularly involved in this 'team' effort.

The teaching programmes

Four visits were made to the school, lessons were observed, and staff and students were interviewed. The observer also accompanied staff and students on a visit to the Houses of Parliament and interviewed the students there.

The selected lessons: A

<u>Simulation Game *Tea-break*</u> The class was regarded as a factory. One teacher appointed three students as foremen and divided the remainder into three approximately equal groups, each representing a shop producing different components. Each shop was asked to choose a shop-steward. Another adult (an invited 'outsider'), who remained concealed in another room, took the part of factory manager. He used the foremen to take messages to the three shops to the effect that their tea-break would be reduced from ten minutes to five minutes because the workers had been taking longer than the ten minutes allowed. Messages passed back and forth between shops and manager, via foremen, shops were treated differently, meetings were held; and eventually there was confrontation between the shop stewards and the manager. The lesson concluded with an analysis of the events.

<u>The setting*</u>
1. A large room (30m x 15m approx.) with easy chairs which doubled as a senior students' common room, with coffee and music, and as a teaching base. It had a generally neutral atmosphere with neither the common room or classroom atmosphere dominating. (It was the room which was usually used for this course).
2. Although there was a blackboard on one long side there was no consistent focal point and the easy chairs were casually arranged and continually rearranged. On this occasion they were in three groups of about fifteen during the game and then turned towards the 'back' of the room for the concluding analysis.
3. The lesson commenced with a teacher, standing in the middle of a disarranged and barely attentive group, giving the introductory instructions. No formalities preceded this and the activity got underway promptly. For most of the lesson there was no adult fulfilling the usual teacher's role. The three adults in the room sat with the three groups to 'help things along' if necessary (see 6). The proceedings were directed mainly by the foremen and subsequently by the shop-stewards. The concluding session was chaired by the manager who sat in the middle of the class.
4. Clearly the teaching style was 'democratic' in that the students were enabled to shape the material of the lesson. The student participation and interaction was the resource material which was eventually analysed jointly by students and adults.
5. The general atmosphere was one of intense activity with all students involved for most of the time. The relationship between students and between students and adults was extremely relaxed.
6. Most (of the teacher) interaction took place between students. The adults present in the groups assumed three roles. They either answered students' questions such as "Can we go on strike without the approval of the union?" or they prompted consideration of various aspects of the issue. They also encouraged participation from the otherwise shy or relunctant members of the group. The concluding session involved as much inter-student discussion as teacher-initiated questions.
The numbering in the commentaries on Schools A to E follows the format of the schedule reproduced on page 207.

Table II Schedule for analysis of field notes*

The setting	The lesson content
	(a) Consistency with project specif-ication & proportion of lesson
	(b) Summary of subject
	(c) Examples of typical lesson activity - teacher behaviour
	(d) " student/class behaviour
1. Characteristics of room	1. Mention of political Issues a. b. c. d.
2. Seating arrangement	2. Coverage according to P.L. Tree cols. 1-3: Knowledge a. b. c. d.
3. Teacher station	3. Coverage according to P.L. Tree cols. 4-7: social responsibility and action Skills a. b. c. d.
4. Teaching style	4. Use made of political concepts a. b. c. d.
5. Classroom atmosphere	5. Use made of procedural values a. b. c. d.
6. Lesson interaction	6. Residual category a. b. c. d.

*This schedule is derived in part from Table III which appears on page 242.

The teaching programmes

<u>The lesson content</u> (The observer chose to remain with one group throughout the game. This schedule therefore represents a partial, though probably representative, view of the lesson).

1. (a) All was consistent albeit mostly concerned with a simulated issue.
    (b) The general issue was industrial democracy. The dispute was initially over the method, the way in which the origin decision was taken. This developed into disputes about goals and values. The whole lesson was concerned with these topics for the students continually discussed the way in which they should act out the simulation.
    (c) (The 'teacher' in this analysis is both the teacher who sat in with the observed group and the other adult who led the concluding discussion.) Apart from the initial stimulus, it was not necessary for the teacher to identify more than a few aspects of the issue as they mostly arose naturally.
    (d) Students identified the issues. The reaction to the initial stimulus was for example "It isn't right that he (the manager) should make that decision without consulting us first".

2. (a) Over 90 per cent of the lesson was consistent and most of the specifications were covered.
    (b) Most attention was given to the appropriate ways and means of influence for the particular issue, although all but one of the other items were adequately covered. There was no consideration of alternative procedures, industrial systems and ways of looking at industrial disputes. They were only enabled to have two views from within the given frame of reference.
    (c) The teacher answered questions concerning the usual procedure or raised the question of the efficacy of particular decisions.
    (d) The students suggested different procedures. They simulated usual procedures without any prompting, for example, a shop stewards committee with a convenor.

3. (a) 100 per cent of the lesson was consistent assuming that a stimulated issue qualifies.
    (b) The lesson was dominated by expressions of self-interest at first. Communication with other groups produced compromises and a common interest. The concluding analysis provided a full consideration of the interests of the management.
    (c) The role of the teacher in this respect was mainly to encourage expressions of justification for feelings and actions.
    (d) Following on from above, the prompted views of the less extrovert students was instrumental in clarifying these justifications. Such students usually counselled caution or expressed sympathy for the management's position.
    In particular, within its own limitations, the simulation provided ample opportunity for experience of conflict and for participation.

4. (a) About 80 per cent of the lesson was consistent. This remarkably high proportion appeared to be a direct consequence of the nature of a simulation whereby a political issue is 'brought alive' and consequently so also are political concepts.
    (b) All concepts except 'Individuality' were implicit at various stages.
    (c) The concepts of 'Force' and 'Order" were introduced by the 'factory manager'. 'Force' was concerned with a threatened lockout and 'Order' was considered in the concluding discussion.
    (d) All the other concepts were implicit or explicit in the students' discussion.

208

5. (a) About 50 per cent of the lesson was consistent. This high pro-
    portion was probably a consequence of the subject matter and the way
    it was handled, that is to say, by a process of role playing,
    discussion and analysis which, in the concluding session, involved
    all four adults. No Episodes could be regarded as inconsistent.
    (b) 'Freedom' and 'Reasoning' predominated in the lesson. 'Fairness'
    and 'Toleration' were occasionally implied but were restricted to the
    fairly narrow context of the simulated issue. There was no observed
    consideration of 'Truth'.
    (c) Both 'Freedom' and 'Reasoning' were facilitated by the teacher
    who led the concluding analysis.
    (d) On one occasion the group debated the fairest procedure to adopt
    about the threatened strike action in order to obtain consultations
    with management.
6. (a) All residual Episodes were neutral and occupied less than 5 per
    cent of the time.
    (b/c) These included the introductory and the intermediary instruct-
    ions by the teacher and the giving of information about or discussing
    exclusively industrial matters.
    (b/d) The students were also involved in discussing industrial
    matters and, occasionally, their own affairs while arranging chairs
    or awaiting the outcome of discussions between shop stewards, fore-
    men and management.

The selected lessons: B

'Young People's Charter' The class was to discuss and prepare a charter
of rights which young people should have in relation to the family, local
community and society at large. This was explained by a teacher in the
first ten minutes and some initial ideas given. The class was then divided into three groups. (A concluding session was to follow a week
later).
The setting
1. The same room as for lesson A.
2. Three groups of about ten students throughout.
3/4. A fairly formal beginning with one teacher taking control from the
'front' of the class. This was followed by informal discussion groups.
The initial role of the teacher was that of dictating instructions. The
discussion groups each had one adult present whose role developed into
that of chairman (see 6).
5. The atmosphere was that of interested, though not heated or particularly enthusiastic, discussion.
6. The intention had been that the groups should produce their own
chairman and that the adults should, as in lesson A, merely 'help out'.
As chairmen did not materialise and as discussion flagged the adult
assumed this responsibility. Most of the interaction focussed on the
chairman and only a small proportion took place between students.
The lesson content (The observer chose to remain with one group throughout the lesson)
1. (a) All was consistent although the topics discussed ranged from the
    immediate and practical to the remote and theoretical, even hypo-
    thetical.
    (b) The subject matter (even within one group) ranged widely from
    family issues of privacy and holidays to national issues of the fran-
    chise. Here also the central debate was over procedures but this
    extended to considerations of values and then goals. Much of the
    subject matter was not wholly political but only political in part

or by positive analogy with similar political issues.

(c) The teacher elicited issues from time to time by asking, for example, "What sort of things that affect you in school do you think are not fair?"

(d) Students provided examples and furthered the discussion in response to the teacher's or other students' prompting.

2. (a) About 40 per cent of the lesson was consistent and most of the specification was covered, albeit briefly.

(b) More attention was paid to the appropriate ways and means of influence for each issue raised. This became more generalised when school-based issues were considered.

(c) The teacher introduced various aspects of the specification into the discussion by asking, for example "How does the headmaster normally deal with that?" or "What is the law on this matter?"

(d) The students provided evaluation of various procedures for influence from their own experience.

3. (a) Over 90 per cent of the lesson was consistent. Indeed, the lesson was devoted almost entirely to considerations of self-interest and social responsibility.

Here, it was particularly notable that parts of the lesson were potentially and actually inconsistent. Although the central issue concerned young people's rights, there was no provision for the practical exercise of rights. As could have been anticipated discussions generated strong views and a sense of injustice among some students. It was as if the teachers had expected these feelings to stop when the lesson stopped. When some students wanted to take action (regarding the reduction of the morning break and availability of rooms), they were gently discouraged from expressing their views outside the 'make-believe world' of the classroom.

(b) There was a rough balance between considerations of self-interest and the interests of others. There was as much determination to represent and understand the interests of parents, teachers and other adults in authority as to assert young people's interests.

(c) The teacher's role was minimal, mainly extending to regulating contributions.

(d) The students were very forthcoming in representing all sides to each issue which was considered. Most were able, for example, to give an opinion as an elder or younger brother/sister and even as an uncle or aunt – usually very conservative views.

4. (a) Over 70 per cent of the lesson was consistent, although most of the incidents were inevitably concerned with the popular concepts and, interestingly, 'Individuality'. All the relating concepts were used although 'Pressure' received surprisingly little attention. 'Authority' was used frequently in a wide range of contexts. 'Power' and 'Order' were used only in the context of school-based issues.

(b) Most of the consistent Incidents concerned 'Rights', 'Freedom', 'Welfare'.

(c) The concept of 'Law' was introduced by only the teacher when he had to refer to the body of rules which proscribed the rights of young people and adults in relation to young people.

(d) All the other concepts arose in the students discussions.

5. (a) About 30 per cent of the lesson was consistent. However, at least 10 per cent could be regarded as inconsistent as intimated in 3(a) above.

(b) 'Toleration' and 'Reasoning' were implied most frequently. 'Fairness' was often invoked as a substantive value but only barely featured as a procedural value. There was no observed consideration

of 'Truth'. 'Freedom' was conspicuous by its explicit negation: the lesson was restricted to a hypothetical exercise and growing demands by students for a voice in certain matters were skilfully dissipated.
(c) The teacher was largely responsible for substaining 'Reasoning' as a value, but also responsible for denying 'Freedom'.
(d) The students' contributions were mostly concerned with 'Toleration' and 'Fairness'. Although 'Freedom' was blocked they (the few involved) appeared to exhibit characteristics of political literacy by their 'proclivity to action'.

6. (a) Residual Episodes took up about 10 per cent of the time. They were mostly neutral but a few tended to be negative.
    (b/c) Mostly they were the process of stimulating discussion. Discussion was inclined to be narrowly based on family and school and there was a disinclination to consider wider issues. Insofar as the teacher attempted to suggest to the students what they ought to be concerned about in the course of a lesson in which they were expected to formulate their own views, this was logically inconsistent with both the lesson and the project specifications.
    (b/d) There was no significant residual student behaviour.

The group of six students selected for interviewing after each lesson were chosen according to 'administrative' criteria. They were all members of one 'community service' option which was to have followed the lesson. This arrangement had its disadvantages in that they were not a friendship group nor were they happy to have the start of their optional activity delayed. Nevertheless, there was no reason to believe that their views were not valid or significant for the purpose of the interviews.

Comment

A particular feature of the school was the status accorded to the senior (fourth- and fifth-year) students. The fifth-year students were afforded privileges and given responsibilities; being expected, in return, to behave responsibly and set an example to younger students. The fourth-year students were continually reminded about and prepared for their roles when fifth formers. There appeared to be a gradual process over successive years of fourth formers winning some of the fifth form privileges for themselves. Thus the list of privileges was enlarged as the distinction between fourth- and fifth-year was continually re-established. This process was probably associated with a particular characteristic of staff attitudes.

The school contained within it some contrasting atmospheres. There was a definite difference between the views of the former headmaster and those of the then deputy headmaster regarding the ways in which discipline should be achieved. The deputy believed that students were all too prone to take advantage of and abuse any privileges granted. The staff were divided on similar lines and probably only a minority, including those involved in the social education programme, held views similar to the headmaster. The senior students, aware of this situation, had mixed and continually changing views of their relationship with the staff. At times they believed that reason and common sense would prevail. At other times they believed, perhaps with some cause, that there was no point in expressing opinions as they would be branded as troublemakers. However, the particular atmosphere in which the programme was conducted was happy, cooperative, vital, innovating and optimistic.

There was a remarkable sense of long-term development rather than a preoccupation with immediate difficulties. It is possible that such an outlook, in a school generally or in individual staff, is likely to lead to curriculum innovations of the kind we are concerned with here. Certainly the teachers involved with the social education programme were preoccupied with moral and social development and regarded this as requiring a significant proportion of the timetable and a wide range of activities.

Staff and students were undoubtedly fortunate to have the use of a room large enough to accommodate a whole year group in comfortable, relaxed surroundings. The arrangement of the room, its other use as a common room and the regular movements of other people (including parents and toddlers) through the room guaranteed a relaxed informal atmosphere.

Other factors contributing to the atmosphere were the flexible and comfortable seating arrangements and the use made of these surroundings by the teachers. No position was consistently designated as the front of the room. A team of about four adults were usually present, and sometimes many more. These being scattered around the room transformed the role of students from that of spectators to that of participants with the adults, a sign of students beginning to be treated, and encouraged to act like, young citizens rather than dutiful subjects.

The style of presentation and language used varied between the adults in the team. Generally, however, the adults did a little less talking than is usual in lessons and virtually no formal lecturing from the 'front'. Most of the talking was in conversation in groups of between ten and fifteen students. Questions were mostly conversational and therefore not closed or merely posed to control the sequence of events. A little use was made of film, or press coverage of local events. Most use was made of dramatisation of real or hypothetical events. Students saw disadvantages in this. They were concerned about the lack of background information or the way in which background information was presented, i.e. not in a permanent form. Their expressed need was in part the consequence of the interest which the lessons stimulated and essentially a product of success, rather than simply a shortcoming of the lesson which could be remedied without much difficulty.

All lessons in the programme featured a high degree of student involvement. The method was indeed student-centred. The teaching was particularly successfully in stimulating the students' interest. Many more girls than boys were resistant to efforts to engage their interest. Part of the success in stimulating interest and involvement and implementing the project specifications was attributable to the first introductory lesson in which the objectives and structure of the course was discussed. Subsequent lessons were explicitly related to the objectives of the course and occasionally analysed in the context of those objectives. Thus there was a recognised framework within which students had a great deal of freedom to determine the content and the pace of lessons. It was also a frame of reference against which they could criticise lessons. The lesson in which councillors discussed a local problem by re-enacting a council committee meeting was heavily criticised because, they said, they "... did not have enough information ... about the opinions and interests of the various people taking part". These opinions had been offered by the students to the teachers after the lesson (and were not stimulated by the observer interview), and they were accepted as a basis for modifying the course in future years.

The fact that the term's course was concerned exclusively with political education freed it from constraints presented by other contexts. The main difficulty was lack of time. There was no obvious part which could be cut, rather there were parts from the other terms' courses which could

usefully be added. It was inevitable that future planning involved extending the course.

Most lessons concentrated on single issues which were dramatised and
with which the students were acquainted or which were deliberately related to the students. Those lessons which covered several issues, for
which the issues were remote, or ill-defined and not well presented, were
distinctly less successful relative to other lessons. They were less
well received by students and less satisfying to the teachers. Thus
for many issues, the students themselves were not adequate sources of
resource material. Much greater attention should have been paid to
briefing student group leaders or to preparing handouts or questionnaires
or other stimulus material.

The analysis of issues according to the political literacy specifications was handled with apparent ease with the exception of two parts. Information regarding who promotes policies was either too difficult to
obtain or too difficult to summarise and so it was either omitted or
glossed over. A consideration of alternatives was thought by teachers
to be too much to add to an already congested course. No doubt it would
also be very difficult to deal with.

The inclusion of particular political concepts appeared to be a chance
occurrence depending on the subject matter being considered and the way
the students chose to deal with it. The way in which concepts were formulated could only be controlled if the teacher dominated the lesson.
This is clearly a disadvantage of the student-centred approach. The
students did not regard this as a disadvantage and the teachers were prepared to sacrifice control in this small respect.

The student-centred method furthered 'Freedom' as a procedural value
and to some little extent 'Toleration' and 'Fairness'. It appeared that
the extent to which the values were present or absent depended mainly on
the teacher leading the lesson or discussion group.

Conclusion

No one factor was responsible for this programme's considerable success
but rather a combination of several factors. It was designed around exclusively political education objectives. It made these objectives explicit and, in particular, they were a part of the course itself. It
depended on a great deal of student involvement, possibly too much so.
It was also taught by a group of teachers with the help of several outside contributors and developed by them in relation to both the school
and the local community. Consequently the programme, even when dealing
with simulated or hypothetical issues, was set in a real and immediate
rather than a remote or make-believe world.

4.4.2   School 'B':   Secondary Modern

This was a co-educational eight form entry 11-16 secondary modern school
located in a small coastal town.

The school was approached by a Development Officer because one of the
staff was contributing to the studies of the History Working Group.

The Teaching Programme: The syllabus appears in full in section 3.2.7 of
this report as one of the suggestions of the History Working Party. This
was taught to a set of about thirty fourth-year students, as part of a
history GCE examinations course, during two double periods each week.

The teaching programmes

The part of the course devoted to political literacy objectives began during the spring term and the experimental syllabus lasted nearly six weeks. However, the issues raised during this part of the course continued to occupy the attention of the group throughout the remainder of the year.

This teacher went further than any other in devising (with our Development Officer) his own methods of assessing the gains in political literacy of his students. These tests, based on stimulus passages, were, like the course itself limited in scope. Nevertheless, they did attempt to measure the understanding of the political ideas and concepts which had been taught. The first test devised is reproduced below.

Read the following passage carefully, and then answer the questions below.

"During the 1920s ... the prospects grew brighter ... The middle class, with its growing number of wealthy factory owners and merchants, began to be more actively anxious to gain a share of political power. To do this it was essential to dislodge the landowners from their control of Parliament. This was the object of working class reformers too, and thus in these years there arose a stronger reform movement based upon an alliance between the middle class and the working class. It was an alliance that carried through the great triumph of the reformers, the Reform Act of 1832". (C.P. Hill, *British Economic and Social History 1700-1964*, p. 161)

(a) What do you think the author means by the term 'middle class'? Give an example of who would be regarded as 'middle class'. What sort of things would lead you to describe a person as 'middle class'?

(b) What do you think the author means by the term 'working class'? Give an example of who would be regarded as 'working class'. What sort of things would lead you to describe a person as 'working class'?

(c) Why was it in the interest of members of both the middle class and working class to join together in the reform movement? Which 'great triumph' did this alliance result in?

(d) What is meant by 'political power' and why was it necessary for reformers to 'dislodge the landowners from their control of Parliament' to get it?'

Five visits were made to the school when lessons were observed and/or staff and students interviewed.

The selected lessons: A

'Recapitulation stage 1a and b' The class of twentysix boys and three girls was, after a brief recapitulation of the previous lesson, asked to prepare answers to the seven questions which are reproduced in the syllabus. After twentyfive minutes there was a discussion of the questions, for the remainder of the lesson, based on the prepared answers.
The setting
1. A fairly large room (15m x 15m) with one side used as a corridor access to other rooms. The other side being windows permitted only parts of the rear and front walls to be used for posters. There was no scope for wall displays for teaching purposes.
2. Four rows of eight desks with a central gangway faced the blackboard. The arrangement was rigid and formal.
3. Although the teacher moved round the room occasionally most teaching was done seated on the desk at the front and the blackboard was used

regularly.

4. The teaching style was formal but relaxed. After administrative pre-
liminaries such as returning books, the class instantly settled to quiet
attention. Information was given both by setting work from books and by
narration and elaboration. Information was checked by use of closed
questions in class and written exercises.

5. The atmosphere although formal was attentive, relaxed and cooperative. There was very little need to check inattentive students.

6. All of the Incidents were teacher initiated and began with clearly
formulated closed-reasoning questions. Student participation was
limited to answering these questions and probably limited by their
assumptions about acceptable behaviour.

The lesson content

1. (a) All the lesson was consistent except the opening revision which
   was neutral.
   (b) The lesson was concerned with the single issue of method, whether
   change should be affected within the existing institutional framework
   or by destroying that framework. The issue was confined to the
   particular historical context of the early nineteenth century.
   (c) The teacher elaborated the issue by means of a limited discussion
   based on each of the seven questions.
   (d) The students reconstructed the answers to the questions from
   information given in previous lessons.

2. (a) 60 per cent of the lesson was consistent, the rest was neutral.
   (b/c) Six of the seven questions relate directly to the political
   literacy diagram columns 1-3. There was a consideration of alternatives, confined to known historical examples, by means of "What other
   methods might the radicals have used?"
   (d) All the students' answers were 'correct' answers from recalled
   information.

3. (a) Only 20 per cent was consistent.
   (b/c) The consistent Incidents were concerned with a consideration of
   the interests of various parts of the radical movement, e.g. "What
   were their attitudes to existing institutions?"
   (d) Again, student participation was confined to correct responses.

4. (a) Although 70 per cent of the lesson was consistent some of the
   concepts were merely present in the questions and were barely elaborated in the answers.
   (b-d) Both 'Representation' and 'Force' were made explicit and fairly
   thoroughly elaborated. 'Pressure' was implicit in the consideration
   of "What methods might they use?" 'Welfare' was briefly mentioned
   among the aims of the radicals and injustice among their grievances.

5. (a) Barely any of the lesson was consistent, although none of it
   could reasonably be regarded as inconsistent.
   (b-d) Certain elements of 'Reasoning'. 'Toleration' and 'Fairness'
   were present but by chance rather than design.

6. 10 per cent of the lesson was neutral and was an explanation intended
   to remedy certain misconceptions which had arisen in the previous
   lesson.

The selected lessons: B

'Legacy' The same class had been preparing written answers, to the
questions in this section, from earlier notes and from text books. They
were first allowed a further twentyfive minutes to complete this work
(which was achieved with very varied success). The rest of the lesson
again took the form of a discussion based on their answers to the

questions.

The setting

This was identical to lesson A in virtually every respect. The only slight but significant change was:

6. The lesson interaction was not entirely teacher-initiated. A few of the more able boys initiated some questions themselves. Some of the teacher questions were open reasoning questions and some called for information which was to be recalled from general knowledge and current awareness.

The lesson content

1. (a) The lesson was not, when taken by itself, strictly consistent in respect of political issues.
   (b-d) For the purposes of the lesson and as a means of evaluating parts of the course the issue of 'the results and the significance of the radical movement' was used for the lesson. But this was neither considered as a political nor as a historical issue. However, two political issues were introduced briefly both in answer to the last question in the syllabus about lessons from the experience of the radicals - Northern Ireland and Proportional Representation.

2-5. Although these two issues were introduced they were merely stated and received as examples and were not analysed. The Northern Ireland issue was seen exclusively in terms of constitutional arrangements of the United Kingdom and apparently not understood to be concerned with problems indigenous to Ireland. Proportional Representation was seen not so much as a political issue with political consequences but as an alternative arrangement of fixed values, rather like metrication perhaps. A small part of the lesson was concerned with general ways and means of influence and their appropriateness for particular purposes today. This was necessarily brief and barely significant.

6. Most of the lesson was residual and neutral with respect to the specifications. (See Section 3.2.6, paragraph 5. for details of points covered).

The group of six students interviewed after each lesson were chosen as comprising two friendship groups. This criteria was used (and generally preferred) in the expectation that they would be more relaxed and would be likely to talk with each other about the lesson during the interview and about the programme at other times. These expectations were fulfilled in the case of this group.

Comment

The atmosphere of the school was in no way distinctive. Being a large school in fairly old buildings it was relatively formal and remote. At the same time it was distinctly happy and cooperative although not enthusiastically so. Although the school representated the lowest ability range of all the schools associated with the project, it did not have the difficulties which a similar school in a large conurbation might have. Discipline and truancy was not a significant problem. The students regarded the staff as reasonable but as typically fusty adults. The staff appeared to be sensitive to the particular needs of below average students. Most of the concerns of the school were with immediate and practical problems to do with, for example, making up for teaching days lost for various reasons.

More than in many schools, the room was a constraint on what could be done with this age group. The room was intended for a variety of uses in

close succession and three other rooms led off it. Therefore movement of
furniture and students or a noisy discussion would have been a distract-
ion to other adjacent classes. Such activity would also have been 'out
of place' generally.

Despite this, the atmosphere in the class was not harsh or oppressive.
Some noise and talking was acceptable provided it was accompanied by
application to set tasks. There was an obvious rapport between teacher
and class. A quiet word with an individual student was sufficient to
maintain order. It was never apparently thought necessary to correct
the class as a whole.

In this atmosphere the teacher could set work and attend to individuals
or other matters without having to be seen to be in control at the front.
The teaching style was relaxed, clear and precise. Information was
provided either by narration or by setting work from books. The understanding of this was checked by means of written questions or by questioning individuals in class.

The method was teacher-centred and the learning was individualised.
Each student was expected to master certain information helped, as an
individual, by the teacher and the texts. Interaction was between
teacher and student and not between students. It was almost entirely
teacher-initiated. Student involvement was limited largely to responses
to questions. Most questions required the recall of one acceptable
answer.

Although it could be concluded, negatively, no great demands were
made on the students, it could equally be concluded that no unreasonable
demands were made on these students with limited ability. For despite
the limitations of the style (and possibly as a consequence of these well
considered limitations), there was considerable interest in and enthusiasm for the subject matter. Not surprisingly therefore there was also
a good understanding of the historical material.

However, their understanding of the historical material could be no
guarantee of an understanding of the political issues involved. There
was undoubtedly a conflict between the basic objectives of the history
course and the additional political education objectives. The additional
fact that this was an examination course meant that the basic objectives
were likely to take precedence. Moreover, as the students were only concerned about the objectives of the history examination they reinforced
this position. Furthermore, a six-week interval in a two-year course
could not be expected to be regarded by the students as being specially
significant.

Despite these drawbacks the course was relatively successful. The full
extent of success is not made apparent in the examples of lessons given
above. This demonstrates a limitation of observing and analysing lessons
as separate units rather than as components of a long term process.
Whereas lesson B is not consistent with project specifications when
looked at apart from the rest of the course, if it is looked at in the
context of the whole course much more of it would be seen to be consistent for it brought together aspects of earlier lessons which had been
based on various parts of the project specification without there being
many lesson references in terms which could be classified as specified
classroom practice. The interviews after the lesson certainly supported
this view.

Taken as a whole, therefore, the course was relatively successful. The
main issue of reform of the franchise was analysed and divided into
various sub-issues. In a limited way an attempt was made to use it as
an analogy for current issues of electoral reform, but it was predominantly viewed as an issue in its own right - as a lesson from the past.

217

It was interesting to students who were interested in history although they were unable to identify themselves with it in any way.

The presentation had been planned with special care to cover as many of the political literacy specifications as possible. Several aspects were not thought possible, such as self interest or action skills. 'Alternatives' were seen, and included, in a very formal way.

The political concepts were faithfully mentioned but the course did not provide an opportunity for the concepts to be used and developed by the students. They were either presented as the classifying tools of the historian (such as 'Pressure') or as the ideas of the historical actors (such as 'Justice').

Student interviews after lesson A revealed no awareness of the political content of the lesson despite a thorough understanding of the historical material. The word 'Representation' had been used five times in lesson A. without any of the interviewed students understanding it. Limited general knowledge was a handicap. However, the interview after lesson B presented a dramatic contrast. Political content was ascribed to the lesson. The lesson was seen as the final part of the course on the radical movement and all comments related the lesson to the course. The course was analysed partly in conceptual terms. For example, after listing freedom of speech as a right, one student elaborated and suggested that "... people would need to be able to speak at meetings on the tele and the radio to really have it ..."

Conclusion

Although procedural values were neglected, in many other respects the programme was successful, and remarkably so given the limited time and other constraints. The main factor contributing to this success may have been the careful and detailed thought which was put into the planning by the history working group and which is apparent from a reading of the syllabus. Also the historical material was concerned with a single political issue which readily lent itself to the recommended analysis. Nevertheless, this success demanded not only much skill but also a great deal of effort which this teacher felt unable to repeat in following years until the project could suggest a structured way of teaching political literacy.

4.4.3   School C - Independent (history emphasis)

This was an independent boys 13-19 school some distance from a small seaside town. Nearly all the 500 boys were fee-paying boarders.

The school was approached by a Development Officer because one of the staff was contributing to the studies of the History Working Party. The school, through the headmaster and several of the staff, was in close touch with recent ideas on curriculum development, more so than many state schools, and was anxious to collaborate with the project.

The Teaching Programme: The first part of the syllabus on the history of the French, Russian and Chinese revolutions (available from the Hansard Society, at cost of replication and postage). This was taught throughout the year to a group of 13-14 year-old boys by the members of the working group who planned the course. The timetable allocation was three fortyfive minute-periods per week.

Five visits were made to the school on which lessons were observed and/

or staff and students interviewed.

The selected lessons: A

Russian Revolution - lesson 2   The class of twentyone boys was asked to
look again at a census of population for Russia in the mid-nineteenth
century and was asked a series of questions about the figures for oral
answers based on information from the book, the previous lesson and
general knowledge.
The setting
1. A small all-purpose room (4m x 10m) in an old part of the building,
not necessarily designed for teaching originally and, if so, then for a
class of about fifteen. It had a high ceiling, high windows and bare
walls.
2. Five rows of four desks faced the blackboard. The spaces between
desks were narrow.
3. The teacher usually stood speaking from the front, occasionally moving halfway down one aisle. No use was made of a blackboard or teaching
aids other than the book.
4. The teaching style was formal and teacher-centred whereby the teacher
both provided the information and checked understanding by means of the
question-response technique.
5. The atmosphere was very formal and fairly attentive. Occasionally
obvious inattention had to be checked but the class was mainly a quiet
passive audience.
6. The lesson was almost entirely a formal sequence of teacher-initiated
closed-reasoning questions followed occasionally by an elaboration on
the answers. There were thirteen such questions in forty minutes and
three elaborations. The only exception was when one student asked in the
middle of the lesson, "Where do Belorussions come from?"
The lesson content
1. (a) About 40 per cent of the lesson was consistent.
    (b) However, the consideration of the problems associated with hete-
    rogenous states, minority groups, racial and ethnic prejudices etc.
    was incidental to the general theme of the prelude to the Russian
    revolution. It was not delineated and analysed as a significant
    issue. Consistency appeared to be fortuitous.
    (c) At three points the teacher made comparisons between nineteenth
    century Russia and Russia today and with other nineteenth century
    experiences. For example, the class were reminded of current press
    coverage of anti-semitic attitudes in Russia today.
    (d) The students provided 'correct' answers to questions thereby
    maintaining the desired progress of the lesson.
2. The identified issue was not analysed according to the political
    Literacy Tree columns 1-3. The issue was presented in a very gener-
    alised form in order to analyse the causes of the revolution and not
    as a topic of study in its own right.
3. (a) Less than 10 per cent was consistent.
    (b/c) The consistent Incidents involved a consideration of the
    interests of minority groups regarding use of a national language.
    "Which groups would resist (the imposition of one national language)
    most?"
    (d) Students provided the expected responses.
4. (a) About 15 per cent was consistent.
    (b-d) All governing concepts were implicit at some point, though only
    briefly. Both 'Order' and 'Authority' were made explicit during a

brief explanation of the problems the Tsarist regime faced in governing a large and diverse state.

5. There was no significant consistency with the procedural values. 'Toleration' and 'Freedom' were implied as substantive values but not elaborated. Parts of the lesson (isolated from the context of the whole course) were inconsistent with 'Respect for Truth' insofar as there was no scepticism about factual claims, nor alternative viewpoints presented. Generally the causes were given as objective historical facts, at least at this stage in the course.

6. (a/b) Most of the lesson fell into the residual category and was a neutral narration or revision of historical data.
    (c) For example Teacher: "What other country expanded its territory rapidly in the nineteenth century?"
    (d) Student response: "The United States of America".

The selected lessons: B

Chinese Revolution – lesson 3   The class had recently read a chapter in the text book about the mid-nineteenth century history of China's relations with the West. This lesson was basically a recapitulation of the work by means of questions round the class and elaborations by the teacher.

The setting
1. A small (4m x 10m) high-windowed ante-room to the library, bright and modernised but bare and cramped.
2. Twelve students sat in relative comfort on three sides of a rectangle of tables, the other nine sat in some discomfort facing the wall down one side of the room sideways on to the teacher.
3-5. Teaching style and classroom atmosphere was similar to lesson A.
6. The interaction was basically the same pattern as in lesson A with more questions and less time spent on exposition from the teacher. There were nineteen teacher-initiated questions in the forty minutes of which nine were followed by elaborations. In addition there were eight student-initiated questions a majority of which were conspicuously off the subject.

The lesson content
1. None of the lesson was consistent. The subject matter touched on numerous historical political issues – the first Opium War, the Russo-Japanese War, the Korean War, the Boxer Rebellion and so on – but these were simply named as events and not treated as issues.
2-5. One procedural value was made explicit and dealt with briefly, – 'Toleration'. There was a very thorough account of the ways in which the West regarded the Eastern cultures with contempt and as 'uncivilised'.
6. (a) In effect all of the lesson was residual and neutral with respect to the project specifications.
    (b-d) There were eight Episodes two of which were sets of four student-initiated questions on barely related topics. Another was concerned to tie up loose ends in the last four minutes. The rest were concerned with China's relations with Britain, France and Japan, with 'westernisation' and with comparisons with Russia.

The group of five students interviewed after each lesson were a friendship group. Perhaps because of their age group and probably because of their institutional environment they were notably less relaxed and forthcoming than the groups in any other school.

Comment

As an old boarding school it had a distinctive atmosphere. Both staff
and particularly students were conscious of being part of a common community for most of their normal daily activities - eating, leisure, wor-
ship, as well as learning. Nevertheless, the atmosphere was, although
friendly and cooperative, certainly very formal and a discreet courteous
distance was judiciously maintained by both staff and students. This
atmosphere was manifest in all observed aspects of the school, including
the teaching programme under consideration.

Although two rooms were used for the observed lessons (and a further
room on another occasion in the week), they were all similar and used in
a fairly similar way. One room which was regarded as a history room,
housed history resources and the lesson in that room was often devoted
to work set from books and other material. It would have been difficult
and certainly 'out of place' to conduct lessons other than with the
fairly formal arrangement described.

The class atmosphere, although formal, would not necessarily have inhibited a more adventurous style of presentation. Whereas it was suggested that the limited style and interaction in School B was probably
fairly well suited to the ability range, the same justifications could
not be claimed in this case for a similar style (see page   ). In comparison with School B, the teaching depended on a much greater frequency
of closed-reasoning questions formulated and answered spontaneously.
Learning was particularly individualised. Just under half the students
made no contributions to the observed lessons. The greatest possible
involvement open to a student was to answer a few questions and to ask a
few himself.

The students interviewed were interested and intelligent enough to retain a great deal of the historical content of the lessons. They had a
fairly good general knowledge about political issues obtained from their
families and the media. Despite this, they displayed little awareness
of or particular interest in the potential political content of the observed lessons: and this state of affairs did not appear to change
during the teaching programme.

As has been remarked in the case of School B, isolated lessons do not
always present a fair account of a whole course. However, that remark
in the case of School B applied to a course concerned with one political
issue. Here the course was concerned with 'revolution', but treated exclusively as an historical concept. Lessons seen in this overall context
were no more consistent with the project specifications than when viewed
in isolation. The basic difficulty was therefore the absence of any
clear use of political issues which could be analysed on the recommended
lines. Inevitably numerous issues were mentioned in the course of
lessons. They were not, however, the objects of study but rather were
numbered among the motive forces of history.

The political concepts were made explicit and discussed in class. Certain issues in the French Revolution were directly related to the concepts, as indicated in the syllabus. The concepts were partly regarded
as the ideas held by historical actors and were not made to relate to
present-day issues.

Procedural values were not an evident concern of the course. The students were not enabled to become acquainted with the self-interest or the
action skills aspects of political literacy and the consideration of
alternatives was largely confined to comparisons between the three revolutions.

Conclusion

The decidedly restricted success, in project terms, of this course was
mainly attributable to the nature of the subject matter. This limited
experience suggests that political literacy is difficult to diffuse
through a course which is political only in a very general sense (see
also School D). The political literacy recommendations are specific and
as such have to be applied specifically rather than generally otherwise
they are no guide at all, either for teaching or assessment. Here also
were the competing objectives of history teaching. In contrast to the
political literacy element, the basic history course was very carefully
and precisely structured. Consequently there was a 'no contest' between
the two sets of objectives. Also the historical events were being used
as analogies rather than as issues. Problems inherent in the use of analogies is discussed on page

4.4.4 School D: Independent (Government and Politics emphasis)

This was an independent boys 13-19 school located in a small country
town. Most of the 600 boys were fee-payable boarders. The sixth form
included a few girls.
　The school was already known to have a reputation for being alert to
current ideas for curriculum development and when approached by a Development Officer was very willing to collaborate.

The teaching programme: The syllabus reproduced below will be recognised
as Paper II of the Oxford and Cambridge Schools Examination Board
advanced level examinations in Political Studies. This was taught,
alongside Principles of Economics, to one first-year sixth-form set, ages
16/17. In the second year the students were to have the option of sitting the examinations in either Economics, or in Economic and Political
Studies. The politics teaching occupied four forty minute periods per
week. The examination syllabus provides some guide to the teaching programme in that lessons were devoted to such topics as 'The Cabinet',
'Civil Service', etc. However, in addition to these there were a number
of lessons at the beginning of the course directly and exclusively concerned with 'Power', 'Authority', 'Opposition', 'Representation' etc.
(Lesson observations are selected from both types of lesson).

Representative Government

　British Government: Parliament - working of Commons; the Lords;
　Prime Minister and Cabinet; The Monarchy; Civil Service; Law Courts;
　Local Government, Party System.
　American Government: The Constitution; President, Congress; the
　Supreme Court; distribution of power in a federal system; White House
　office, Cabinet and agencies; Civil Service; Law Courts; Party
　System.

Five visits were made to the school on which lessons were observed and/
or staff and students interviewed.

The selected lessons: A

Opposition. The class of twelve boys and one girl were asked to jot down

in five minutes any ideas which they associated with the word
'opposition' (used as a political concept). They were further asked to
consider what might be meant by a distinction between institutionalised
and uninstitutionalised opposition. These notes and the discussion which
followed were intended to be based on recent reading. The last ten
minutes of the lesson were devoted to a discussion of opposition with the
school society being used as an analogy.

The setting
1. A small (4m x 8m) room, in the Economics/Politics suite situated in
a modernised part of an old building. There were windows high on one
wall allowing use of all four walls for posters, cuttings, book displays
and resource storage. The suite of rooms was a very well equipped,
business-like setting which included an audio-visual resources room and a
periodicals, pamphlets and cuttings resources room, both open-access.
2. Seating was around tables arranged in an 'E' pattern.
3. The teacher made extensive use of the board and also moved to all
parts of the room in the interstices of the 'E'.
4. The teaching style was very informal, lively and engaging. The
teacher's own enthusiasm for the subject was evident and infectious.
5. The atmosphere was very relaxed and both friendly and respectful.
Lessons were obviously enjoyable because the material was shown to be
relevant to students' interests and experiences.
6. The interaction was basically that of teacher-question and student-
response but the questions were both open-reasoning and open questions.
All answers were (by definition) acceptable and were incorporated into
the lesson. The lesson content appeared to be a discussion between
equals and the direction dictated by the logic of reasoning. A great
deal of value appeared to be placed on the students' own opinions.

The lesson content
1. (a) For the purpose of analysis it is assumed that the lesson was
    generally consistent rather than neutral throughout. This is in fact
    very doubtful.
    (b) There were two issues - 'How should we set about opposing
    (government policies)?' and 'How should you set about expressing your
    views in school?' The second was the analogy occupying the final ten
    minutes. The first is really an academic issue of political science
    and was analysed as such. The second, although a real and immediate
    issue, was only political by analogy and again analysed as such.
    Thus, according to project criteria, neither were obviously political
    issues.
    (c) There were eight question-initiated Incidents in forty minutes.
    A question typical of those used to draw out other aspects of the
    analysis was, "Some governments claim that they 'cannot afford the
    luxury of an opposition'. What do you think they might mean by that?"
    (d) All student behaviour made useful contributions in the form of
    factual answers, statements of opinion or further questions which ex-
    tended the analysis.
2. (a) Over 30 per cent of the lesson was consistent (if the issues are
    regarded as political).
    (b) Most of the consistent material was concerned with customary
    ways of dealing with things and with who promotes which ideas. There
    were no genuine alternatives considered, only variations on the theme
    of institutionalised/uninstitutionalised opposition.
    (c) The closest to a genuine alternative was the question, "In some
    states opposition is suppressed 'for the sake of ideology'. What sort
    of state would that be?"

(d) There was a general consensus. Students did not challenge any given information but sought further justifications.

3. (a) About 25 per cent was consistent (again if the issues are regarded as political).
(b) This was concerned with the expression of views in school and therefore related to self-interest and thinking about action skills (and deploring lack of opportunity).
(c) Only two initial questions were necessary to set off extensive discussion. "If you have got a housemaster who does not allow discussion of an issue, what could you do?" and, "Are there any other ways?"
(d) A wide range of answers and concrete examples were given all of which were accepted as analogous.

4. (a) About 50 per cent of the lesson was consistent. However, most of this was hazy and ill-defined.
(b) All the governing concepts were implied in various references to government. Similarly the popular concepts and 'Representation' were implicit in the brief reference to the school analogy. Only 'Pressure' was present throughout much of the lesson but the closest this came to being explicit was when terms such as suppression and repression were used.
(c/d) The concepts were encountered and passed over, usually without comment. For example, Teacher: - "If opposition is repressed, what happens? How do people express opposition?" Response: - "Riots?"

5. No significant part of the lesson was consistent. Too few aspects of the project specification were present to sustain any one of the procedural values.

6. (a) Less than half of the lesson Incidents were residual and neutral.
(b-d) The residual parts included the introductory instructions and two factual ('what?') questions Incidents, - for example "What does 'institutionalise' mean?", which received factual answers.

The selected lessons: B

The Cabinet

1-3. The same conditions prevailed as for lesson A. The only notable changes were in the wall displays which still featured topical cuttings and posters and were necessarily different.
4-6. An outline of the lesson interaction is included here, this being the only effective means of conveying a little of the style and atmosphere and of the content upon which the later analysis is based.

Minutes
Elapsed

0 (Teacher:) 'Jot down on a scrap of paper any problems and issues which you associate with the Cabinet'
(Teacher walks round class discussing work of individuals)

6 (Teacher writes on blackboard:)
(a) Why have a Cabinet?
(b) Is it necessary?
(c) What other questions follow these?'

8 (Students:) 'Surely (b) is assumed in (a)'
(T) 'Yes and also ...
(T. writes on blackboard:)
(d) Is the Cabinet necessary? If so - for what?'

10 (S) 'Are you questioning the Cabinet or are you giving us the facts?'

(T and S discuss rationale of teaching method – analysis based on set reading etc.)

16 (T) 'What are the reasons given for having a <u>large</u> Cabinet?'
(S) 'To be representative'.
(S) 'But this function is performed by the House of Commons'.
(Detailed discussion between several S about the relationship between Cabinet size and the idea of representation with clarification and elaboration provided by T).

23 (T) 'What are the arguments for a <u>small</u> Cabinet?'
(S) 'Efficiency'
(S) 'Less chance of conflict'
(T) gives an account of the power relationships between Prime Minister and senior members of the Parliamentary party)

29 (T) 'What do you understand by Collective Responsibility?'
(S gves an acceptable answer and there follows an informal discussion)
(S) 'I think they should agree in private as well as in public'
(S) 'I don't think it is even necessary to agree in public'
(T) 'Don't you think that would affect the credibility of the Cabinet?'
'Which Minister resigned recently? 'What was the effect of her resignation?'
(S) 'But you can't expect them to agree on absolutely everything!'
(T) 'No, of course not – just on major policy statements'.

35 (T) 'What are the <u>functions</u> of the Cabinet?'
(In the final five minutes functions were enumerated and discussed).

40

The lesson interaction was basically the same as in lesson A. However, the question-initiated Incidents were slightly longer and certainly more complex. Some would be more accurately regarded as Episodes. More Incidents were student-initiated. Student behaviour was directed generally to fellow students as well as to the teacher. With more student-initiated behaviour there was more acceptance of student opinions by the teacher, either expressed or implied in silence which invited further student opinion. The atmosphere was therefore more like a 'seminar' than a 'lesson'.

The lesson content

1-3. It is difficult to stretch the definition of a political issue to include the subject matter of the lesson. As in lesson A political science issues, such as 'What do we understand by Collective Responsibility?', were present. There were five major themes and numerous minor ones, none of which were analysed in the prescribed way.

4. (a) Over 30 per cent of the lesson was consistent.
(b) 'Power' was made explicit in a few ways and was implicit in much of the discussion. 'Authority' was also implicit. 'Representation' was briefly defined as a political science concept when a little confusion arose.
(c) In connection with the size and composition of the Cabinet the teacher explained the Power relationships with the Cabinet.
(d) One student attempted to correct another in his use of the word 'Representative'. Both explained their particular usages of the word.

5. As in lesson A, no significant part of the lesson was consistent as no aspect of the project specification was present. However, the

early Incident in which one student asked for an explanation of the
teaching method being employed suggests a consciousness about procedure and the possibility of 'Freedom'.
6. About 80 per cent of the lesson was residual and neutral.

A group of ten of the fourteen students were interviewed. This was
made possible by selecting a lesson which fell immediately before two
timetable periods allocated to these students for private study. This
group did not include the girl (who was Maltese) and three boys who were
much less enthusiastic about the subject than those who were interviewed.

Comment

Being located in a small town, the school community was not quite as
closed or inward looking as may otherwise be the case with boarding
schools. The atmosphere was much closer to the state schools in the
sample than to School C. There was barely any feeling of the cloistered
monastic community which would have been expected from the age and
architecture of the buildings. The atmosphere was however distinctly
formal and, with the exception of a few departments such as Art, and
Economics and Politics in particular, the formal polite distance between
staff and students was maintained.
The whole suite of rooms offered versatility rather than simply the
room in which lessons were observed. Teachers in the department made
ad hoc arrangements in order to make use of, for example, the audio-
visual room. This potential versatility was only exploited for greater
efficiency in teaching to examination objectives and even this within a
traditional framework. Students learned individually within the whole
class. There was no collective learning or small group exercises.
The teaching style and classroom atmosphere became more informal and
more seminar-like over the course of the year. The style was similar to
that in Schools B and C but most of the questions were open or open-
reasoning. This facilitated student involvement and produced a more relaxed atmosphere. The students very much preferred this style of teaching to that which they experienced elsewhere in the school. In geography,
students claimed, no student-initiated behaviour was permitted and all
questions were closed-reasoning. "He's really old fashioned, you know.
He won't let you say anything till he speaks to you, will he. He just
tells you things, then asks things like, 'You. What's a rift valley?'.
You never discuss anything ..." The teacher was conscious of this contrast with his colleagues and was able to exploit these features of the
school for the purpose of analogies with political institutions which
always interested the students.
The method of teaching, learning and note-taking was introduced as a
subject for consideration by the teacher at an early stage. In so doing
he was remarkably successful in inhibiting a linear form of note-taking
and conceptualisation of the subject by the students and in fostering an
understanding of the complex nature of interrelationships in politics
with the use of pattern diagrams for example. He also raised the consciousness of most students about the events and interaction of the
lesson. A lot of use was made of audio tapes and video tapes of Open
University programmes, radio discussions and commercially prepared tapes
on British and American Government and Politics. For example aspects of
the Civil Service were taught using a commercial tape of a discussion
between two academics. Students made notes on the power relationships,
they enlarged on the discussion each time the tape was stopped and they
were asked to consider the way in which political concepts were being

used by the speakers.

Despite the quality of teaching and the enthusiasm in lessons political science objectives were made explicit and not political literacy objectives. It appeared that, by the end of the year, these students were equipped with a technical language of political science, having been "brilliantly introduced to one burning and controversial <u>constitutional question</u> after another, but were still of low political literacy" (see document 2.1 paragraph 8). The examination syllabus objectives were enhanced by this approach and these objectives excluded coverage of political literacy objectives.

This was not necessarily inevitable. The concepts of 'Opposition', 'Power', etc. could have been made explicit through a particular political issue. In a lesson on Power the power relationship between trade unions and the Labour Government was discussed in a four-minute Episode. There was another five-minute Episode in which the power of the monarchy in Spain was mentioned. Either of these, then topical, issues could have been the basis of the whole lesson. For the lesson on the Cabinet the well documented 'Chrysler Affair' was a suitable issue upon which to base several lessons (College F, lesson A). In the absence of such an approach there was no opportunity to apply the basic political literacy specification.

This did not prevent some consideration of political concepts. The application of these concepts was necessarily to a much narrower range of political material than would have been the case had political issues been considered. The concepts were given some wider application by means of carefully chosen analogies but the concepts were consequently understood to be political science concepts rather than those which "occur in ordinary people's talk about politics" (document 2.3 paragraph 4).

Absence of the political literacy analysis implied an absence of the recommended procedural values, although similar procedural values were probably present concerned with perhaps 'interlectual rigor', 'curiosity', or the importance of 'precise expression'.

Conclusion

As with School C the success of this course was limited despite the very high quality of teaching in this case. The limitation was not inherent in the course but in the method of application. The subject was largely conceived of, and therefore taught in, conventional textbook terms. That is to say, in terms of the nature of and relationships of the institutions of the state rather than as a study of political activity. It was probably taught in such terms because, for examination purposes, it had to be learned and reproduced in such terms.

4.4.5 College E: Further Education College

This was a Further Education College with approximately 850 full-time and 3000 part-time students. It provided a full range of examination and liberal studies courses and the various departments were split between three buildings on separate sites. The Business Studies department, with which we were concerned, was accommodated in the main building located in an inner-city area.

<u>The teaching programme</u>: The syllabus was extracted from the RSA Certi-

ficate of Office Studies which in its second year has an unusually
enterprising syllabus in government covering: an introduction aimed at
achieving some understanding of the nature and importance of politics; a
project revolving around the use and nature of some government service
used by the public; how central government policies are decided, how
legislation is approved and the institutions associated with both processes; similarly, local government; and central control over local
government.

There were five part-time students aged 16+ following this course which
was held on only one afternoon per week from 3.15 p.m. to 5 p.m. and
taught by one lecturer.

Four visits were made to the college on which lessons were observed
and/or staff and students interviewed.

The teaching on this course was the most interesting of all the programmes observed. It presented more difficulties for observation even
than the completely informal setting of School A because the proposed
method of study was not really appropriate to the particular type of
lesson interaction observed. A problem for description, observation and
analysis arises, not because of an eccentric or involved teaching style
but, because description and analysis is unlikely to convey adequately
the qualities which enriched the lesson above what may be regarded as
mere group discussion.[4]

All the lessons observed were carefully prepared and planned with
detailed supporting and follow-up handouts and materials. A copy of the
plan was made available to us, indeed, several days before the lesson.
The plans were extremely flexible sometimes to the extent of including
two alternative lessons. Each lesson plan included a broad strategy
for detailed and specific objectives.

The selected lessons: A

(i) The Leadership of the Labour Party   (ii) The Cabinet/Chrysler Affair

A discussion was initiated by the question "Who do you think is going to
succeed Wilson as Leader of the Labour Party?" The discussion moved on
to consider, on the basis of a handout, the methods used in the three
main English parties for choosing leaders. It ended by considering the
meaning of the terms 'left-wing' and 'right-wing'. The last half hour
of the lesson was a preliminary to a discussion of the Cabinet the
following week. This involved an explanation and discussion of two handouts on the 'Chrysler Affair'. (The lesson the following week involved
a simulation of the Cabinet meetings which made the controversial decisions, based on roles taken from the Granada TV reconstruction of the
events).

The setting

1. A fairly large room (10m x 10m), in an old building, with a high ceiling and windows on two sides. The view in one direction was of basement
walls and in the other of students passing by in the corridor. All walls
were bare.

2. The desks and chairs were arranged in about six rows of six. Only a
small semi-circle of desks round the front table were used.

3. The teacher posed the initial question from the front but had moved

---

4 For an example of a similar style to parts of the observed lessons see
   the description of a Latin lesson by Britton in Barnes, D. Britton, J.
   and Rosen, H., *Op. Cit.*, P. 85

to the back of the room within five minuts and sat alone for nearly
thirty minutes silent for most of that time. For the remainder of the
lesson he joined the discussion in the semi-circle at the front.
4. A little use was made of the blackboard both to pose questions and
record relevant information as it emerged. Handouts providing summaries
of information or intended to stimulate discussion were referred to frequently.
5. The atmosphere was particularly informal and relaxed. A more apt
description, attributable to the fact that the students were part-
timers, would be 'mature'.
6. The interaction varied considerably. At the beginning of the lesson
it was entirely discussion between students. After sixteen minutes one
student turned round to the teacher and asked, "What do you think
Mr. ...?" and received the reply, "What views have you come to?", thus
gently turning the onus back on them. After twenty minutes the teacher
introduced a few factual questions. Teacher involvement became more
frequent as the lesson progressed and his contributions eventually included corrections of misunderstandings and summaries of progress made.
The students acted as fellow learners and instructors. Those who had
little understanding of certain points learned from those with a deeper
understanding. The latter improved their own understanding by experiencing the difficulties of others and by being challenged to explain what
they claimed to understand intuitively.

The lesson content
1. (a) The last parts of the lesson were certainly consistent. The
   first part does not fit the specification well but merits recognition
   as a political issue. It is therefore possible to assert that all of
   the lesson was consistent.
   (b) The first issue was 'who should lead the Labour Party?', and the
   second, which was introduced briefly, was 'should the Chrysler Company be subsidised out of public funds?'.
   (c) The handouts on the Chrysler issue summarised all the background
   information extending well beyond most of the project specifications.
   These points were introduced briefly.
   (d) In contrast to this method of providing information the students
   themselves provided or recalled most of the information for the
   leadership issue.
2. (a) At least 80 per cent of the lesson was consistent.
   (b) The consistent material from the leadership issue was largely
   concerned with the customary procedures and institutional arena. In
   the case of the Chrysler issue the emphasis was on who promotes what
   policies.
   (c) In addition to the prepared material, the teacher provided information on such aspects as the various ways and means of influence.
   The alternatives were confined to alternative government procedures
   and policies and did not extend to considerations of alternative
   ideologies or a consideration of the reliability or significance of
   the information provided.
   (d) In the discussion of the labour leadership, the students were
   more inclined to consider alternatives. In one exchange they considered the possibility of ways in which the whole procedure might
   have been rigged by Wilson.
3. (a) Only about 10 per cent of the lesson was consistent.
   (b) This involved a brief mention of the interests involved in the
   Chrysler issue.
   (c-d) The teacher explained the various interests in the localities
   of the various Chrysler factories as part of the briefing for the

planned simulation.
4. (a) Less than 10 per cent of the lesson was consistent.
(b-d) There was a brief mention of 'Authority' implicit in the
student discussion of the leadership issue and a consideration of
'Pressure' by the teaching in connection with the Chrysler issue.
5. (a) At least 70 pr cent of the lesson was consistent.
(b) The most evident procedural value was 'Reasoning'. 'Fairness'
and 'Freedom' were also probably present. 'Toleration' and 'Truth'
could not be regarded as being present as the lesson lacked the
specified range of alternatives and range of experience.
(c) The features of 'Reasoning' were mainly provided by the teacher
through information on policies, institutions, means of influence
etc.
(d) Many of the features of 'Freedom' were prevalent in the student
discussion on the leadership issue.
6. No significant part of the lesson could be regarded as residual.

The selected lessons: B

(i) The 'Conditional' Budget (ii) Facilities for the Disabled
(Government Services)

The first part of the lesson occupied twenty minutes and was a consideration of that splendidly controversial issue, Mr. Healey's first 'conditional' budget of 1976. The rest of the lesson dealt with local and
central government policy for the disabled. One of the students was confined to a wheelchair and had been so for about seventeen years. She
depended on the help of the other students. A newspaper article was read
out about the lack of suitable facilities for the disabled on the liner
QE II. She was asked about her recent experience on a college staff/
student committee which had considered the matter in connection with the
college. The students discussed all aspects of the issue, particularly
concerning whether the disabled should be treated as people with special
needs or as normal people. During the discussion the teacher listed on
the blackboard, 'Income, Work, Mobility, Housing, Education, Social,
Care/Medical', after which he asked a few factual questions and then
directed the discussion to a consideration of the political machinery for
providing facilities. One handout, a comprehensive newspaper article on
the issue, was provided.
The setting
1-2. The same room and arrangement as in lesson A.
3. Although the teacher remained at the front, the disabled student was
to one side at the front and for most of the lesson was the focus on the
discussion.
4. Use was made of the blackboard as indicated and, in addition, to record factual details of government services.
5-6. The atmosphere was as relaxed and as mature as in lesson A. The
interaction during the first part was a straightforward teacher-directed
discussion. However, the second part was quite different. The lesson
was directed by the disabled student alone for twenty minutes. Even
after the teacher entered the discussion, the disabled student remained
at the centre of the exchanges. The teacher asked four factual questions
and three closed-reasoning questions. The disabled student provided
almost all the information and elaborated on it in response to further
student questions and opinion.
The lesson content
1. (a) Both parts of the lesson were 100 per cent consistent with res-

230

pect to issues.

(b) The first issue about the budget concerned goals, values and methods. The second issue concerned goals, values, methods and re-sults.

i. (c) The teacher provided details of the conditions of the budget offer and the machinery for negotiation.

(d) The students widened the scope of the discussion by intelligent questioning. For example, one student introduced a consideration of values by suggesting that the principles and priorities were wrong.

ii. (c/d) The teacher's list of factors on the blackboard merely sum-marised the goals of the issue which, together with values, methods and results, had all been introduced by students. To give an example, one student recommended that special communities should be constructed for disabled people, to which another student commented that such a provision would amount to "segregation, and that's wrong."

2. (a) Both parts were again 100 per cent consistent and most parts of the specification were covered.

(b) The budget issue was only covered superficially in twenty minutes, but it was used to illustrate what had been covered already concern-ing the financial policies of central government. Alternatives received little attention. The issue of the disabled was thoroughly covered. Alternative arrangements in other societies were not mentioned. In common with other issues which concern minorities, this was hardly a political problem. Consequently there was little scope for debating different ideological positions. Nevertheless it was a real and immediate issue which involved all the students.

i. (c) The teacher had to provide a lot of the details about who promotes what policies, different ways and means of influence etc.

(d) The students provided some information, particularly about their own union's views (NALGO), and asked questions themselves.

ii. (c) The teacher had to provide some details but a few questions were sufficient to enable the disabled student to introduce all the necessary information. For example, "Is the ... (Local Council) ... required to provide special housing?". "How are they required to do this; what makes them?"

(d) Almost all the political literacy specification was covered by the students asking questions, such as "How can we ensure that facil-ities in this College are suitable?"

3. (a) Between 70 per cent and 80 per cent of the lesson was consistent (it is difficult to be precise as nearly half the lesson compromised Episodes of informal discussion).

i. (b-d) Two Incidents by the teacher were consistent in the first part: one concerned with the effects of the budget negotiations on the students; and the other with the effects on and likely reactions of other trade unionists. No opportunity for action was presented.

ii. (b-d) All but four Incidents (the four factual questions) were con-sistent in the second part. The lesson was dominated by the inter-ests of both the disabled and the others on the issue. Only the dis-abled student could refer to first-hand experiences, the most relevant of which was as a member of the staff-student committee.

4. (a) Between 50 per cent and 60 per cent of the lesson was consistent.

i. (b-d) The concept of 'Representation' and the governing concepts were introduced by the students. One student commented about the procedures for the conditional budget negotiations, "Isn't that the wrong way round? This is what democracy is all about. They (*the TUC*) are making decisions for their members". Another student asked:

"When the budget has been approved by the TUC what happens if the trade unions demand more?" A discussion then followed which included the concepts of 'Power', 'Authority', 'Force' and 'Order'.

ii. (b) The second part of the lesson referred to all the popular concepts as well as 'Law', 'Representation' and 'Justice'.

(c) The teacher introduced the concept of 'Law' in respect of the facilities for the disabled by giving details of the provisions of and background to the Chronically Sick and Disabled Persons Act 1970.

(d) Consideration of all the popular concept arose in the students' discussion. (A re-reading of the definitions given in document 2.3 will indicate how especially suited this topic is to a consideration of these concepts!) With regard to 'Welfare' one student asked, "What provisions are there (for the disabled, in this college) in the event of a fire?"

5. (a) At least 80 per cent of the lesson was consistent. It is possible to regard the few neutral parts dealing with factual material as being in some way consistent with 'Reasoning'.

(b) 'Toleration' and 'Freedom' were clearly evident although 'Freedom' did not amount to making effective decisions except in the case of the disabled student. 'Reasoning' did not include 'scepticism about factual claims' and, as neither of the elements of 'Truth' were present, 'Fairness' was limited.

(c/d) Virtually all of the elements of the procedural values depended on the interaction of student discussion although 'Reasoning' was supported by deliberate but restrained and only occasional teacher involvement.

6. Only one Incident was residual and neutral, the returning of marked essays at the beginning of the lesson.

All five students were interviewed after each lesson and occasionally in the students' common room before the lesson commenced.

Comment

The college was probably a fairly typical example of an FE college. The students were on average older than those in school. The air of greater maturity was enhanced by, in the case of part-timers, their experience of the world of work; and, in the case of full-timers, by their antipathy to the atmosphere of secondary school. Compared with secondary school students they had a keener sense of their personal 'rights' and were more willing to express and assert these 'rights'. The college staff were more sympathetic to the views of students than might generally be the case in secondary schools. There were a significant number of students who were older than the staff and had a first-hand experience of the subject matter of college courses. The atmosphere was harmonious.

Without doubt, the college rooms were uninviting and uninspiring; but this appeared to have no adverse effect. The age or wider experience of students may have been a compensating factor. The kind of teaching which was possible was very restricted, especially in contrast to the facilities available for the similar programme in School D. Nevertheless, the teacher took the students outside the college as much as possible, to council meetings and rent tribunals etc.

The small class size was an advantage in that any seating arrangements were informal and only the most traditional teacher could have succeeded in establishing a formal lecturing stance. The small class had its disadvantages. There was a narrow range of opinion and source of experience, for which the teacher had to go to considerable lengths to compensate. This was partly done by means of well prepared handouts and partly by skilful exploitation of the experiences of the students. The teacher's questions were a careful mixture of factual and open-reasoning intended to draw out new information rather than to repeat taught material. At least as many classroom questions were student-initiated, none of which could be regarded as tangential and all of which helped establish which material interested them. (See the introductory remarks about the teaching style and the footnote reference on page   to group learning experiences).

The students had mixed feelings about the style. They found the lesson extremely interesting and enjoyable but they were very worried about the apparent neglect of the examination syllabus as the exams were drawing closer. "Well, for example there's the Law Lecturer, he just dictates notes all the time and we'll just have to learn them for the exam. But with Mr. ... you don't really know what you're supposed to learn." (In the event, all but one, a persistent absentee who failed all the examinations, obtained good passes and two obtained credits.)

The teacher had no such worries about apparently abandoning the examination syllabus and teaching through issues. At the time there were two encouraging features of the new approach. He claimed it was far more enjoyable to teach and that the heightened student interest was both stimulating and reassuring. The good examination results were a later bonus.

The lesson planning began with political issues and continued to focus on them. At no time was the impression given that issues were merely the dressing and that the examination syllabus was the more serious stuff which was, for some reason, being overlooked. The issues were given the highest status and, as a result, understanding of those institutional factors which were relevant to the issues was thereby enhanced.

Only a few issues were considered. They were carefully and thoughtfully selected and prepared. As a consequence of this, most of the political literacy specification was covered without too much difficulty. Political concepts seemed to arise naturally although there did not seem to be any inevitability about this. However, given the wide coverage of the political literacy analysis the presence of some of the procedural values probably was inevitable.

Conclusion

The course was very successful, the main reason undoubtedly being the priority given to political issues. The additional factor was the way in which the students were enabled to become involved and interested in the chosen issues. The only scope for improvement was in respect of procedural values. Here the political literacy objectives in this respect would probably have to be made explicit by the teacher rather than the teacher merely providing opportunities for the values to emerge.

4.4.6 School F*: Comprehensive and Community College

This is a mixed Comprehensive School and Community College, formed some years ago from a Grammar School and two Secondary Modern Schools, and

* This report was made and written by G.S.V. Petter whereas the others
  in this section are by Alex Porter (*Editors*).

The teaching programmes

serving a coastal and inland area. Many evening activities involve parents and students, and this institution is clearly a focal point for social and educational activity in the town and its surrounding districts.

The teaching programme:

The following syllabus was devised for a group of less able boys and a group of less able girls in the fourth year, and for two similar groups in the fifth year. For those in the fourth year all nine lessons (of seventyfive minutes each) were to be included; for those in the fifth year, eight periods were allotted, this because the timetable of public examination impinged on the school curriculum.

This syllabus has been fitted into a General Studies course which is taken by students in the fourth and fifth years. Other subjects included health and careers guidance.

POLITICIAL EDUCATION TOPICS

1. What does the future hold?
   In what direction is mankind developing?
   Can all peoples of the world anticipate improving living conditions?
   Is there quite simply enough food to go round?
   If resources of the world have to be husbanded, what measure of national and international control will be necessary?
   What are the dangers in the future? - independent nationalism - international communism - regional poverty - mass destruction - automation.
   Where does this leave the individual who is probably seeking personal happiness and security?
   Can he find it himself? Is the happiness of individuals tied up with the dangerous elements that seem almost beyond individual control?
   What do you think about war?
   What do you think about centralised government control over personal issues?
   What do you think about international resource control?
   What do you think about automation? - decisions being made by machines about your personal life.
   Who will make these decisions that will determine your future?
   What say will you have?

2. How can I have a say when no one will listen to me?
   What is the position of young people in society today?
   Is their role simply to be a pressure group?
   What measure of consultation should we afford young people? - in the home - in the school - in society.
   When should they be independent - what does independence mean? ...
   Consultation in school and community college - why not decision-making? Whose responsibility is it?
   What are the responsibilities of parents in relation to young people?
   What do some parents want to decide for their children? - school subjects - friends - hours - money - careers.
   What responsibility do young people have towards their parents?
   Why are generation viewpoints different? Life experience - war - affluence - religion - social acceptance - personal freedom - education ...

3. What are the underlying concepts?
   The basis on which our democracy is founded. What are our rights as individuals? Do we know precisely? How is it established? The Communist has his Red Book, the United States' citizen his Bill of

234

Rights. What do we have? Nothing formally written. Freedoms have
been established by precedent. Rights are determined by law.
Justice is available to all according to a legal pattern. Fairness
exists within a traditionally established framework. The basis of
democracy is corporate decision-making – the will of the majority.
Upholding those decisions is the responsibility of government,
national and local. We need government – the implementation of
rules – in order to live together as a community.
Do we accept the need for rules – in the home – in school – in
society?
Who makes the rules? ...
Which rules would we as young people change? How can we change them?
By operating within the system or by ignoring the system? ...
When is the individual justified in going against the system of
rules? Is he ever justified?

4. Our future part in national decision-making
   The process – Parliamentary election
                  Party system – the responsibility of the member to his
                  constituents, to his party, to his sponsors
                  Government – democratic decision-making
   Pressures upon Parliament and Government,
       Public meeting   Party conferences, Local political
                                  parties
       Protest, demonstration   City
       Lobbying   CIB
       Mass media   TUC
   Referendum – Fact and opinion. Voting.
   Sorting out grievances. Expressing personal opinion. The ombudsman.
   The right to complain and how to do it.
   Keeping oneself informed – a responsible democracy depends upon an
   educated electorate.
   The consumer and Nationalised Industry. Electricity, gas, coal,
   railways, airways, telephones, post.
   Then detail similar to that above was given for the following
   syllabus headings:

5. The local scene
6. You and the law
7. Where do you get the information? Fact and opinion
8. How will you fit in when you leave school? (The majority of this
   session was given over to talk and discussion on Trade Unionism.)
and lastly,
9. What are the values that you will stand for? (Part of this session
   should be the discussion of a questionnaire based upon the personal
   issues.)
   Where do you stand personally?
   How will you determine your success?
   What contribution will you make to society?
   What will your standpoint be? What do you consider the State's
   responsibility is to you? What do you expect?
   Does society owe you a living? What kind of life are you looking
   for?
   How will you assert yourself individually? Will you be a joiner?
   Are you a loner? How strongly do you feel a social responsibility?
   How do you feel about bringing up a family? How good a parent will
   you be? What standards will you set for your children?
   Where do you stand on major personal issues?
       Marriage & divorce, abortion   Euthenasia

The teaching programmes

Homosexuality	Capital punishment
The Church & the State	Vivisection
Population control	Censorship
Overseas Aid	The right of the individual to pay
Caring for the aged/handicapped	for his privilege – health, education, home.

What personal prejudices do you have?
Where did they come from? – parents – education – experience – fear
How fair-minded are you?
How unbiassed will your political opinion be?

All the teaching was undertaken by the headmaster who said that he was taking full responsibility himself because of the sensitivity of his staff, some of whom appeared somewhat suspicious of the programme, and to prevent any possible difficulty with parents or governors.

Only two visits to the school were possible because of shortage of funds and the long distance which had to be travelled. But the visits, though they yielded of necessity only impressions, were valuable because they included far more than mere observation of lessons. It was possible to take part in evening activities, to observe members of the school and of the community college going about their normal business and sense the atmosphere. It was also possible to have extended conversations with the headmaster both about the problem of introducing political literacy for the first time and about the difficulty of mobilising the interest of pupils. As will be seen, the problem of introducing political education proved less difficult to solve than might have been expected; but the matter of enlisting the interest and enthusiasm of pupils, particularly girls, presented difficulties which the headmaster feels have still to be overcome.

An interesting feature of this school's participation in the project was the fact that the first visit included lessons observed in two groups of boys, one in the fourth-year and the other in the fifth; the second visit, which took place in the next school year, was devoted to a class of fifth-year girls who had been involved in their fourth-year with the syllabus set out above. The comments which follow therefore are concerned with reaction of boys to the syllabus in its first year of operation; the second visit was devoted to some investigation of the reaction of fifth-year girls who had already taken part in the programme during the previous school year.

The selected lessons – A

Topic 8. "How will you fit in when you leave school?"

The setting was the normal classroom of standard size. The boys sat at desks arranged in the traditional manner with the headmaster facing them. The style of teaching was socratic, based, that is, on question and answer with good use of information distributed for students to see. In this case the documentation included legislative procedures concerning employment.

A trade unionist, a post office worker had been invited to make a small presentation to the boys about the trade union movement and to answer questions. The atmosphere of the classroom was relaxed from the start and the lesson gained momentum as it went along. Seventyfive minutes seemed initially to be too long a stretch of time, but this preconception proved false. One did not notice the passage of time, and discussion was more eager and strenuous after an hour than one would have expected.

236

The lesson content

The lesson was divided into two parts, the first dealing with getting a job and the second concerned with membership of trade unions. Though the political content seemed remote when proceedings were opened, it was in the centre of the picture after one hour and a quarter.

The first part of the lesson might well have been labelled 'careers education'. It was concerned with the future of individual boys, their reasons for choosing the job that they in fact chose, and the general prospect of employment in the immediate vicinity and elsewhere. All this had the effect of making pupils feel that the matter in hand was one in which they were necessarily involved.

Hence, when the trade union worker was asked to speak about trade unions and the responsibilities and rights of membership, there was very close attention. The issues involved concerned relations between workers and employers, and the operation of individual trade unions in relation to the movement in general as well as to the government. It also covered the status of individual members of a union and their rights and duties. Skills, attitudes and participation produced very strong reactions. It appeared that there was considerable doubt in the minds of some boys about whether it was necessary to join a union at all, and equal doubt about the duty of members to take strike action when advised to do so. The trade union worker stressed the importance of a collective stand by members in order to protect individuals, but some boys were doubtful about the wisdom of this. They wanted to know whether it would not be better for a dissatisfied worker to approach management direct and make his own peace. On the matter of strikes, even stronger reactions were manifest. The headmaster expressed himself as not in favour, as a teacher, of strike action, the trade union worker being adamant that it was a necessary weapon.

Direct reference to political concepts (as set out in document 2.3) was not specifically made. But 'Power' and 'Authority' were clearly contrasted; 'Freedom' and 'Welfare' were also featured. The flavour of political concepts was clearly distinguishable to the observer; how much they were recognised by the boys is difficult to say.

Values stood out strongly; they were perhaps treated rather more as substantive values than as the procedural values described in document 2.4. Certainly 'Freedom' and 'Toleration' came through strongly, also 'Respect for Truth'. But underlying all the discussion, and emphasised strongly by the headmaster, was the notion of 'Obligation' as the counter weight to 'Freedom'.

The selected lessons: B

Topic 7. "Where do you get the information? Fact and Opinion"

This was a lesson to a group of twentythree fifth-year boys.

The setting and the teaching style were traditional; the classroom atmosphere relaxed. Clearly the relation between the boys and the head was one of mutual respect.

The lesson was not concerned with political issues as such; rather with information available from the media, the way it is presented and the degree to which it has an impact on the ordinary citizen.

Although the official title of the lesson indicated that it was concerned with the media, the second part of it in fact was devoted to a shortened version of a questionnaire put out by the Political Education Research Unit at York. Thus, though the basis of the lesson was knowledge rather than issues, the knowledge embraced basic knowledge about

membership of the Cabinet, the TUC, devolution and international affairs.
The lesson content
It is not possible to analyse this lesson on the lines set out in the
Appendix because the objectives were restricted. But the effect of producing four popular newspapers was to enable the headmaster to find out
which papers the parents took and how many boys in fact read them. In
the event, seven out of twentythree boys read newspapers every day, but
not the pages concerned with political matters. No one could say what
the political slant of the four newspapers was.

Of the twentythree boys, six were regular subscribers to magazines, but
these included *Angling Times, Shooting Times, Farmers' Weekly* and
Motor Cycle News. It is a point of interest that though all boys paid
out of their own pockets for these weekly magazines, no boy bought his
own newspaper.

There appeared general ignorance about the radio. Nobody knew the
popular names given to radio news programmes, e.g. *The World at One.* Out
of twentythree boys, two only listened to news broadcasts every day,
though twentytwo out of twentythree owned a radio. Nobody listened regularly to any radio programme.

Television produced much the most lively response. Two boys said that
there were four television sets in their homes; no one was without television. Out of twentythree boys, seven watched TV for less than two
hours a day, one for less than three hours, eight for less than five
hours, but two for more than five hours; two watched for more than six
hours. Of the two boys who watched most television, neither proved to
have much elementary political knowledge. No one appeared to watch do-
cumentary programmes, but everyone watched some national and international news every day. One or two discussed or argued political
matters with their parents.

Television rather than radio or newspaper appeared to be the medium
through which boys learnt most, and if they were to learn about politics,
it would be through TV that they learnt.

The questionnaire from York produced some interesting results. In the
fourth-year group to whose members the questionnaire had previously been
put, correct answers to twenty questions had ranged from six to nineteen,
the average being between ten and twelve. In the fifth year lesson which
is now being described a very similar result was obtained. On the other
hand, the headmaster had been requested to put the questionnaire to a
group of 'O' level candidates, and he arranged to do this with a group
of fifteen. Of those fifteen pupils, the lowest score was seven (by
one pupil); two pupils scored sixteen, two eighteen and the remaining
ten, nineteen out of twenty.

This session was only concerned with issues in as much as the media,
in particular the newspapers, were a means by which political points of
view could be put. Nor was it an occasion on which many political concepts could be used. 'Freedom' and 'Pressure' were explicitly mentioned, but there was no concern with 'Power' and 'Authority' as such.

Procedural values played a major part, particularly 'Respect for
Truth', 'Fairness' and 'Freedom'. But, as in the fourth-year lesson, the
object of the exercise was not so much to introduce procedural values in
the context of the project papers as to suggest certain substantive
values which the press, the radio and newspapers brought into play.

The selected lessons: C

This was a lesson to a group of about thirty fifth-year girls who had,
in the previous year, been through the syllabus. The purpose of the

headmaster was, on this occasion, to find out how much impact the fourth year's work had made. Initially, the result appeared to be disappointing. Girls could with difficulty be induced to say anything at all, and when they did start to talk, they gave the impression that they felt that very little of what they had done in the previous year was their concern.

Very wisely, the headmaster took up the matter of 'concern', and devoted the period to eliciting from the girls what they considered did concern them, and what the concern of the world would be over the next quarter of the century.

The issues raised in discussion were race, the population explosion, and world food shortage. Of these issues, the only one which caused more than a flicker of reaction was that of race, and here prejudice was strong. On the issue of population explosion and the problem of food supply, both introducing the Third World, the general reaction was that these matters were too far removed from the experience of the girls to warrant their taking much interest in them. By the end of the lesson, a small number were evidently convinced that they had some responsibility to know at any rate something about the problems which had to be faced.

Comment

These lessons illustrate both the opportunities and the difficulties which face teachers introducing political literacy as a specific element in the school programme for the first time. The opportunity is that a skilful teacher can reassure pupils by reminding them of knowledge that they already possess, the relevance of which they had previously not understood. The difficulty that the teacher faced was that of harnessing knowledge to the literacy tree and to the political concepts. The introduction of procedural values was relatively simple; the introduction of certain issues and concepts was not difficult. What proved difficult with the boys and girls on this occasion was to make a systematic application of the literacy tree, bringing in all its aspects.

In as far as the literacy tree and the arguments of document 2.2 could be used in the lessons observed, it was manifest that both boys and girls tended when faced with an issue to ask how it would affect them personally before they asked where the issue would be settled. Most difficult of all was to make both boys and girls – and particularly the girls – feel involved. There was no lack of interest; pupils were prepared to listen and listen attentively. There were signs of growing confidence in that, very gradually, both boys and girls were made to realise that they already possessed some of the knowledge necessary to help them to understand political issues and to participate in settling them. But there was still a great though understandable gap between an awareness of the issue in question and any realisation that active participation was either possible or desirable.

Conclusion

The technique of adopting a module of six to eight lessons succeeded within the limits imposed upon it. In this school and community college, the time, in the view of the observer, had been well spent in that the initial interest of pupils had been enlisted.

Appendix: Research design and procedure

The data for these studies were collected in accordance with a carefully
predetermined set of criteria derived for the most part from the recommendations of the project documents. As far as possible the criteria and
the methodology were adapted from those appearing in accounts of similar
studies. Our objectives were like those predominant in studies which
have been classified as Comparative Studies[5]. Specifically the studies
were intended to be Matching Studies which were designed to compare
actual classroom practices with the behavioural objectives of the project
- that lessons should be conducted according to the specifications of political literacy in the project documents. The studies were also, to
some extent, to be a mixture of both 'formative' and 'summative' studies.
By formative studies in this context we mean that feedback from the observer was intended to bring classroom practice closer to the project
specifications. The studies were to be summative to the extent that
measurements of achievement in implementing the project specifications
were to be introduced and comment was to be made on how well the specifications were implemented in different settings.

The techniques I devised for the comparative work were based on those
described by Wright (1959)[6] in a process study, and by Smith (1970)[7] in the
only example of a matching study quoted by Eggleston, Galton and Jones
(1975). For the purposes of recording classroom practices I decided to
use the 'stimulus-response' Incident[8] unit of interaction. In practice
this meant a single question and answer sequence. This was chosen because it was likely to be the smallest division of classroom behaviour
which could include a reference to political concepts. (Reference to
political concepts was likely to be the briefest example of specified behaviour). It was anticipated that longer and more complex units of interaction were more appropriate to categories of behaviour concerned with
either political values or political issues and that such 'Venture' or
'Episode' units could be built up from recorded Incidents when observation schedules and field notes were later analysed. The relationship
between Incidents and Episodes was derived from Smith (1970)[9]. The proposed method was to record the full content of all question-initiated
Incidents. The data was later to be analysed according to predetermined
categories of specified practice to decide the extent to which classroom
practice had been 'consistent' with the behavioural objectives of the
project.

5 Eggleston, Galton and Jones, "A conceptual map for interaction studies"
  in Chanan, G. and Delamont, S. *Fontiers of Classroom Research* (NFER
  1975)
6 Wright, E.M.J. "Development of an instrument for studying verbal be-
  haviours in secondary school mathematics classrooms" *Journal of
  Experimental Education* Vol. 28, No. 2 (1959)
7 Smith, J.P. "The development of a classroom observation instrument
  relevant to the earth sciences curriculum project" *Journal of Research
  in Science Teaching,* Vol. 8, No. 3, (1970)
8 Nuthall, G.A. and Lawrence, P.J. *Thinking in the Classroom* (New Zealand
  Council for Educational Research, 1965)
9 Smith, B.O. & Meux, M.O. et al, *A study of the Logic of Teaching,*
  (University of Illinois Press, 1970)

In practice, the observation technique turned out to be very useful as a frame of reference but in many circumstances too restricted if applied rigidly. The technique assumed a model of teacher-managed interaction. Where there was a very high proportion of student participation, as in Schools A, E and F, the proposed method could not have recorded all significant data. At the other extreme, where student participation was very low and the lessons largely comprised formal lecturing, as in School C, there would have been too few question-initiated Incidents to record. In these cases a longer, Episode, unit of observation was necessary to record sufficient data for analysis.

The categories of specified practice, subsequently used to analyse the collected observation data, are set out in table III. These I derived from the project documents reproduced in Section 2 and, for further clarification, they should be checked against the detailed accounts in the documents. The categories refer to the overt behaviour of the teachers and students; i.e. a 'Category 1.1 practice' was manifest when a teacher or student asked, in the context of discussing a political disagreement, what purpose a given action should serve.

Table III

1. Mention of political Issues, i.e. mention of disagreement over:
    - Goals (what purpose should a given action serve?)
    - Values (in what way should we act or not act?)
    - Methods (how should we do it?)
    - Results (was it the right outcome?)

    4 Categories

---

2. Mention of:
    - who promotes various policies
    - the institutional arena for conflicts
    - how existing institutions help or hinder settlement
    - different ways and means of influence
    - appropriate ways and means for particular purposes
    - alternative political arrangements, sources of information and ways of looking at given information

    9 Categories

---

3. Mention of the effects of disputes on oneself and on other people. Opportunity given to express individual interests and to justify the pursuit of those interests
    Mention of the interests and the justification of others

    Provision made for first-hand experience of conflict of values and of choice
    Student insistence on taking part, being heard etc.

    12 Categories

---

4. Use made of Political Concepts of Power, Force, Authority, Order, Law, Justice, Representation, Pressure, Natural Rights, Individuality, Freedom and Welfare

    12 Categories

---

5. Use made of Procedural Values of Freedom, Fairness, Toleration, Respect for Truth and Respect for Reasoning (as illustrated in document 2.4)

    19 Categories

Total Number of Categories Prescribed
Project Documents - 56 Categories

The first stage of analysis, therefore, involved my checking through all the recorded data to decide whether there had been any mention of political issues, and, if so, in what form (the four section 1 categor-ies). Any mention of a political issue was identified on the lesson transcripts and marked as being 'consistent' with project specificat-ions. If, say, five recorded Incidents were 'consistent' out of a total of twentyfive lesson Incidents, the lesson was classified as being 20 per cent 'consistent' in respect of section 1 categories.
The procedure was then repeated for the 'Political Literacy Tree co-

lumns 1-3 specification' (the nine section 2 categories) and yet again
for columns 4-7 (the twelve section 3 categories). So, for example, if
an Incident included reference to 'Knowledge of alternative types of
societies' it was marked as 'consistent'. Incidents could be classified
as 'inconsistent' with these categories if they represented a total negation of the specified objectives, such as wrong information being given
or the topic being ruled as inadmissible.

This procedure was repeated for a fourth time and the recorded data was
checked against each of the twelve section 4 categories. Either the
contextual use of the word or the use of a 'definition' or an 'account'
of the concept was regarded as sufficient to mark that the Incident was
'consistent'. Incidents which did not employ the specified political
concepts were classed as 'neutral'. No Incidents were to be classed as
'inconsistent'.

The analysis for the 'Procedural Values' (Project document 2.4) was
difficult and unsatisfactory. The values and the document suggest a
<u>general direction</u> that classroom practice ought to take but proved not to
give an adequate guide to the <u>form</u> it ought to take. The only clues to
the form are given by locating the values in the political literacy diagrams "to show the kinds of factors ... which might best combine to illustrate the actual working of the (*values*)" (see paragraph 11). But
these do not in practice amount to a specification of the form of classroom practice. It has not been made clear how many parts of the political literacy tree are sufficient for a value to be present or whether the
values could be present if none of these parts featured in a lesson. As
no other basis of judgement was provided, the assumption made for the
purpose of analysis was that a lesson could be classified as more or
less 'consistent' with the specified procedural values according to how
many Incidents corresponded to those parts of the political literacy
tree (i.e. the nineteen section 5 categories) and which were combined as
specified in the diagram given in document 2.4 There could be 'inconsistent' practice if wrong information was given or if any Incidents
amounted to a negation of the specification of the political literacy
tree.

Lesson Incidents which were 'neutral' with regard to all 5 components
of the analysis were grouped together in a 'Residual' category. As a
large proportion of the data did fall into this 'Residual' category a
lot of effort had been expended in constructing and using the framework
of analysis with little by way of 'consistent' practice to show for it.

The above scheme formed the basis of the work involved in monitoring
what was going on in the six schools, of presenting five of the
teaching programmes, and of measuring the 'success' of teachers in
implementing project objectives.

In addition to the observation of lessons a considerable amount of data
was collected about the teaching programme, the school, and the views of
teachers and students. Students were interviewed after the lessons had
been observed and we tried to gauge the extent to which they were aware
of those characteristics of the lesson which were related to the project
specifications. These interviews with students were also useful in providing additional details of the unobserved parts of the teaching programmes and of the school setting. Their opinions of the teaching
programme and their changes in opinion as the course progressed were
noted and have been taken into account in the commentaries and conclusions. The changes in their apparent attitude to and awareness of political issues were also of similar interest. These interviews and the
events of the lessons we observed were discussed with the teachers. This

experience, together with details of the experience with other participating schools, was in part intended to encourage innovations and modifications towards, where appropriate, a greater consistency with project specifications.

The accounts of the teaching programmes are intended to be more qualitative than quantitative. The studies aimed at describing and illuminating as fully as possible those aspects of the programmes which concerned the project in their particular settings. The accounts are attempts to describe the observed relationship between the estimated 'success' of the programmes and a wide range of other factors. These factors include such things as the general characteristics of the school setting and the students involved; the immediate teaching environment; the style of teaching and the lesson interaction; and the form in which the programme was included in the curriculum. Only those details have been included which were deemed to be relevant to this 'success' as much of the work undertaken in accordance with the planned methodology, especially the student interviews, produced data which appeared to be of no particular consequence.

The word 'success', wherever it appears, has been used in a strictly limited sense. Naturally it does not extend to include any educational objectives beyond the scope of the project. More importantly , it does not include an evaluation of the extent to which the teaching led to gains in the political literacy of students. The responsibility for such evaluation belonged to the independent Political Education Research Unit at the University of York and an account of their work will appear separately. Success in this particular study involves, initially, the ability to implement those project recommendations which I selected and summarised for the purposes of analysing lesson practices. It additionally involves the teacher having prepared and planned to implement the project recommendations and some students having become aware of the project-based content of the lessons. The more the teacher and some students were satisfied with the progress of such a lesson the more successful it was considered to be. We may not, however, infer any forms of success beyond that which was defined for the purposes of these studies and which is confined to those events observed by a Development Officer or those described by teachers or students. Even very successful programmes in these terms may not necessarily lead to longer-term results, such as gains in the political literacy of students or a continuing programme of political education in a school or a wider take-up of the ideas of that programme.

Two further charactersitics of the work must be appreciated. Throughout the studies all participants, both teachers and students, were kept fully informed about the objectives, procedures and progress of the studies. They probably knew as much about what we were doing and what we were looking for as we ourselves did. Consequently there was a process of continual adjustment of procedures in the light of the views of the participants.

As a direct consequence of the limited resources available, all the work of observing each lesson and analysing the related data was the responsibility of one person working alone. There are, therefore, no measurements of inter-observer reliability. All the accounts are one person's subjective impressions, the intended theoretical basis of which has been described as fully as possible in order to provide some means whereby the reader may form his/her own conclusions.

Alex Porter

5

APPENDIX

A. PARLIAMENT, THE PUBLIC AND POLITICAL EDUCATION*
   by John Sutton (the Chairman of the Politics Association)

"If the people can't trust their government, the whole works will fall
 apart." (Harry S. Truman)

1. It has been widely asserted that the confidence which the British
people place in their political institutions, and especially Parliament,
has declined in recent years. The Politics Association believes that
such a trend is less to be associated with failings within the institutions themselves than with a failure to present, not simply Parliament
but the broad principles and practice of Parliamentary politics to the
public, and especially the younger generation, in a systematic and pur-
poseful way. The Association seeks to end the long neglect of political
education as the best long-term means of ensuring that 'the whole works'
does not fall apart and, in looking at the particular problem of the
presentation of Parliament, it is conscious that this is only one part,
albeit a vital one, in 'the whole works'.

2. The Politics Association is in no doubt that schools and colleges
should support the principles and practices of parliamentary politics in
a broad sense, but would not wish to exclude from political education
the consideration of alternative ways of doing things both within and
without the system. Simply to promote the virtues of the existing order
without regard either to its short-comings or to alternatives is as educationally sterile as it is unimaginative and unrealistic.

3. In considering the presentation of Parliament in the broader context of political education, the Association deliberately avoids discussing Parliament in isolation because it is precisely by presenting
Parliament in isolation in the past that it has been too frequently seen
by the public as 'boring' and irrelevant to their lives.

*This was originally prepared as a submission to the Hansard Society's
 working party on 'Public and Parliament' as part of their Future of
 Parliamentary Institutions in Europe Programme. But it was communicated
 to the House of Commons Committee on Services of the House which led to
 Mr. Sutton giving evidence to that committee.

The background

4. Most industrialised countries make some provision for political education. In many, a programme of political instruction is seen as a vital and compulsory part of the curriculum. In some, including England, political education has traditionally been seen as peripheral and incidental. In England there has been, until recently, a total neglect of political education sustained by a marked reluctance even to face the issues which it might raise.

5. From 1870, when Robert Lowe saw in the Elementary Education Act the need 'to educate our masters', successive governments have acknowledged the duty of the school system to instil respect and acceptance of the established political order. Such instillation, however, was always seen as indirect, proceeding on unwritten assumptions and pious hopes. Indeed, such pronouncements on the subject as emanated from official sources tended to stress the importance of duty and conformity.

6. The 'School Government edition of the Manual of the Code and 'suggestions' for the consideration of teachers and others concerned in the work of Public Elementary Schools, 1909-10' spoke of "the high function of the teacher .... to prepare the child for the life of the good citizen" but clearly saw such preparation as the product of the general character development of children in schools through the promotion of "loyalty to comrades, loyalty to institutions, unselfishness and an orderly and disciplined habit of mind."

7. In spite of the attempts of some eminent political and social scientists in the 1930s to arouse public concern over the lack of political education, the official view continued to be hostile to any direct approach. The Spens Report in 1938 again favoured the indirect method:

"The importance of history, and in particular recent history for its own sake is obvious; moreover, since with pupils under 16 the theoretical discussion of economic questions is impracticable, and the objections to the direct discussion of current political questions are considerable, recent political and economic history is the best introduction to the study of politics. Not only does it supply the necessary information, but it can also be taught so as to induce a balanced attitude which recognizes differing points of view and sees the good on both sides ... it is in this way, by precept or still more by the breadth of their own sympathies, that teachers can best educate pupils to become citizens of a modern democratic country."

8. The Norwood Report of 1943 laid even more emphasis on the importance of good citizenship but was explicit in its denial that politics could be taught, except incidentally, in any systematic way before the age of sixteen.

"Nothing but harm can result, in our opinion, from attempts to interest pupils prematurely in matters which imply the experience of an adult - immediate harm to the pupil from forcing of interest, harm in the long run to the purpose in view from his unfavourable reaction ..."

"In this connection we wish to consider one of the many topics which have been brought to our attention for inclusion in the curriculum, namely education for citizenship. From what has already been said we hope it is clear that we regard it as of vital importance that education should give boys and girls a preparation for their life as citizens. We agree with the contention of the evidence which has reached us that British men and women should have clearer conceptions of the institutions of their country, how it is governed and administered centrally and locally, of the British Commonwealth and its origins and working, and of the present social and economic structure, and that they should realise their duties and responsibilities as members of these smaller and greater units of society. Of all this we have no doubt. But we remind ourselves that the growth from childhood to adolescence and so to citizenship is a gradual process and that, if the later stages are to be sound, the earlier stages cannot be forcibly hurried through. The practical problem is to discover how much can appropriately be taught to children at different stages of their development and how that teaching can best be given. Our own belief may be shortly put, thus. Teaching of the kind desired can best be given incidentally, by appropriate illustration and comment and digression, through the ordinary school subjects, particularly history, geography, English and foreign languages and literature. Nevertheless lessons devoted explicitly to public affairs can suitably be given to older boys and girls certainly at the sixth form stage, and probably immediately before this stage. The most valuable influence for developing that sense of responsibility without which any amount of sheer information is of little benefit is the general spirit and outlook of the school - what is sometimes called the 'tone' of the school."

9. Even after the 1944 Education Act, which specifically referred to the need for preparation for 'the responsibilities of citizenship', official publications of the Department of Education and of the Schools Council have continued to avoid the challenge of how that pious intentions of promoting good citizenship should be implemented in the classroom. The Newsom Report (1963), dealing specifically with those who left school at the earliest opportunity, stated the problem with admirable clarity:

"A man who is ignorant of the society in which he lives, who knows nothing of its place in the world and who has not thought about his place in it, is not a free man even though he has a vote. He is easy game for 'the hidden persuaders'."

Alas, the Report did not go on to say how that ignorance should be remedied.

10. Where political education has occurred at all, it has been in one or two forms:

(a) Civics: Many courses have been provided under this heading, particularly for senior pupils in the now disappearing Secondary Modern Schools. Typically, they are concerned with a description of the mechanics of central and local government and prescriptive of the conformist and deferential participation of the good citizen as a voter. So long as such participation was at some distance removed from the school-leaving age and the institutions described were remote and seemingly irrelevant anyway, such courses were doomed to achieve only very limited success.
(b) British Constitution: In many Grammar Schools, Comprehensive Schools and Colleges of Further Education, 'O' and 'A' level courses have been offered as options. Indeed, until it was to some extent supplemented by sociology in the last few years, British Constitutions was a major growth

subject, useful at 'O' level for the increasing numbers reaching the fifth year of Secondary Education without a foreign language, and equally at 'A' level as a further choice for pupils who wished to avoid the more traditional 'A' level subjects. Frequently, it was seen as a 'soft option' or 'make-weight' subject, valuable more as a ticket to the next educational staging-point than for its intrinsic value.

The nature of the syllabuses offered was not dissimilar to the Civics approach already described. Too often, the syllabuses and the examination papers reflected a concern with procedural minutiae and institutional description which were far removed from the real world of politics. The good teacher, who put political flesh and blood onto his dessicated skeleton, did so in the knowledge that his pupils found it interesting even if the examiner would not ask them to reproduce it!

11. The neglect of political education which has been such a feature of the English system has created a situation in which the majority of pupils leaving school at the age of sixteen are ignorant of even the most basic political issues. A research project, sponsored by the Leverhulme Trust and promoted by the Hansard Society for Parliamentary Government, looked at the level of political knowledge among school-leavers and confirmed the impression of those who worked in the field that very little was being done in schools to prepare young people for even a minimal involvement in political activity.

Reasons for the neglect of political education

12. The lack of effective political education may be ascribed in the first place to timidity. Local authorities and headteachers have been very conscious of the need to avoid any suggestion that political indoctrination might occur in schools. While Civics might be admissible, the very word 'politics' was inclined to arouse suspicion and evoke a defensive reaction. The Department of Education and Science, maintaining its position of non-involvement in curricular matters, has also tended to view this as a 'difficult' area.

13. A second reason for the neglect is undoubtedly the long-held assumption that appropriate political knowledge, skills and attitudes are somehow absorbed by the pupil in the course of the traditional school curriculum. It is doubtful whether this were ever true, except perhaps for a very small minority, and it is demonstrably not true today.

Indication of change

14. The initial impetus for the promotion of political education came from teachers. In 1969, a group of teachers formed the Politics Association, which has been active in assessing the nature of the problem and advocating appropriate remedial action. It has been able to suggest important modifications in the syllabuses in political subjects and examination questions of a number of the examining boards, and has been the focus for informed discussion on the wider question of political education for all. It has also sponsored the publication of a series of textbooks on *Political Realities*.

15. Specifically relating to Parliament, the Association, in 1973, was instrumental in negotiating and drawing up an agreement between the three major political parties on a code of practice to be adopted in the arrangement of sixth form conferences and talks in schools, to which

politicians were invited.

16. The Programme for Political Education with which the Politics Association has been closely associated, has received a limited degree of support from the Schools Council and the Department of Education and Science has appointed one of its Staff Inspectors to be an assessor of the Programme.

17. The Department of Education and Science recognised the work of the Association by making a grant to promote its activities over a period of three years.

18. The Schools Council has invited the Association to nominate a representative to its Social Sciences Committee.

19. Two Universities have recognised the particular importance of political education by making direct provision. The University of York has set up the Political Education Research Unit, under the direction of Professor Ian Lister, and has established a Joint Honours Degree in Politics and Education. The University of London Institute of Education had decided to establish a Lectureship in Education with particular reference to political education.

20. The BBC has given some recognition to the importance of political education by putting out a series of radio programmes *Teaching Politics: Problems and Perspectives* on Radio 3 in 1975 (repeated 1976), and a television series, *Politics Now* on BBC 1 in 1976.

21. A number of leading politicians of all parties have supported the work of the Politics Association by speaking at conferences and meetings. The Rt. Hon. Reginald Prentice, M.P., when in office as Secretary of State for Education and Science, strongly supported the promotion of political education. Speaking at the Association's Annual Conference in 1974, he said that he perceived a dangerous degree of disillusionment with politics:

"We cannot put it all down to apathy and mental laziness on the part of the electorate. Millions of people are not apathetic. They are deeply concerned about the future of our country but they do not feel very much enthusiasm for politicians of any party."

The Rt. Hon. Sir Keith Joseph, M.P., addressing a similar gathering in 1975, added his support:

"Very impressed I am by the efforts to define a framework of explanation that pays full respect to tolerance, truth, reason, freedom and civilized values. I acknowledge the honourable search by partial men and women for impartiality."

Politicians of all parties have recognized the disillusionment with politicians and with Parliament to which Mr. Prentice referred, and have seen in the development of political education on a sound basis the best hope of finding remedies.

Present and future needs in political education

22. The Politics Association believes that any official endorsement of

political education, such as exists, for instance, in the Federal German Republic or in the USA, would be both undesirable and out of keeping with the educational structure and traditions of this country. At the same time, it feels that there is great scope for official encouragement of local initiatives and for the creation of a climate of official opinion in which such initiatives can take place.

23. The Association would like to see the Department of Education and Science go forward from its initial support of political education by its grant to the Association, to promote in-service courses both for secondary teachers and for those in further education.

24. The Association would welcome the appointment of one of Her Majesty's Inspectors as a specialist in the field of political education.

25. The Association recommends that the Department of Education and Science should consider the promotion of in-service courses in the Youth Service and the exploration of other means by which political education might be advanced in the Youth Service.

26. The Association believes that urgent attention should be paid to the subject of political education in the training of teachers. A national conference in this field would be a first step towards appropriate developments.

27. The Association would like to see more resources than are at its disposal, or allocated to the Programme for Political Education, devoted to a national survey of the provision made for political education in schools, colleges of further education and teacher-training establishments.

The promotion of Parliament

28. Although the Association sees the problem of the presentation of Parliament in the wider context of political education generally, there are a number of recommendations which it wishes to put forward which relate specifically to Parliament.

29. Parliament has an important educational role to play in presenting itself which has been totally neglected in the past. Almost every famous national institution does more to present itself to the public than Parliament does, although the opportunity to do so is obvious and easy to grasp. If it is thought that the dignity of Parliament makes it either unnecessary or inappropriate for it to play such a role, the position should be reconsidered.

30. Educational visits to Parliament are very popular, but fall drastically short of achieving any but the most limited educational objectives. The following recommendations are made:
(a) That an Education Officer with appropriate staff should be appointed to promote the educational presentation of Parliament.
(b) That educational visits should be handled quite separately from other party visits (e.g. constituency groups, etc.)
(c) That guide-book material appropriate to young people should be made available.
(d) That the task of guiding and explaining the work of Parliament should be given to trained teachers. The present Custodians have an admirable

respect for Parliament and an encyclopaedic knowledge of its buildings
and customs, but have little to offer which could be described as political education.
(e) That a lecture-room should be provided at Westminster where educational parties can be appropriately briefed, with modern visual aids, and
where Parliamentary debates may be seen 'live' on closed-circuit television or (when Parliament is not sitting) in suitable recorded excerpts.
(f) That the booking of educational visits should be handled by the Education Officer and not by M.Ps. The Education Officer should, however,
inform Members of projected visits so that they might, if they wished,
make an appropriate contribution to the programme for the visit.

31. The Association believes that Parliament has also a general responsibility to present itself in a way which will positively help teachers
in the general work of political education. The following recommendations are made:
(a) That, linked with the promotion of educational visits, a general
public and educational information service should be set up which would:
  i.   provide a general information service, backed up by appropriate
       publications.
 ii.   answer public queries.
iii.   produce summaries of important parliamentary papers, including
       summaries of key debates.
 iv.   produce materials on Parliament suitable for educational use.
(b) That Her Majesty's Stationery Office should have many more outlets
to the public than at present, so that HMSO publications are readily
available 'over the counter' in all major centres of population. Teachers would thus have much better access than at present to materials
vital to good up-to-date teaching.
(c) That HMSO publications should be on sale at Westminster.

32. The Association is convinced that the presentation of Parliament
could be dramatically improved in return for a very modest expenditure
of capital and an equally modest annual budget. Such an improvement
would serve the cause of Parliamentary government and would be a practical step towards the provision of adequate political education in
Britain.

B. POLITICAL COMPETENCE
    John Slater and R.A.S. Hennessey*

1. Although the idea of political education is suspect to many people,
there are nevertheless compelling reasons for asserting its importance in
the 11-16 curriculum. It is of course already present in many subjects
of the curriculum: in history, geography, economics, even English and
religious education classes; work done under such headings as 'social'
and 'environmental' studies is often concerned with issues that are political. So political education does not necessarily mean the addition of
a new subject to the curriculum. But its importance to society requires
a clearer definition of its objectives, and of the knowledge and skills
and attitudes which are necessary to support it. We are not always confident that classes called 'politics' or 'government' are sufficient to
meet the requirements. Frequently they emphasise political machinery,
usually limited to that of central and local government, or political
philosophy, at the expense of real issues. Some schools would argue
that class teaching is less important than the development of school
councils in helping pupils to develop political competence. We would
not deny this, but would be doubtful whether this experience alone
transfers directly to make participation in society beyond the school
more effective. However it is true that political understanding for
11-16 year old pupils is affected by more than classroom learning.
Everything that is formally intended in the school is part of its curriculum. Schools are themselves political institutions in that they involve power and authority, participation, and the resolution of different opinions. Children's perception of these are arguably a strong influence in the development of their political attitudes.

2. There has always, of course, been a case, which has been accepted
by many teachers, that one of the functions of the curriculum is to give
young people an appreciation of the nature of government. Pressure to
give this more reality in terms of understanding political behaviour has
obviously been given great emphasis by the lowering of the voting age
to eighteen. More than that however there is an increasingly democratic temper in our society. This recognises that inevitably in human
society there will be diversity of objectives, and considerable disagreement as how best to achieve them. One of the tasks of government
is how best to resolve these differences. A democratic society seeks to
involve in this process of resolution all points of view in such a way
that they will all survive. However since the enfranchisement of the
majority, and in recent years, the rapidly increasing complexity of political decisions, often involving technical, scientific and economic
considerations, the ability of individual citizens to understand, much
less actively to influence the decisions of central government appears
to be diminishing. Thus there has been a rapidly increasing pressure
for participation in smaller, often local, units of decision-making;
trades unions, factories, schools, and pressure groups. People are
seeking, and claiming, their right to discuss and to choose. The school
curriculum would be wise to recognise this and to increase the likeli-

*The authors are HMIs, but wish to make clear that the paper is simply
a discussion document intended to pose certain questions not to provide
answers, and while it shows that the inspectorate see the field as
important, the opinions expressed are personal.

hood of <u>responsible</u> participation by supporting it with knowledge and
an informed understanding of the potential, and the limitations, of the
contribution of individuals to their own government.

3. <u>Content</u>

Content involves three areas. First there must be an understanding of
the machinery, not only of central and local government, but also industrial relations, the education system and the contribution made by
pressure groups. Second it must include an understanding of issues over
which the people disagree. Disagreement may be over <u>goals</u> (where are we
going? what purposes would a given action serve?); over <u>values</u> (in
what way should we act or not act?); over <u>methods</u> (how should we do
it?); or over <u>results</u> (was it the right outcome? the fairest? the
best?).* For young people aged 11-16 issues must be related to concrete examples, e.g. the <u>welfare state</u>, <u>motorways</u>, <u>comprehensive</u>
<u>schools</u>, <u>capital punishment</u>, <u>abortion</u>, <u>strikes</u>. Third there must be
knowledge of the groups who are involved in political decision-making,
e.g. political parties, the trades unions, the CBI, the press and interest groups. It must examine the effect on political aspirations and the
effectiveness of, for example, regional, economic, and ethnic differences. In order to have some insight into these areas it is also necessary to see them in some historical perspective which will demonstrate not only the potential, but the limitations of political action.
It will assist us, if not to predict, at least more intelligently to
anticipate political developments. But political understanding in the
end must evolve from an awareness of the close interaction of political
machinery, with issues, and the likely groupings of those who support
or oppose them.

4. <u>Concepts</u>

Political knowledge is often categorised conceptually. Political concepts, are as much tools of analysis as glossaries of technical terms,
and are a necessary bridge between mere political knowledge and political understanding. They help categorise our knowledge and experience
through such general concepts as <u>power</u>, <u>authority</u>, <u>welfare</u>, <u>freedom</u>,
<u>liberty</u>, through those associated with democratic machinery, e.g.
<u>elections</u>, <u>bills</u>, <u>pressure groups</u>, to those describing particular be-
liefs and ideologies, e.g. <u>socialism</u>, <u>conservatism</u>, <u>communism</u>,
<u>capitalism</u>, <u>anarchism</u>, and to those associated with specific issues,
e.g. <u>nationalisation</u>, <u>comprehensive reorganisation</u>, <u>pacifism</u>, <u>devolution</u>,
<u>women's rights</u>, <u>racism</u>. This list is meant neither to be prescriptive
nor exclusive. Which concepts are present in a syllabus will depend
upon the particular objectives of the teacher and of the issues that
are of current importance. Nor will it always be possible, or necessary,
for the pupils explicitly to understand them. Political concepts should
however assist teachers to select their material and define their objectives. If the concepts remain implicit for many pupils, they should at
least be introduced to concrete examples of them.

*We are indebted to Robert Stradling and Alex Porter for these categories
which they identify in their paper 'Issues and Political Problems'.
(Discussion document 2.5)*

5. Attitudes

The very richness and complexity of these concepts implies disagreement. The fundamental political question is 'what happens when people disagree?' If this is related exclusively to the machinery of central government, or even local government, such decisions will still seem distant from the lives of citizens. However the resolution of differences is part of the world of work, the school, clubs and societies, and indeed the family. If we recognise that political competence may affect attitudes at these familiar levels, the encouragement of political education will often produce suspicion, even antipathy. The attitudes which seem to us to be necessary accompaniments to responsible political competence may go some way at least to reassuring those who are worried at the prospects of an increasingly politically literate population. The attitude of political competence in a democracy is based above all on toleration. By this we mean not only the acceptance, but the welcoming, of diversity in society. This means neither indulgence nor indifference. It can mean neutrality, if we recognise it as inactive commitment, but commitment nonetheless. Another political attitude is an acceptance of compromise. There are of course other ways of resolving political differences: by war, imprisonment, censorship, and other forms of force. We are not suggesting that there may not be justifications for these other means on occasions, but they are not political in the sense that we have defined it in this paper. Political education must include an awareness of these alternatives, but political decisions within our own society inevitably involve compromise, and even acceptance of the second best. This does not mean that convictions should be constantly changed to meet circumstances, but it does mean that they should be held with open-mindedness – another essential political attitude in a democracy. As Bertrand Russell put it; 'When you come to a point of view, maintain it with doubt. This doubt is precious because it suggests an open-mind. I do not mean to argue that we should confuse an open-mind, with an empty mind.'

It is not only those who are politically dogmatic who may assist those forces which theaten democracy, it is also those who are politically indifferent. 'The only thing necessary for the triumph of evil is for good men to do nothing' (Edmund Burke). Young people and parents too quickly spot the weaknesses in the theme of 'universal toleration'. 'Are all views to be tolerated?' is a challenge that open political education must face. Here again, the institutions in a free society which determine the curriculum have to decide for themselves where the line must be drawn. Some views and attitudes are arguably unacceptable in our democracy: racism, suppression of opinion, exploitation of the defenceless. These are anathema to most people in our society. Education which identifies the evils we must resist, and suggests how we may resist them, is quite proper and likely to command wide support.

What we have been saying in this section on attitudes is that it is not enough for political education to talk in terms of the virtues of democratic society; in addition we must provide intellectual weapons to resist those who oppose it.

6. Skills

In order to develop these attitudes, certain skills and abilities are necessary. They have much in common with those described in the appendix on history: the ability to find evidence and to evaluate it, to identify slanted interpretation and bias, the ability to understand and appreciate the predicaments and points of view of other people. These

skills must be applied not only to texts, documents, and political literature, but more particularly to the media - press, radio, television
and the cinema. Another important skill for people who will be drawn
into decision-making is the ability to make a sound argument based on
evidence and to express a given case clearly. Reason and logical thinking must be at the heart of much political behaviour. These skills
must not only be practised and refined in writing, but verbally - in
argument and dispute, in presenting a case, in defending a point of view.

7. The areas of the curriculum

Although some schools offer 'politics' or 'civics' as a subject for a
time-table this is not a common arrangement. As with technology (see
separate paper) politics can, in fact, be offered as a curricular item
without requiring its own subject area or departmental organisation.
Therefore the curriculum needs to be clear as to the kind of knowledge
and skills and attitudes that it thinks sixteen year olds ought to enjoy, and through what subjects, activities and organisation these ends
may be achieved. We have already alluded to the need for clear language
in order to understand and express political matters. In particular,
informed reading of the newspapers, watching the television, listening
to the radio and talking about current events and problems offer diverse
and accessible contexts for the development of language skills. But
it must never be forgotten that political competence depends more on
oral than on written communication. The understanding of number is part
of political competence more and more. Statistics offer a main source
of data in political discussions because economic matters are a chief
concern of political debate. There is also the more refined study of
'psephology' - the quantification of political behaviour notably of
elections, but this is a more specialised interest.

Whilst the emphasis and careful observation and interpretation of
given data is as important a political skill as it is a scientific one,
there are ways in which politics and science connect. The paper on
technology deals with these at some length when it referred to the tech-
nological basis of our lives, the options this has presented, the conflict it has generated - all of these are potentially political, or have
already become so.

Politics is also deeply concerned with ethical questions and moral
problems. Although some people would argue that the morality grows
out of material considerations, others would dispute this. However both
schools of thought tend to express much of their politics in moral and
ethical terms.

8. Final considerations

Those who claim that politics ought to be 'kept out of' whatever it may
be are being ingenuous (or, on occasions disingenuous and politically
skilful). Wherever there is disagreement, there lies a potential for
politics; for aggregating issues, organising support, arguing, pro-
pagating, settling difficulties. There is 'politics' in this wide sense
in every club, society or classroom if we did but see it. Possibly
those who are coy about 'politics' mean 'party politics', but British
democracy is parliamentary and rests on national parties, which are
inevitably enmeshed with major issues, a fact more readily understood
by the politically literate.

Political education does not come merely through certain lessons in
history, geography, English, economics or politics as such. That part
of school organisation which we call, broadly, 'pastoral' is also

involved in that its organisation is a statement of the degree of seriousness and care with which personal and group problems are taken. Similarly, the pedagogy employed throughout the school has political implication. For example do we train young people to live in a democracy by talking to them excessively rather than inviting their views? Does repeated copying from textbooks on worksheets produce autonomous citizens? Do such arrangements as a few prefects but many non-prefects, or the employment of corporal punishment, prepare for life in a democracy? Is the curriculum in general, and each syllabus in particular, actually explained or justified to pupils at any stage? Are 'options' really informed choices?

It is not the task of political education to recommend particular political opinions, but on the other hand this paper does not claim to be value free. Its values are those of an open society, which accepts diversity of belief, participation, and the rights of individuals to assess evidence and to come to their own conclusions. The aim is to give pupils knowledge and tools for <u>informed and responsible political participation</u>. The late John Whiting in his play *Marching Song* has one of his characters say: 'you will forgive my contempt for men who think they fulfil their obligations by expressing an opinion'. Political education might also do something to restore a respect for political activity and attitudes, and rescue them from the worrying trend of current cynicism about the place of politics in society.

(22 February 1977)

C. REPORT ON LOCAL DEVELOPMENTS ARISING FROM THE SCHOOLS COUNCIL FUNDING
Geoffrey Petter

*Mr. Petter was, for his second year's work, funded by the Schools
Council. So his report to them was written for their purposes and con-
tains much narrative detail and repetition of matters already set out in
Section I of this Report. We extract only the sections on the
possibility of diffusion of our Report and the background to his work.
The numberings are those of his original report which is with the
Schools Council (Paper number SC77/36 September 1977). Editors.*

(The Report began by summarising the aims and organisation of the
Programme for Political Education)

4   In the school year 1974/75 the task of the Development Officer was
to foster working relations with LEAs showing interest in the Programme
and prepared to cooperate; to establish contacts with head teachers,
with teachers' unions and professional Associations concerned with work
in schools and in Further Education, as well as with the TUC and CBI;
to assess the working groups, and in particular, to help them to identify
schools which might be associated fully or partially with the project;
finally, to attempt to focus the exploratory work whenever possible, on
teachers' centres.

4.1 The original plan was for the work to be handed over to Alex Porter,
then head of Social Studies, Solihull VIth Form College, in the late
summer of 1975. It became evident during the first year of the
Programme, that in order to maintain momentum two full-time workers
during the second year would be needed, in addition to the Political Education Research Unit in York.

5   The grant of £5,600 from the Schools Council enabled the project to
have, in effect, two co-directors: one (Alex Porter, with Nuffield
funds) devoting his time to curriculum advice and development in close
touch with six of the experimenting institutions, (the other six being
closely monitored by York); the other co-director (Geoffrey Petter with
Schools Council funds) being free to devote his time to three tasks:
a. offering advice and help where asked to schools who could not be
catered for in our formal monitored-trial programmes
b. meeting where possible requests by LEAs and teachers' centres to or-
ganise seminars and short courses to decide or coordinate methods of
political education; but above all
c. exploring the possibility of local centres or even groups of
authorities undertaking some longer commitments or developments in these
fields when the Nuffied Programme had ended.

Paragraphs 6-12 then summarised the theoretical basis of the Programme

13.1   It was necessary during the early months of the school year to
help the co-director (Nuffield) and the Political Education Research
Unit to complete the selection of schools and colleges to take part in
experimental work in the classroom. (Plans for ten schools and two
colleges of Further Education to take part in the project had been completed before the end of the Christmas term 1975). Some of the institutions identified for trial work volunteered as a result of preliminary

liaison with the appropriate Education Authority. In some cases, the school eventually took part because of previous contact with a member of the Working Party or with one of the team of PERU. When schools were suggested by Local Authorities, the participation depended on whether local circumstances in individual schools made this possible.

14   Meanwhile, Geoffrey Petter's own plan of operations involved three stages: first, discussion with Officers of the LEA; second, a meeting with Advisers and/or Wardens of teachers' centres; third, a meeting at a teachers' centre at which the purpose of the Programme for Political Education would be explained. The objective, as an outcome of the third stage, was the setting up of a working group to consider possible syllabuses based on the arguments and guidelines of the project documents.

15   The importance of establishing a good and fruitful relationship with an LEA at the highest level cannot be over-emphasised. Crucial to the success of any venture of this kind is the blessing not only of the Chief Officer but of the Chairman and, indeed, the Shadow Chairman of the Education Committee.
15.1   In the summer of 1974 all LEAs in the country had been sent the Explanatory Paper. Some twenty replied; of these only one expressed a firm intention to take no part in the exercise. The others all indicated a wish to be further informed.
15.2   Already, during the first year of the project the responses from six Authorities had been encouraging. It seemed therefore sensible to make further approaches where preliminary contacts had given ground for optimism. The early Autumn was spent in probing further those areas where early response has been good.

(Paragraphs 16-17 summarised early approaches to the six LEAs who had expressed interest)

18   The most important development before Christmas 1975 was the arrangement which was made for a conference of the Working Party, representatives of Schools Council, participating schools, LEA Advisers and others to meet for twentyfour hours to discuss the project, its problems and its prospects.
18.1   The conference held at Easthampstead Park in January 1976 considered three aspects of the Programme: first, the place of politics in the curriculum; second, the role of Local Authorities and, in particular, their advisory services in the development of the work; third, assessment. The forty members who attended represented most of the institutions taking part in experimental classroom work, members of the project's Working Party, representatives of the Schools Council and a number of heads and teachers who were attracted to the work.
18.2   Concentration on three aspects of the work made it possible to achieve three objectives: first, to give teachers an opportunity to describe in the discussion groups what they were actually doing, what proportion of which age group was involved, what specialised staff were being used and what methods were used; second, to provide the three discussion groups with the chance of debating among themselves whether politics should be a module in a Social Science course or in a Humanities course, or whether it should be a matter of 'infusion', i.e. built into syllabuses in English, History, Geography, Sociology, etc; third, to put into perspective the role of the Monitoring Unit at York ....

19   Bearing in mind the fact that the project was envisaged as one designed to produce various kinds of ground plan for a syllabus worked out for local groups of teachers, it seemed sensible to concentrate attention on those authorities in which groups of teachers were most likely to be active. The LEAs chosen were Kirklees, Northamptonshire, Suffolk, ILEA, London Borough of Brent, East Sussex, West Sussex, Wiltshire, Gloucestershire, Avon and Devon.

19.1   The objective was to identify six LEAs willing to make a reasonably firm commitment as follows:
a. to set up a working party of not less than six teachers to construct curricular models based on PPE papers working over an extended period of some two years; b. to base the work on a teachers' centre or on a College of Education; c. to offer continuing support to the working parties by Advisers or Centre Wardens; d. to hold a course or workshop at the end of the two-year period in order to give other teachers in the area the benefit of the Working Party's thinking and conclusions. It was envisaged that there would be some kind of coordination at the centre, and that some members of the original Nuffield Working Party would be available as consultants, on a purely voluntary basis, if working groups needed help.

(Paragraphs 20-28 then detail the mixed fortunes of the negotiations with particular LEAs. The best progress was made with the help of Mr. Rex Beddis, Senior Advisor for Humanities of the County of Avon, who encouraged groups of teachers in Local Studies to consider 'political literacy'. The warden of the Filton Teachers' Centre, Mr. Robert Philpott, set up a working group whose activities are worth describing in detail as an example of what could happen at centres).

The Filton Teachers' Centre

29   The initial meeting, held in July 1976, was attended by five teachers from three comprehensive schools and by a lecturer from (a) technical college. Even at this stage, teachers from thirteen other comprehensive schools in Avon had expressed an interst and a desire to be kept in touch with the group's activities. Basic subject areas of the teachers concerned were History, English and Geography, and the personal interests of individual members ranged from first year secondary to A level. Members of the group readily agreed that 'since our country took political democracy too much for granted, without working at it, we might lose it almost without realising it.' At the same time there was agreement that programmes sometimes labelled as 'Citizenship' tended to be purely descriptive, lacking any kind of analysis of where the real power lay. There was also a fair measure of agreement that the inclusion of a political module in a General Studies course as part of the common core in the fourth and fifth years, might well be appropriate; some members felt that there was genuine scope for development in the lower half of the secondary school ....

29.1   The second meeting in October was attended by two members of the original group, by four teachers from comprehensive schools attending for the first time and by Derek Smith of the Bristol University Extra-Mural Department. This link with the Extra-Mural Department of this University was to lead to a further link with the University's Politics Department.

29.1.1 This second meeting began to look in more specific terms at the possibilities of political education within the curriculum. History, English and General Studies were each thought to provide a way in. A level syllabuses had in the past tended to be unhelpful because of the strong emphasis on descriptive rather than analytical work. The problem for the curriculum designer was to attempt to preserve a balance between the legitimate demands of academic subjects and what was described as a 'social commitment'. Some considered that the academic commitment could well be followed by a social commitment: for instance, French by European Studies, History by Civics, Geography by World Studies etc. But the majority view was that these two commitments could well be fused. The real balance was twofold: between present and past and between moral and social.

29.1.2 The upshot was that it was decided to compile a rough checklist of aspects of Political Literacy which must somehow be included. This checklist contained the following:

1. the local dimension - the national dimension - the European dimension - the rest of the world - the world dimension;
2. trade unions - political parties - pressure groups - the media - welfare state - population pressures;
3. rights and duties of the citizen - responsibility of active citizens towards the aged and the young - elections - democracy and totalitarianism and shades between.

29.2   At its third meeting, the group decided to concentrate on five areas:

1. political education related primarily to the local area;
2. political education related primarily to the national sphere - focussed on 6th-form teaching;
3. political education related primarily to the contemporary European scene;
4. political education related to contemporary China;
5. the global political scene: relationship of the rich to the poor, the outbreak and control of wars, etc.

29.2.1 The warden stressed that the aim should be a limited number of small teaching units which, while geared to a specific situation, could be of use in roughly parallel situations. He emphasised that the aim is not to provide prescriptive recipes; rather to offer examples of what might work in various situations.

29.3   About this time four sets of teaching material were circulated for general consideration.

29.4   The fourth meeting, in February 1977, explored further the five areas decided upon during the previous Autumn. In the 'local' section, interest focussed on two areas: a project related to the development of Lulsgate Airport and another concerned with what might be called 'community politics' stemming from a project already in operation at Hartcliff School, Bristol. The 'national' input came from two directions: from a teacher at Whitfield School who introduced some work on British Parliamentary Representation, a subject on which another group had been working for some time; also from the Filton group itself, whose members sought to bring the problems and tensions related to political decision-making directly into the classroom.

29.4.1 The Filton group's approach was to prepare and direct a case study based on decision-making on the Fast Breeder Reactor. A five-stage programme was envisaged:

   i. the production of a series of 'Energy Cards' for class role play on each of the five major areas detailing type of energy source, comparative costs, development costs, polution and conservation problems, etc;

ii.   in addition to these was a further set of cards representing the
major lobbies, identified as:
a.   Organised groups (Friends of the Earth, Half-Life);
b.   Local people living near power stations;
c.   Unions
d.   Influential individuals in science and public life;
e.   Local Authorities
iii.   A further input would then be based on the questions - 'Who makes
the decisions?' and 'How can they be influenced?' The group wanted to
define three areas of decision-making: Government (Departments - Cabinet
Committees - Cabinet); Parliament (particularly significant on free vote
issues); the People (either through a Referendum or through an issue
significant at a General Election).
There was no agreement about the form in which this particular input
should be; it might be a matter of wall charts, a foldout leaflet, separate cards, overhead projector transparences, in a booklet or simply
material put on a blackboard.
iv.   It was also envisaged that a further step, to be taken at sixth-
form level in General Studies or in Politics, would be to set the class
up with Cabinet Cards, detailing briefs, personalities, interests of
various Ministers, into which context a case study could be introduced.
v.   After initial trials had been carried out by members of the group,
work could then be completed on 'pasting up' information cards with
cuttings and further information for teachers and classes where required.
It was emphasised that in all this work, the aim would be direct impact.
Even the least able must, if possible, be made politically literate.
29.4.2 Following conversations at the Hansard Society, correspondence
with the Sussex Institute of Contemporary European Studies and discussion
among members of the group, it had been agreed that the 'European dimension' should be treated by taking the Fishing Dispute as a material for
study. This question had certain advantages:
a.   people's livelihoods concern;
b.   'European personality'
c.   The question involved internal reactions among all of the nine
members, and external relations in Europe (Norway) and beyond (Russia);
d.   Questions in European Parliament.
A tutor at Filton Technical College had prepared a comprehensive brief
for developing the theme, and other members of the group were working on
teaching proposals. It was agreed that direct illustration of the
various factions involved could be most widely produced in an audio-
visual presentation of some sort.
29.4.3 China and 'The World Dimension' did not produce definite plans.

30   There are five observations to be made about the activities of
the Filton Teachers' Centre. First, it illustrates the result of the
combination of several local initiatives and the stimulus of the working
papers of the Programme for Political Education. The concern of the
Warden that the European dimension should be given significance was put
into a new focus by the Working Party's papers; at the same time, the
working papers by themselves would not have generated the activity which
ensued without some individual initiative. Second, the Filton Centre
became the instrument by which a network of communication was set up
between more than a dozen schools in conjunction with an Extra-Mural Department and a College of Further Education. Third, the brief description of four meetings, spread over a period of six months, illustrates
the way in which thinking can lead to action. At the first meeting a
general strategy was devised; at the second, more specific terms of re-

ference were decided upon; at the third, areas of study were positively identified and some teaching materials were produced; at the fourth meeting three out of five areas of study were planned in some detail. Fourth, and very important, the activities of the group illustrate the way in which enthusiasm can generate not only wider involvement of schools in an area but an expansion and elaboration of topics to be studied. Lastly the group's activities illustrate the way in which new thinking in fact tends to lead to the discovery of effective work already being done, for instance, at Filton High School.

Both Henbury and Blackwell schools have decided to incorporate a module of work in politics in the non-examination time in the fourth and fifth years - between a hundred and one hundred and eighty minutes per week; other schools are beginning to think along the same lines, relating the work to an extension of moral and social education.

31   The present thrust in the direction of inculcating political literacy is indicative not of any process of innovation but rather of an attempt to delineate and highlight an essential element in the process of education which is too often vaguely implied at the moment when it should be explicit. There is reason to hope that the enthusiasm of teachers will create a momentum at Filton Teachers' Centre which may be self-perpetuating....

32   Can it be argued from what is happening at Filton that all that is necessary is to produce a worked-out hypothesis and leave it to teachers in the locality to treat it as they will? Is it perhaps the most economical plan to provide materials for thought and leave teachers to work out syllabuses and materials without making provision for any cooperative action between Local Authorities? After all, the experience at Filton may well be repeated in a number of parts of the country. Filton has been cited as one of several examples in Avon; there may be others equally significant. But the answer is surely that important though it is to encourage local enthusiasm to generate local action, some consolidation of the work of the Programme for Political Education on a cooperative basis, involving several Authorities, is essential if real progress is to be made.

IV Possibilities for the future

33   Five Local Education Authorities have made a declaration of intent to be further involved with the work - Avon, Brent, Devon, Kirklees and Northamptonshire; the ILEA and Wiltshire are possible additions to this list. The Authority areas prepared to cooperate have in common: a. an Adviser and teachers prepared to pursue the matter further; b. either a school or a teachers' centre suitable as a base for activities; c. some sympathy with the working documents of the Programme for Political Education as a hypothesis on which to proceed.

34   If to the Authorities which have given a reasonably firm commitment can be added the ten schools and two Colleges of Further Education in which trial syllabuses have been implemented in the classroom, a (promising) geographical picture emerges....

35   By the end of the school year 1976/77 the work both of the London and York ends of the Programme for Political Education will have finished; but important beginnings will have been made and, equally important, firm foundations for further work will have been laid. It

remains to be decided what further assistance the work of inculcating political literacy merits over the next decade.

36   On the national level there is no lack of interest. Teachers Associations are watching cautiously the progress of events. These Associations have many commitments and many problems on their minds at the present time. They have the difficult task of deciding on priorities, and it is no part of this report to suggest what those priorities should be, only to stress that if literacy matters, it is incomplete without its political dimension. Meanwhile the Society of Education Officers has shown sympathy, given encouragement and offered advice. The Geographical Association and the Economics Association both emphasise the important role that each has to play in any course, General Studies or otherwise, in which a political element enters. Historians and teachers of English have a clear interest and, many of them, a clear commitment to be involved in the work. Finally, the Politics Association, and the Association of Teachers of Social Sciences are both strongly convinced of the importance of political education and anxious to play their part in it. Their aims do not always coincide, but their objectives have in common the fact that each Association wishes to see citizens fully motivated. Differences of philosophical approach by no means preclude the possibility of friendly cooperation.

37   The significant fact about the work so far done in an effort to inculcate political literacy is that, by and large, discussions in teachers' centres and work done in schools and Colleges of Further Education have, for the most part, been multi-disciplinary. As the report to the Nuffield Foundation will show, the idea of infusion, that is of using an individual subject discipline as a medium for political education where appropriate, has not always proved appropriate or popular.
   The historians undoubtedly believe in it; indeed there is a tendency on the part of all subject specialists to assume that political education can be successfully undertaken through the medium of, say, sociology, economics, geography, English or history. But experience so far suggests that progress is most likely to be made where subject specialists, instead of staking a claim to monopolise the field, pool their resources and show willingness to make a contribution to a general programme. This is especially appropriate where a module for the inculcation of political literacy is included, as it has been in a number of the trial schools, as part of a General Studies course preferably forming part of the core curriculum. It is not without significance that in discussions in Brent, Exeter, Swindon, Filton and elsewhere, the participants represented the principal disciplines associated with the Social Sciences.

38   It is envisaged that political education, if it is to be regarded as essential to the secondary process, will demand in-service training courses for those who undertake the work. What has been achieved by the Programme for Political Education, sponsored by the Hansard Society and the Politics Association, has been foundations laid of three kinds:
a. preliminary experiments with teaching materials, inspired by working papers but devised by teachers;
b. systematic monitoring of six and self-evaluation and external assessment of the other six institutions undertaking experimental teaching;
c. the genesis of small groups of teachers in a few Authorities prepared to think and plan both approaches and materials, using the project papers as a working hypothesis.

38.1   The setting up by the Institute of Education (London University) of the Centre for Political Education with Alex Porter as its director, is an indication, on the one hand of the Institute's conviction that the inculcation of political literacy is a matter of importance and, on the other hand, of its equal conviction that in-service training of teachers demands high priority. The Centre for Political Education will be in a position to act as a focal point of reference for those groups in Local Authorities which are working out schemes, and also for those schools and Colleges of Further Education which have undertaken experimental teaching, if they so wish it.

38.2   Meanwhile it is to be hoped that the valuable work of the Political Education Research Unit at York University, a highly individual and pioneering contribution to the Programme for Political Education, can be continued.

39   In view of the favourable response by Local Authorities, of the willingness of a few of them to give active cooperation and of the keen interest shown by a number of professional associations, this report (to the Schools Council) ends with one single recommendation: that the foundations laid be built upon, and that work started by a small and enthusiastic body of men and women be carried on both by them and by those they have inspired to join them.

40   Guidelines

1. The importance of establishing a good and fruitful relationship with an LEA at the highest level (para. 15).
2. The need to strengthen the structure of the project and to establish centres of activity in LEA areas (18.3).
3. The significance of interest or support on the part of Teachers' Associations and other potentially interested bodies (31).
4. The part played by courses and conferences (18.3, 24, 27).
5. The role of the teachers' centre (29 *et seq*).
6. The possibilities of the inter-disciplinary approach (36).
7. Political Education, regarded as essential to the process of secondary education, will demand in-service courses for those who undertake the work (38).
8. The need to consolidate the work of monitoring and assessment in schools which have taken part in experimental teaching (38, 38.2).
9. In view of the declaration of intent made by five LEAs, the need to build on foundations already laid (33, 39).

We thank the following bodies for their cooperation in aspects of Mr. Petter's work: the Association of Assistant Mistresses, the Association of Head Mistresses, the Assistant Masters Association, the Association of Teachers in Technical Institutions, the Confederation of British Industry, the Headmasters Association, the National Association of Head Teachers, the National Association of Schoolmasters, the National Union of Teachers and the Trades Union Congress. *Editors*